THE POEMS

OF

Charlotte Smith

WOMEN WRITERS IN ENGLISH
1350–1850

GENERAL EDITOR
Susanne Woods

MANAGING EDITOR
Elaine Brennan

EDITORS
Patricia Caldwell
Stuart Curran
Margaret J. M. Ezell
Elizabeth H. Hageman
Elizabeth D. Kirk

WOMEN WRITERS PROJECT
Brown University

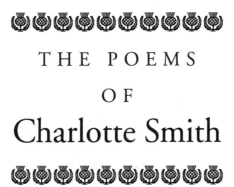

THE POEMS
OF
Charlotte Smith

EDITED BY

Stuart Curran

New York   Oxford

OXFORD UNIVERSITY PRESS

1993

Oxford University Press

Oxford   New York   Toronto
Delhi   Bombay   Calcutta   Madras   Karachi
Kuala Lumpur   Singapore   Hong Kong   Tokyo
Nairobi   Dar es Salaam   Cape Town
Melbourne   Auckland   Madrid

and associated companies in
Berlin   Ibadan

Published by Oxford University Press, Inc.,
198 Madison Avenue, New York, New York 10016-4314

Oxford is a registered trademark of Oxford University Press

Library of Congress Cataloging-in-Publication Data

Smith, Charlotte Turner, 1749–1806.
[Poems]
The Poems of Charlotte Smith / Charlotte Smith:
edited by Stuart Curran.
p.   cm. -- (Women writers in English 1350–1850)
I. Curran, Stuart. II. Title. III. Series.
PR3688.S4A6   1993   821'.6--dc20   92-14882
ISBN 0-19-507873-X (cloth)
ISBN 0-19-508358-X (paper)

This volume was supported in part by the
National Endowment for the Humanities,
an independent federal agency.

Printing (last digit):
9   8   7   6   5   4
Printed in the United States of America
on acid-free paper

To the Hon. Martha W. Griffiths,
who taught me much
and
to Andrea Mitchell,
who helps me teach others

CONTENTS

The Emigrants

Uncollected Poems

Conversations Introducing Poetry

Beachy Head, Fables, and Other Poems

FOREWORD

Women Writers in English 1350–1850 presents texts of cultural and literary interest in the English-speaking tradition, often for the first time since their original publication. Most of the writers represented in the series were well known and highly regarded until the professionalization of English studies in the later nineteenth century coincided with their excision from canonical status and from the majority of literary histories.

The purpose of this series is to make available a wide range of unfamiliar texts by women, thus challenging the common assumption that women wrote little of real value before the Victorian period. While no one can doubt the relative difficulty women experienced in writing for an audience before that time, or indeed have encountered since, this series shows that women nonetheless had been writing from early on and in a variety of genres, that they maintained a clear eye to readers, and that they experimented with an interesting array of literary strategies for claiming their authorial voices. Despite the tendency to treat the powerful fictions of Virginia Woolf's *A Room of One's Own* (1928) as if they were fact, we now know, against her suggestion to the contrary, that there were many "Judith Shakespeares," and that not all of them died lamentable deaths before fulfilling their literary ambitions.

This series is unique in at least two ways. It offers, for the first time, concrete evidence of a rich and lively heritage of women writing in English before the mid-nineteenth century, and it is based on one of the most sophisticated and forward-looking electronic resources in the world: the Brown University Women Writers Project textbase (full text database) of works by early women writers. The Brown University Women Writers Project (WWP) was established in 1988 with a grant from the National Endowment for the Humanities, which continues to assist in its development.

Women Writers in English 1350–1850 is a print publication project derived from the WWP. It offers lightly-annotated versions based on single good copies or, in some cases, collated versions of texts with more complex editorial histories, normally in their original spelling.

The editions are aimed at a wide audience, from the informed undergraduate through professional students of literature, and they attempt to include the general reader who is interested in exploring a fuller tradition of early texts in English than has been available through the almost exclusively male canonical tradition.

SUSANNE WOODS
General Editor

ACKNOWLEDGMENTS

Producing a book is always a cooperative project; producing a series of books such as Women Writers in English becomes more of a cooperative crusade. What began as a small specialized research project has developed into an adventure in literature, computing, and publishing far beyond our initial abstract conception.

At Brown University, many administrators have given the Women Writers Project invaluable support, including President Vartan Gregorian, Provost Frank Rothman, Dean of the Faculty Bryan Shepp, and Vice President Brian Hawkins. Vital assistance has come from the English Department, including chairs Walter Davis, Stephen M. Foley, and Elizabeth D. Kirk, and from staff members at Computing and Information Services, particularly Don Wolfe, Allen Renear, and Geoffrey Bilder. Maria Fish staffed the Women Writers Project office through crises large and small.

At Oxford University Press Elizabeth Maguire, Claude Conyers and Ellen Barrie have been patient, helpful, and visionary, all at the same time.

Ashley Cross, Julia Deisler, and Lisa Gim shared with me their excitement about teaching early women writers, as have many other faculty members and graduate students at Brown and elsewhere. My friends and colleagues locally in Brown's Computing and the Humanities Users Group and internationally in the Text Encoding Initiative, especially Michael Sperberg-McQueen, have stimulated my thinking about texts and the electronic uses and encoding of texts. Syd Bauman and Grant Hogarth have sustained me in the computer and publishing aspects of the project.

Students are the life's blood of the Women Writers Project, and all of the students who have passed through our offices are part of this volume. Most particularly, among those who worked on *The Poems of Charlotte Smith* were Stephanie Bell, Lisa Billowitz, Sarah Finch Brown, Ashley Cross, Julia Flanders, Laelia Gilborn, B. Jessie Hill, Deborah Hirsch, Daniel J. Horn, Jason R. Loewith, Katherine Lott,

Deborah Lowe, Carole E. Mah, Leslie Stern, Susan B. Taylor, Michele Tepper, and Amanda Zabriskie.

Other students who have especially contributed to the spirit and vitality of the WWP office include Carolyn Cannuscio, Elizabeth Carroll, Lisa Chick, John Fitzgerald, Sharon Garrick, Jennifer Hofer, Mithra Irani, Anthony Lioi, Elizabeth Weinstock, and Andrea Weissman. Benjamin Plotkin deserves a sentence all his own.

My personal thanks go especially to Sarah Finch Brown and Julia Flanders for their meticulous scholarship and their support through the final production details.

ELAINE BRENNAN
Managing Editor

ACKNOWLEDGMENTS

Throughout this project I have been grateful for the active encouragement of a number of scholars whose interest in Charlotte Smith's writings has whetted my own and on whose knowledge I have been fortunate to rely. I record particular debts to David Blewett, Isobel Grundy, Margaret Maison, Mitzi Myers, Judith Pascoe, Richard Sha, Judith Stanton, William St Clair, and Laura Zimmerman. The exemplary Singer-Mendenhall collection of the Van Pelt Library at the University of Pennsylvania has allowed me instant access to virtually the entire corpus of Smith's writings, and Daniel Traister in his oversight of it has been unfailingly committed to the value of this endeavor. The Huntington Library has been a special resource for this volume, as it has for the entire effort of the Women Writers Project. The edition has benefitted as well from the resources of the Folger Library, the Library Company of Philadelphia, the New York Public Library, and the Library of the University of California at Los Angeles.

STUART CURRAN

INTRODUCTION

Charlotte Smith was the first poet in England whom in retrospect we would call Romantic. Influential among her contemporaries, through the popularity of her verse over nearly a quarter century she established enduring patterns of thought and conventions of style that became norms for the period. Her most direct beneficiary among the more canonical male poets was William Wordsworth, who seems to have felt her impact from the first. At least he implicitly suggests an affinity when, upon attaining his majority in 1791 and stopping in Brighton on his way to France, he sought Smith out to secure from her an introduction to another important influence in early Romanticism and the subject of his first published poem, Helen Maria Williams, then resident in Paris and beginning her series of *Letters from France* on the course of the Revolution. As a literary elder in 1833, a generation after Smith's death, Wordsworth looked back from a double perspective of unstated debt and rueful survivorship, reflecting that Smith was a poet "to whom English verse is under greater obligations than are likely to be either acknowledged or remembered." Absorbed in style and thought into the mainstream of Romantic poetry, Smith's fate was to encourage the creativity of other poets and become herself by the second half of the nineteenth century largely forgotten by literary history.

That was a destiny to which many women writers have been subjected, and perhaps the events of Smith's life should have inured her to expect it. For with dashed expectations she lived her entire existence. She was born into a world of genteel elegance not far from St. James's Palace on 4 May 1749, the second daughter of Nicholas Turner and Anna Towers, and with the exception of her mother's death in the birth of her brother three years later, her youth was idyllic, lavishly situated between her father's London townhouse and Sussex estates, and indulged with the best of what then passed for a girl's education. Sent to school in Chichester at age six, she was instructed in art by George Smith, a noted landscape painter, a tutelage somewhat frustrated by a near-sightedness that would have important consequences for her later poetry. By eight she was in a girl's school in London's Kensington suburb, adding dancing and acting to her public accomplishments—she was remembered as the best actress in the school—and in her private moments reading everything she could lay her hands on. She grew quickly into a accomplished young woman, so quickly indeed as to draw an advantageous proposal of marriage when she was but fourteen. This her father spurned, but the sign of the approaching end of her childhood should have been a portent to her. Neither her father's good intentions nor his indulgence of her independent development was to last long.

After twelve years as a widower Nicholas Turner, whose principal claim to attention was as an independent man of fashion, took an interest in a Miss Meriton, whose principal claim to his attention was her potential contribution to that stylish image, a dowry of £20,000. A headstrong adolescent daughter was in these circumstances rather a hindrance, particularly given the jealousy of the new bride, and largely through the machinations of her maternal aunt, who thought she was securing Charlotte's happy independence, a match with suitable prospects in life was found. On 23 February 1765 the pampered Charlotte Turner, ten weeks shy of her sixteenth birthday, was married off to a pampered Benjamin Smith, twenty-one years old and heir to a West-Indian commercial enterprise he would prove incapable of managing. It was a mistake on all sides, and the originally dutiful and self-sacrificing Charlotte in short time came to see its full dimensions. Her sister, the distinguished children's author Catherine Anne Dorset, quotes from a letter describing Charlotte's awakening to her plight while still an adolescent: "No disadvantage could equal those I sustained; the more my mind expanded, the more I became sensible of personal slavery; the more I improved and cultivated my understanding, the farther I was removed from those with whom I was condemned to pass my life; and the more clearly I saw by these newly-acquired lights the horror of the abyss into which I had unconsciously plunged." Smith's biographer, Florence Hilbish, concludes from the less than reliable expedient of tracing similar circumstances in her novels that Nicholas Turner, who died in 1775, was appropriately unhappy with his second wife. Certainly it was the case that his daughter, though the oldest child, was effectively disinherited by his remarriage. And she discovered herself effectively ruined by her own.

As long as Benjamin's father remained alive and they lived in his vicinity, he exerted a measure of control over his son's spendthrift ways. But Charlotte, for the sake of her burgeoning family, successfully urged a move to the Hampshire countryside in 1774; and two years later her father-in-law died, leaving a large estate and the last will of a self-made man of affairs. It was written without benefit of appropriate legal advice, and so scrupulous was it in its complicated attempt to preserve the patrimony from the son's dissipations that its various terms were actually incompatible. The estate was thus plunged into a litigation of Dickensian intricacy whose principal issues took twenty-three years to sort out, and both Benjamin and Charlotte were long dead before the final settlement actually took place. The bulk of the estate was siphoned off into legal fees, and, incredible as it may seem, the four surviving children of Charlotte Smith who had been the main objects of her father-in-law's protective codicils were unable until 1813, thirty-seven years after his death, to claim their shares in his estate.

A sense of the legal system as an arbitrary machine of power operating without any essential relation to equity runs deep in Smith's writing. It is augmented by her recognition that the law is a social code written by men for a male preserve, and that the principal function of women within its boundaries can only be to suffer consequences over which they have no control. This reflects Smith's long years of effort, unable herself to join in litigation, to enlist help from powerful male allies in order to provide for her children's education. In the end her hectoring alienated most of these men, and what means of advancement, from education to employment, could be found for her children—all ten of them—she provided herself.

For a time, after her father-in-law's death, the disaster inherent in legally tying up the estate was averted by Benjamin's securing a lucrative government contract through prominent connections. But the contract came to its end along with the American war in 1782, and a host of unpaid creditors could no longer be put off. In December 1783, leaving her children with her younger brother at Bignor Park, the Sussex estate where she had herself grown up, Charlotte Smith encapsulated the original error of her marriage, joining her debt-ridden husband in the King's Bench Prison. It was she who by the summer of 1784 secured his release in a short-term settlement of his affairs, but by the fall he was again so deeply involved that there was no recourse but to have him absent himself from England. Because Benjamin spoke no French, Charlotte accompanied him to Dieppe, saw him decently set-tled, then returned the same day to continue her efforts to satisfy his creditors. But having no success and pregnant with her twelfth child, she gathered them all in October 1784 and moved her family to France. There she found her husband, with his customary extravagance, ensconced in a dilapidated chateau twelve miles from a market town and in the midst of a rude and uninviting peasantry. With the spring Charlotte Smith returned to Sussex and secured the necessary agree-ments to resolve her husband's debts and enable his return. Hilbish, on the strength of a much later short story, surmises that he came back with a French mistress, which provoked a separation between husband and wife. Whatever the case, in 1787 Benjamin Smith returned to France, and Charlotte, legally separated without having secured a cru-cial power over her own financial affairs, was left to provide for eight children on her own.

The way to do so was clear to her. Immediately upon accompanying Benjamin to the King's Bench, Charlotte Smith had attempted herself to find an independent means to relieve the family from debt. By May 1784, still resident with her husband in prison, and through the offices of her neighbor, the highly successful man of letters William Hayley (whom at that point she had never met), Smith printed in Chichester and published in London a small and elegant volume whose full title testifies alike to her sorrows and her irreducible self-esteem: *Elegiac Son-nets, and Other Essays by Charlotte Smith of Bignor Park, in Sussex*. Smith would not hide her name behind a cloak of anonymity, nor would she deny herself the estate where she grew up and where her children remained under her brother's protection, so far distant from the actual prison to which marriage had reduced her. Her success was immediate, and a second edition of the *Elegiac Sonnets* was called for. The reception was obviously more heartening than it was remunerative, but, though she soon saw that the means to financial independence lay in prose,

Smith's sense of her genteel heritage and her claims to artistry never allowed her to abandon a commitment to poetry. Over the next sixteen years there would be eight further, continually expanding, editions of these poems: by 1800 they were housed in two ample volumes adorned with engravings by a major contemporary illustrator, Thomas Stothard.

Before one turns to the nature of these and the two other volumes of her poetry, it would be useful to delineate Smith's other career as a professional writer. In the decade between 1788 and 1798 she produced ten novels that in their aggregate constitute perhaps the major achievement in English fiction during those years and certainly establish a forceful expansion of the arena circumscribed by women's fiction between the novels of Burney and those of Edgeworth and Austen. Her range of character and style testifies to a general inventiveness that sustains her novels even when the plots begin to creak. Her heroines are almost always the central figures of the novel, and, though their virtue may seem too generally insisted on and may appear to surmount only the kinds of tests that are conventional to fiction of the period, it is plain from Smith's concentration on these figures and on the nature of the threats to them that survival is indeed a real issue.

This is doubly clear from the translations with which Smith initiated her education in fiction, which, though undertaken sheerly for profit, reveal an element essential to the accurate measure of her mind and achievement. During the winter of 1785 she spent in Normandy, she began what she assumed was the first English translation of the Abbé Antoine-Francois Prévost's scandalous novel, *Manon Lescaut*. It had actually been redacted in a disguised form into English twice before, which, when the point was raised to dispute her publisher's claim to originality, drove Smith in 1786 to withdraw the edition shortly after its publication. But that the issue was publicly raised in the first place almost surely stems from Smith's not having observed the implicit gender codes of late eighteenth-century British culture. For a priest to have written such a tale of illicit passion and upward sexual mobility was what the English might expect of a country like France, but for a woman to have translated it—even with a silent diminishing of its libertine atmosphere—was to step across the bounds of common propriety. And yet, the fact that Manon, with the Marguerite of *Faust*, stands as a tragic heroine of more than one distinguished nineteenth-century opera (Massenet's *Manon* and Puccini's *Manon Lescaut*) suggests how mythic is the character she upheld for a modern bourgeois society reared on a double standard of sexual morality. Smith's translation of such a work alerts us from the first to the strong feminist element in her writing, a reality principle nurtured by her sense of having already been in life twice at the mercy of men who used her and cast her off. Her second translation from the French, a series of legal cases from *Les causes célèbres* she called in English *The Romance of Real Life*, has been generally dismissed as simple hack work. But the fact that among these stories is the first appearance in English of what the later twentieth century has come to see as a primary document about the status of woman within early bourgeois culture, known through Natalie Zemon Davis's title as *The Return of Martin Guerre*, once again might remind us of Smith's abiding conviction that in "real life" women are often victims of the men who possess them and of the male system that sanctions such control.

In her private poetry, particularly in the bulk of her ninety-two *Elegiac Sonnets*, that external system is an unspecified but pervasive, ominous presence that threatens the autonomy of the self that records it. In her most sustained public poem, *The Emigrants*, the system is disintegrating of its own tyrannical impulses around both her and the outcasts of fortune she surveys. The fact that there is so little difference between its French and British victims, between those observed and the sympathetic but powerless observer of their plight, underscores the universal anarchy that passes for law and the helplessness of mere persons before encoded systems of public power. In terms of its sheer craft, *The Emigrants* is the finest piece of extended blank verse in English between Cowper's *The Task* (1785) and Wordsworth's unpublished initial version of *The Prelude* (1799), which like her poem he projected in two books. Its reappearance after two centuries, however, provides more than a missing artistic link; for in its interweaving of the public and private, the political and the personal, its meditative absorption of and sometimes by its surroundings, and its sense of a universal existential crisis, *The Emigrants* establishes a weighty touchstone against which to measure the major poetic voices of the 1790's: both those, from Anna

Barbauld and Samuel Taylor Coleridge to Mary Robinson and Robert Southey, who reveal themselves as, like Smith, highly politicized in their vision and those conspicuously not so, Wordsworth perhaps being the principal example.

There were those in her own day who found Smith's reiterated legal tribulations annoying. Anna Seward, continually exuding a manifest envy of Smith's success, called her sonnets "a perpetual dun on pity," and the public reviews generally found her diatribe against the law in *The Emigrants*, as well as at various points in the novels, intrusive on their artistic independence. A later critical perspective might wish in *The Emigrants* to accentuate the link between the law and arbitrary state power as instruments of an interiorized exile and to engage the complex political indictment that results from this comprehension. As for the sensibility whose unalterable pain drives Smith's sonnets through fifteen years of expanding popularity, both a historical understanding of the cult of feeling and a contemporary feminism should allow readers two centuries later a more sophisticated grasp of the personal and cultural dynamics at work than is expressed by Seward's dismissal. More particularly, later readers will be able to recognize the imperatives against which Smith as a professional poet had to position herself and the subtle shifts in literary history enacted by her as a result.

It is clear that unrequited love, as it is expressed in the Petrarchan system, would scarcely be thought an appropriate sentiment for a female voice in the first place, or at least for this female who was trying first to bail her husband out of prison and, later, having secured an agreement of separation from him, to maintain her precarious independence. That in the very first edition of the *Elegiac Sonnets* Smith produced studied variations on Petrarchan themes, and that later she headed her second volume with an epigraph from Petrarch, should alert the reader to her awareness both of the conventions of the traditional sonnet sequence and of the effect of her reversing its traditional gender roles. It is undoubtedly the case that Smith's reiterated sorrows are somewhat numbing, but if modern readers of poetry sat down to a complete course, stretching across centuries and cultures, in Petrarchan sexual frustration they might find themselves persuaded that Smith's contemplation of a threatened and unfulfilled life is less dependent on formula than are the dozens of poetic sequences spawned by Petrarch in the clubbish atmosphere of Europe's masculine renaissance. Her own accent on the isolated sensibility struck a responsive chord in her readers and her numerous followers, provoking a remarkable number of sorrowful sonnets in the ensuing decades. It might be justly claimed, however, that only when Wordsworth turned to the form in 1803, publishing his results in his 1807 volumes the year after her death, did any contemporary surpass the polished formal surface of her sonnets. The revival of the sonnet in British Romanticism was driven as much by Smith's dexterous artistic craft as by her themes.

One feature of the expanding editions of the *Elegiac Sonnets* that deserves accenting is the degree to which Smith attempts to position herself midway between the realms of art and reality. On the one hand, she celebrates her art as spontaneous: she is like the legendary nightingale in transmuting her personal sorrow into the brief liquidity of mellifluous song. But on the other hand, she emphasizes again and again that she belongs to a long tradition of singers and that her poems transmit a number of ventriloquized voices. The three sonnets after Petrarch in the first and second editions are joined in the expanded third by another, and the unity is immediately followed by a rendition of a Metastasio lyric; three sonnets taken from incidents in Goethe's *Werther* in the 1784 collection are likewise expanded to five in the third and fourth editions. With the fifth Smith adds three sonnets originally included in her first novel, *Emmeline*, and in the sixth another five from its successor, *Celestina*. Ten further sonnets from six other works would adorn later editions. When the two-volume sequence of *Elegiac Sonnets, and Other Poems* had attained its final state in 1800, there were in all thirty-six poems in the collection distinguished as not being her personal expressions. From such evidence one is led to observe how truly fitting was Smith's reputation as the best actress in her Kensington school.

That her epitaph recalled "a life of great and various sufferings" is not wholly owing to the effect of her writing in publicizing it; Smith's monument in Stoke Church, Guildford, Surrey, was, after all, erected by her surviving family. But in order to take the full measure of her art, it is important to hear the balancing voice of her sister, Catherine Anne

Dorset, who in her memoir emphasizes "the playful wit and peculiar vein of humour which distinguished her conversation," and who, calling to mind the happy vitality exemplified by her carefree youth, remarks: "Cheerfulness and gaiety were the natural characteristics of her mind." Although these qualities do appear in some of the poems attached to the editions of *Elegiac Sonnets* (namely, "The Origin of Flattery" and "Thirty-Eight"), perhaps they show to their finest effect where least to be expected, in the series of bird fables derived from Fontaine that Smith included, when crippled with a terminal illness, in the last of her naturalist books for children, *The History of Birds*, published after her death in 1807.

That same year saw the printing of her last volume of verse, *Beachy Head and Other Poems*, which, though clearly projected by her, was not left wholly ready for publication and to some extent reveals the intrusive hand of others: perhaps Mrs. Dorset, whose career as an author of imaginative children's books was just beginning; perhaps Joseph Johnson, the venerable publisher of England's liberal voices during the first phase of English Romanticism, to whose good offices this last volume was consigned. Since there are varying standards of punctuation and capitalization evident in the volume, one can presume the surviving manuscripts were left in different stages of finish. Unfortunately, the resulting textual problems may be insoluble. According to her sister, "Mrs Smith left no *posthumous* works whatever. The sweepings of her closet were, without exception, committed to the flames." It is unlikely, then, that we will ever be able to determine whether her masterpiece *Beachy Head* was as unfinished as the introductory note to the volume assumes it to be. From a modern experience of Romanticism, nurtured by the sometimes oblique narrative strategies of its major poets, a work that begins atop a massive feature of the landscape and ends immured within it bears a remarkable coherence, the more so since in no poem of the period can one find so powerful an impulse to resolve the self into nature. In its multitudinous, uncanny particularity, nature in "Beachy Head" represents a counter reality to that of human society and history. In a sense the whole volume, with its variety of natural treatments—from the opening meditative reminiscence through fable to allegory to didactive moralism and religious exemplum, all attended by an array of botanical, geological, and ornithological learning—testifies to an alternate Romanticism that seeks not to transcend or to absorb nature but to contemplate and honor its irreducible alterity. In both its psychological and ecological timbres Smith's final volume strikes distinctly modern chords.

None of the canonical male Romantic poets who lived long enough to grow old got better. Thus it may come as something of a surprise (though the experience is replicated among a number of women poets of the period) to observe Charlotte Smith, in her fifties and crippled by illness, attaining a technical mastery in her final volume that qualifies her to sit among the most select poets of this age. When she died on 28 October 1806 she was widely lamented, particularly by other women poets. They testified at once to her personal struggle for independence in the midst of misfortune and to the public position she so long sustained as a beacon to writers who emulated her popularity. Despite what Catherine Anne Dorset could memorialize as "a life so peculiarly and so invariably marked by adversity," there was in this poet whose first signature was "Charlotte Smith of Bignor Park, in Sussex" a seasoned professionalism that made her one of the exemplary writers of her age.

Note on the Text

The texts of Charlotte Smith's poetry are drawn from the last edition over which the author exercised editorial control, with modest emendations from other lifetime editions where comparison suggests a printer's error or idiosyncrasy in the copy text. Over the nearly quarter-century in which she published and reprinted her poetry, its punctuation varied with the fashion of the year and of the printer; so the variables are considerable in this respect. Variants in punctuation are noted, however, only where they materially affect the sense. Such accidental features of the copy text as capitalization are generally preserved; but other usages that are period oddities, such as the long s and repeated quotation marks at the beginning of each line, are quietly modernized. Smith's copious endnotes have been printed as footnotes, separated from the text by a short rule, with editorial interpolations inserted within brackets, and, where pertinent, variants or additions from other printings recorded. Punctuation interpolated by the editor has likewise been placed in brackets. Editorial footnotes are separated from the text and authorial notes by a full-width rule. The poems are printed according to the chronology of the volumes where they appear, which is roughly the chronology in which they are written, with the exception that Volume II of Smith's *Elegiac Sonnets,* issued in 1797 four years after the publication of *The Emigrants,* is here contiguous with Volume I, and the complete set of sonnets, originally divided at number 60, is thus grouped as a whole, with the miscellaneous poems that accompanied them in both volumes printed in sequence thereafter.

The base text for Sonnets 1 through 59, inclusive, and for the sequence of poems between the "Ode to Despair" and "Verses intended to have been prefixed to the novel of Emmeline" is the ninth edition of *Elegiac Sonnets,* Volume I (London, Cadell and Davies, 1800); Sonnets 60 through 92, and the sequence between "The Dead Beggar" and "Lydia," derive from the second edition of *Elegiac Sonnets,* Volume II (London: Cadell and Davies, 1800). Manuscript texts for *What is She?* (LS1253) are published by permission of the Henry E. Huntington Library. Smith's "Prologue" to *Antonio* was not published with the printed text; it too is printed here, by permission, from the manuscript (LA1306) in the Henry E. Huntington Library. Other manuscript variants are printed here by permission of the Berg Collection, New York Public Library. Cited editions and specific variants are listed in the Textual Notes at the end of this volume (page 313).

Elegiac Sonnets
and Other Poems

{ 1784–1797 }

EPIGRAPH TO VOLUME II.

Non t' appressar ove sia riso e canto
Canzone mio, nò, ma pianto:
Non fa per te di star con gente allegra
Vedova sconsolata, in vesta nigra.

PETRARCHA.

Epigraph. The conclusion to Petrarch's Sonnet 268: "Fuggi 'l sereno e 'l verde, / Non t'appresar ove sia riso o canto, / Canzon mia, no, ma pianto: / Non fa per te di star con gente allegra, / Vedova sconsolata, in vesta negra." [Flee serenity and renewal; approach not, my song, where there be smiles or singing, no, only tears: it will not do for you to remain among happy people, disconsolate widow, clothed in black.] Throughout her frequent citations of Petrarch Smith quotes loosely, a practice open to opposing interpretations, indicating an Italian either insecure or so fluent as to be stored in her memory.

TO WILLIAM HAYLEY, ESQ.

Sir,

While I ask your protection for these essays, I cannot deny having myself some esteem for them. Yet permit me to say, that did I not trust to your candour and sensibility, and hope they will plead for the errors your judgment must discover, I should never have availed myself of the liberty I have obtained—that of dedicating these simple effusions to the greatest modern Master of that charming talent, in which I can never be more than a distant copyist.

I am, Sir, Your most obedient and obliged Servant,

Charlotte Smith

Dedication. William Hayley (1745–1820), of Eartham, Sussex, Charlotte Smith's wealthy neighbor and one of the most popular of late eighteenth-century English poets, identified himself with liberal causes and patronized literary and artistic talent, including, besides Smith, William Cowper and William Blake.

PREFACE TO THE FIRST AND SECOND EDITIONS

The little Poems which are here called Sonnets, have, I believe, no very just claim to that title: but they consist of fourteen lines, and appear to me no improper vehicle for a single Sentiment. I am told, and I read it as the opinion of very good judges, that the legitimate Sonnet is ill calculated for our language. The specimen Mr. Hayley has given, though they form a strong exception, prove no more, than that the difficulties of the attempt vanish before uncommon powers.

Some very melancholy moments have been beguiled by expressing in verse the sensations those moments brought. Some of my friends, with partial indiscretion, have multiplied the copies they procured of several of these attempts, till they found their way into the prints of the day in a mutilated state; which, concurring with other circumstances, determined me to put them into their present form. I can hope for readers only among the few, who, to sensibility of heart, join simplicity of taste.

PREFACE TO THE THIRD AND FOURTH EDITIONS

The reception given by the public, as well as my particular friends, to the two first editions of these poems, has induced me to add to the present such other Sonnets as I have written since, or have recovered from my acquaintance, to whom I had given them without thinking well enough of them at the time to preserve any copies myself. A few of

---

Preface to the first and second editions. Line 5. **for our language**: a commonplace deriving from the definition of "Sonnet" in Dr. Johnson's *Dictionary of the English Language* (1750) as "not very suitable to the English language."

Line 15. **taste**: The original Preface concluded with a final paragraph omitted from the ensuing editions where Smith supplied notes: "The readers of poetry will meet with some lines borrowed from the most popular authors, which I have used only as quotations. Where such acknowledgment is omitted, I am unconscious of the theft."

those last written, I have attempted on the Italian model; with what success I know not; but I am persuaded that, to the generality of readers, those which are less regular will be more pleasing.

As a few notes were necessary, I have added them at the end. I have there quoted such lines as I have borrowed; and even where I am con-   10
scious the ideas were not my own, I have restored them to the original possessors.

PREFACE TO THE FIFTH EDITION

In printing a list of so many noble, literary, and respectable names, it would become me, perhaps, to make my acknowledgments to those friends, to whose exertions in my favor, rather than to any merit of my own, I owe the brilliant assemblage. With difficulty I repress what I feel on this subject; but in the conviction that such acknowledgments would be painful to them, I forbear publicly to speak of those particular obligations, the sense of which will ever be deeply impressed on my heart.

PREFACE TO THE SIXTH EDITION

When a sixth Edition of these little Poems was lately called for, it was proposed to me to add such Sonnets, or other pieces, as I might have written since the publication of the fifth[.]—Of these, however, I had

---

Preface to the third and fourth editions. Line 6. **Italian model**: The Italian sonnet, deriving from Petrarch's usage, uniformly rhymes the opening octave *abbaabba*: only two of Smith's follow this pattern. She is much more drawn to the Shakespearean model, whose three independently rhymed quatrains and final couplet structure forty-four of her sonnets. The rest are in various experimental hybrids, of a type then called "irregular." In the revival of the sonnet during the late eighteenth century the propriety of its rhymes and metrics was much debated.

Preface to the fifth edition. Line 1. **list ... names**: The fifth edition (1789), printed by subscription to help Smith support her children (see her note to Sonnet 82 on page 71) bears a subscription list of 817 names, strongly weighted to the aristocracy and the cultural and political establishment. It marks Smith's arrival in contemporary estimation as a poet of note.

only a few; and on shewing them to a friend, of whose judgment I had
an high opinion, he remarked that some of them, particularly "The
Sleeping Woodman," and "The Return of the Nightingale," resembled
in their subjects, and still more in the plaintive tone in which they are
written, the greater part of those in the former Editions—and that,
perhaps, some of a more lively cast might be better liked by the Pub-
lic—"'Toujours perdrix,'" said my friend—"'Toujours perdrix,' you 10
know, 'ne vaut rien.'—I am far from supposing that *your* compositions
can be neglected or disapproved, on whatever subject: but perhaps
'toujours Rossignols, toujours des chansons tristes,' may not be so well
received as if you attempted, what you would certainly execute as suc-
cessfully, a more cheerful style of composition." "'Alas!' replied I, 'Are
grapes gathered from thorns, or figs from thistles?' Or can the *effect*
cease, while the *cause* remains? *You know* that when in the Beech
Woods of Hampshire, I first struck the chords of the melancholy lyre,
its notes were never intended for the public ear! It was unaffected sor-
rows drew them forth: I wrote mournfully because I was unhappy— 20
And I have unfortunately no reason yet, though nine years have since
elapsed, to *change my tone.* The time is indeed arrived, when I have
been promised by 'the Honourable Men' who, *nine years ago,* under-
took to see that my family obtained the provision their grandfather
designed for them,— that 'all should be well, all should be settled.' But
still I am condemned to feel the 'hope delayed that maketh the heart
sick.' Still to receive—not a repetition of promises indeed—but of

---

Line 4. **friend:** According to Smith's sister, Catherine Anne Dorset, this friend is probably
Bryan Edwards, himself a poet.

Lines 10–11. **Toujours ... rien:** a saying attributed to the popular Henri IV, king of France,
to the effect that a daily diet of partridge is tiresome.

Line 13. **Toujours ... tristes:** "Always nightingales, always sad songs." The nightingale, in
legend, having been deserted in love, pressed her heart against a thorn and lamented her
fate in song.

Lines 15–16. **Are grapes ... thistles?:** Matt. 7:16.

Line 25. **settled:** an allusion to the Chancery suit to recover the moneys left in trust to her
children in her father-in-law's will; it was settled to Smith's advantage in 1798, but not
finally resolved until a few months before her death in 1806; the actual estate was legally
closed in 1807.

Lines 26–27. **hope ... sick:** "Hope deferred maketh the heart sick: but when the desire
cometh, it is a tree of life" (Prov. 13:12).

scorn and insult when I apply to those gentlemen, who, though they acknowledge that all impediments to a division of the estate they have undertaken to manage, are done away—will neither tell me *when* they will proceed to divide it, or *whether they will ever do so at all.* You know the circumstances under which I have now so long been labouring; and you have done me the honor to say, that few Women could so long have contended with them. With these, however, as they are some of them of a domestic and painful nature, I will not trouble the Public *now;* but while they exist in all their force, that indulgent Public must accept all I am able to achieve—'Toujours des Chansons tristes!'"

    Thus ended the short dialogue between my friend and me, and I repeat it as an apology for that apparent despondence, which, when it is observed for a long series of years, may look like affectation. *I shall be sorry,* if on some future occasion, I should feel myself compelled to detail its causes more at length; for, notwithstanding I am thus frequently appearing as an Authoress, and have derived from thence many of the greatest advantages of my life, (since it has procured me friends whose attachment is most invaluable,) I am well aware that for a woman— "The Post of Honor is a Private Station."

                                    London, May 14, 1792.

PREFACE TO VOLUME II

It so rarely happens that a second attempt in any species of writing equals the first, in the public opinion, when the first has been remarkably successful; that I send this second volume of small Poems into the world with a considerable degree of diffidence and apprehension.

    Whatever inferiority may be adjudged to it, I cannot plead want of

---

Line 46. The advice of Cato to his son Portius on survival in a wicked world: "'Content thyself to be obscurely good. / When vice prevails, and impious men bear sway, / The post of honour is a private station" (Joseph Addison, *Cato,* IV.iv.140–42).

Preface to Volume II. This preface, whose angry and defensive tone reflects the extremity of Smith's helplessness before the protracted legal process of the Chancery suit, was suppressed upon publication of the second edition of this volume in 1800.

time for its completion, if I should attempt any excuse at all; for I do not forget that more than three years have elapsed since I reluctantly yielded to the pressing instances of some of my friends;* and accepted their offers to promote a subscription to another volume of Poems—I say, accepted the offers of my friends, because (with a single exception) I   10 have never made any application myself.

Having once before had recourse to the indulgence of the public, in publishing a book by subscription, and knowing that it had been so often done by persons with whom it is honourable to be ranked, it was not pride that long withheld my consent from this manner of publication; and, certainly, the pecuniary inconveniencies I had been exposed to for so many years, never pressed upon me *more* heavily than at the moment this proposal was urged by my friends; if then I declined it, it was because I even at *that* period doubted, whether from extreme depression of spirit, I should have the power of fulfilling (so as to satisfy   20 myself) the engagement I must feel myself bound by, the moment I had accepted subscriptions.

Could any one of the misfortunes that so rapidly followed have been foreseen, nothing should have induced me to have consented to it—for what expectation could I entertain of resisting such calamities as the detention of their property has brought on my children? Of four sons, all seeking in other climates the competence denied them in this, two were (for that reason) driven from their prospects in the Church to the Army, where one of them was maimed during the first campaign he served in, and is now a lieutenant of invalids. The loveliest, the most   30 beloved of my daughters, the darling of all her family, was torn from us for ever. The rest deprived of every advantage to which they are entitled;

---

* Particularly those of Joseph Cooper Walker, Esq. of Dublin, by whose friendly and successful applications in Ireland I am particularly obliged. [Walker (1761–1810), a long time friend of Smith's, was a Dublin antiquarian who wrote a volume of memoirs of early Irish bards as well as studies of Italian drama.]

Line 30. **invalids**: Charles Dyer Smith (born February 1773) suffered the amputation of his leg in the siege of Dunkirk in 1793.

Lines 30–32. **The loveliest ... for ever**: Anna Augusta De Foville, Smith's favorite daughter, died in April 1795. Smith refers to this melancholy event throughout this volume of poetry.

and the means of proper education for my youngest son denied me! while the money that their inhuman trustees have suffered yearly to be wasted, and what they keep possession of on false and frivolous pretences, would, if paid to those it belongs to, have saved me and them from all these now irremediable misfortunes.

I am well aware that the present is not a time when the complaints of individuals against private wrong are likely to be listened to; nor is this an opportunity fit to make those complaints; but I know so much   40 has been said, (so much more than so trifling a matter could be worth) of the *delay* of this publication, that it becomes in some measure a matter of self-defence, to account for that delay. Those who have expressed such impatience for it, were apprehensive (indeed they owned they were) of the loss of the half guinea they had paid. I have more than once thought of returning their money, rather than have remained under any obligation to persons who could suspect me of a design to accumulate, by gathering subscriptions for a work I never meant to publish, a sum, which no contrivance, no success, was likely to make equal to one year of the income I ought to possess. Surely, any who   50 have entertained and *expressed* such an opinion of me, must either never have understood, *or must have forgotten,* what I was, what I am, or what I ought to be.

To be suspected even by arrogant ignorance of such an intention to impose on public generosity, has not been the least among the mortifications I have within these last years been subjected to; I place them to the same long account of injuries, where this, however, is almost lost in the magnitude of others! Let not the censors of literary productions, or the fastidious in private life, again reprove me for bringing forward "with querulous egotism," the mention of myself, and the sorrows, of   60 which the men, who have withheld my family property, have been the occasion. Had they never so unjustly possessed, and so shamelessly exercised the power of reducing me to pecuniary distress, I should never, perhaps, have had occasion to ask the consideration of the *reader,* or to deprecate the severity of the *critic.* Certainly I should never have been compelled to make excuses as a defaulter in point of *punctuality* to the *subscriber.* Nor should I to any of these have found it necessary to state the causes that have rendered me miserable as an *individual,* though *now* I am compelled to complain of those who have crushed the poor abilities of the *author,* and by the most unheard of acts of injustice *(for twice seven years)* have added the painful sensations of *indignation* to the inconveniencies and deprivations of indigence; and aggravating by future dread, the present suffering, have frequently doubled the toil necessary for to-morrow, by palsying the hand and distracting the head, that were struggling against the evils of to-day!

It is passed!—The injuries I have so long suffered under are not mitigated; the aggressors are not removed: but however soon they may be disarmed of their power, any retribution in this world is impossible—they can neither give back to the maimed the possession of health, or restore the dead. The time they have occasioned me to pass in anxiety, in sorrow, in anguish, they cannot recall to me[.]—To my children they can make no amends, but they would not if they could; nor have I the poor consolation of knowing that I leave in the callous hearts of these persons, *thorns* to

"goad and sting them,"

for they have conquered or outlived all sensibility of shame; they are alive neither to honesty, honour, or humanity; and at this moment, far from feeling compunction for the ruin they have occasioned, the dreadful misfortunes they have been the authors of, one shrinks from the very attempt to make such redress as he might yet give, and wraps himself up in the callous insolence of his imagined consequence; while the other uses such professional subterfuges as are the disgrace of his profession, to baffle me yet a little longer in my attempts to procure that restitution, that justice, which they dare not deny I am entitled to; and to insult me by a continuation of tormenting chicaneries, perpetuating to the utmost of their power the distresses they have occasioned, and which their perseverance in iniquity has already put it out of the power of Heaven itself to remedy!

Would to God I could dismiss these oppressors from my mind for ever, as I now do from the notice of any future readers, whom I may

---

Lines 89–93. **one shrinks … his profession:** Smith refers to the principal trustees of the estate of Richard Smith, his son-in-law John Robinson and the lawyer Anthony Parkyn.

engage to any work of mine, (though very probably I may now take my
last leave of the public). And let me, while I account for the delay of this
work, and for many defects that may perhaps be found in it, assign the
causes for both, and lament that such have been the circumstances
under which I have composed it, as may rather render it a wonder I
have produced it at all, than that it has been so long in appearing, and
yet appears defective. Surely I shall be forgiven once more for "queru-
lous egotism," when the disadvantages I have laboured under are con-
sidered; complaint may be pardoned when the consequences of what I
deplore, mingle themselves in all my feelings, embitter every hour of my   110
life, and leave me no hope but in the oblivion of the grave.

Some degree of pride which

"Still travels on, nor leaves us till we die,"

makes me somewhat solicitous to account for the visible difference in
point of numbers between the subscribers to this and the former vol-
ume. If I were willing to admit that these Poems are inferior to those
that preceeded them, I know that such a supposition would not have
withheld a single subscription—but I also know, that as party can raise
prejudices against the colour of a ribband, or the cut of a cape, it gener-
ates still stranger antipathies, even in regard to things almost equally tri-   120
fling. And *there are,* who can never forgive an author that has, in the
story of a Novel, or the composition of a Sonnet, ventured to hint at
any opinions different from those which these liberal-minded person-
ages are determined to find the best.

I know, therefore, perfectly well, how I have sinned against some ci-
devant, I was going to say friends, but I check myself, and change the
word for acquaintance,

"Since friendship should be made of stronger stuff,"

acquaintance, who when my writing first obtained popularity, erected

---

Line 113. **Still ... die:** "See some strange comfort ev'ry state attend, / And Pride bestow'd on
all, a common friend; / See some fit Passion ev'ry age supply / Hope travels thro', nor quits
us when we die" (Pope, *Essay on Man,* lines 271–74).

Line 128. **Since ... stuff:** apparently a play against Mark Antony's funeral oration: "Ambi-
tion should be made of sterner stuff" (*Julius Caesar,* III.ii.92).

themselves into patrons and patronesses. To the favor they *then* conferred I am not insensible; and I hope they will accept it as a proof of my perfectly understanding the extent of the obligation, that I have so silently acquiesced in not expecting it to be repeated, and have never suffered them to be put under the painful necessity of avowing their dereliction in 1797, of the writer whom they affected so warmly to patronize in 1787. Ten years do indeed operate most wonderful changes in this state of existence.

Perhaps in addition to the friends, or *soi-disant tel,* whose notice and whose names have for some such causes as these, been withheld, I might add as *another cause,* that for many months past I have been so apprehensive of not having health enough to superintend the publication of even this small volume, that I had desired those few friends who had voluntarily engaged to collect subscriptions, not to persevere in their kind endeavours; and I had written to my elder sons, entreating them, should death overtake me before I could complete my engagements, to place, as soon afterwards as they could, in the hands of Messrs. Cadell and Davies, a sum sufficient to reimburse them any expences they might have incurred, and to repay the subscriptions.

I am at length enabled to send it into the world—and have certainly omitted nothing that was in my power to make it not intirely unworthy the general favor, and of the particular kindness of *those* without whose support I believe it would have been impossible for me to have prepared the few verses I had by me, or to have composed others. That these are gloomy, none will surely have a right to complain; for I never engaged they should be gay. But I am unhappily exempt from the suspicion of *feigning* sorrow for an opportunity of shewing the pathos with which it can be described—a suspicion that has given rise to much ridicule, and many invidious remarks, among certain critics, and others, who carry into their closets the same aversion to any thing tragic, as influences, at the present period, their theatrical taste.

It is, indeed, a melancholy truth, that at this time there is so much tragedy in real life, that those who having escaped private calamity, can

---

Line 138. **soi-disant tel**: such as call themselves friends.

withdraw their minds a moment from that which is general, very naturally prefer to melancholy books, or tragic representations, those lighter and gayer amusements, which exhilarate the senses, and throw a transient veil over the extensive and still threatening desolation, that overspreads this country, and in some degree, every quarter of the world.

CHARLOTTE SMITH.

May 15th 1797.

ELEGIAC SONNETS AND
OTHER POEMS

I

The partial Muse has from my earliest hours
    Smiled on the rugged path I'm doom'd to tread,
And still with sportive hand has snatch'd wild flowers,
    To weave fantastic garlands for my head:
But far, far happier is the lot of those   5
    Who never learn'd her dear delusive art;
Which, while it decks the head with many a rose,
    Reserves the thorn to fester in the heart.
For still she bids soft Pity's melting eye
    Stream o'er the ills she knows not to remove,   10
Points every pang, and deepens every sigh
    Of mourning Friendship, or unhappy Love.
Ah! then, how dear the Muse's favours cost,
If those paint sorrow best—who feel it most! *

II
Written at the close of spring

The garlands fade that Spring so lately wove,
    Each simple flower which she had nursed in dew,
Anemonies,† that spangled every grove,
    The primrose wan, and hare-bell mildly blue.

---

* "The well-sung woes shall soothe my pensive ghost; / He best can paint them who shall feel them most." Pope's "Eloisa to Abelard," 366th line.

† Anemonies. *Anemony Nemeroso.* The wood Anemony.

Sonnet 1. Line 1. **partial**: friendly; beneficial.

Line 8. **thorn ... heart**: alluding to the song of Philomela, the nightingale: see Smith's Preface to the sixth edition.

No more shall violets linger in the dell,   5
    Or purple orchis variegate the plain,
Till Spring again shall call forth every bell,
    And dress with humid hands her wreaths again.—
Ah! poor Humanity! so frail, so fair,
    Are the fond visions of thy early day,   10
Till tyrant Passion, and corrosive Care,
    Bid all thy fairy colours fade away!
Another May new buds and flowers shall bring;
Ah! why has happiness—no second Spring?

III

To a nightingale*

Poor melancholy bird—that all night long
    Tell'st to the Moon thy tale of tender woe;
    From what sad cause can such sweet sorrow flow,
And whence this mournful melody of song ?

Thy poet's musing fancy would translate   5
    What mean the sounds that swell thy little breast,
    When still at dewy eve thou leavest thy nest,
Thus to the listening night to sing thy fate.

Pale Sorrow's victims wert thou once among,
    Tho' now released in woodlands wild to rove?   10
    Say—hast thou felt from friends some cruel wrong,
Or died'st thou—martyr of disastrous love?
Ah! songstress sad! that such my lot might be,
To sigh, and sing at liberty—like thee!

---

* The idea from the 43rd Sonnet of Petrarch. *Secondo parte.* "Quel rosigniuol, che si soave piagne." [With so highly traditional a subject, the specific influence of Petrarch's verse on this sonnet is at most slight.]

IV
To the moon

Queen of the silver bow!—by thy pale beam,
   Alone and pensive, I delight to stray,
And watch thy shadow trembling in the stream,
   Or mark the floating clouds that cross thy way.
And while I gaze, thy mild and placid light   5
   Sheds a soft calm upon my troubled breast;
And oft I think—fair planet of the night,
   That in thy orb, the wretched may have rest:
The sufferers of the earth perhaps may go,
   Released by death—to thy benignant sphere;   10
And the sad children of Despair and Woe
   Forget, in thee, their cup of sorrow here.
Oh! that I soon may reach thy world serene,
Poor wearied pilgrim—in this toiling scene!

V
To the South Downs

Ah! hills belov'd!—where once a happy child,
   Your beechen shades, "your turf, your flowers among,"*
I wove your blue-bells into garlands wild,
   And woke your echoes with my artless song.
Ah! hills belov'd!—your turf, your flowers remain;   5
   But can they peace to this sad breast restore;
For one poor moment soothe the sense of pain,

---

* "Whose turf, whose shades, whose flowers among." Gray [Thomas Gray, "Ode on a Distant Prospect of Eton College," line 8].

Sonnet 4. Line 1. **Queen of the silver bow**: Diana, classical goddess of the moon.

Sonnet 5. Title. **Downs**: the high grassland overlooking the Sussex coast, a frequent site for Smith's poetry.

And teach a breaking heart to throb no more?
And you, Aruna!*—in the vale below,
    As to the sea your limpid waves you bear,   10
Can you one kind Lethean cup bestow,
    To drink a long oblivion to my care?
Ah! no!—when all, e'en Hope's last ray is gone,
There's no oblivion—but in death alone!

VI

To hope

O Hope! thou soother sweet of human woes!
    How shall I lure thee to my haunts forlorn?
For me wilt thou renew the wither'd rose,
    And clear my painful path of pointed thorn?
Ah, come, sweet nymph! in smiles and softness drest,   5
    Like the young Hours that lead the tender Year,
Enchantress! come, and charm my cares to rest:—
    Alas! the flatterer flies, and will not hear!
A prey to fear, anxiety, and pain,
    Must I a sad existence still deplore?   10
Lo!—the flowers fade, but all the thorns remain,
    "For me the vernal garland blooms no more."†
Come then, "pale Misery's love!" be thou my cure,°
And I will bless thee, who, tho' slow, art sure.

---

* The river Arun.

† Pope's "Imitation of the first Ode of the fourth Book of Horace" [line 32].

° Shakspeare's *King John* [III.iv.35].

Sonnet 5. Line 11. **Lethean**: Water from the river Lethe, in classical myth, erased the memory of earlier life for souls returning to earth to be born again.

VII

On the departure of the nightingale

Sweet poet of the woods!—a long adieu!
    Farewel, soft minstrel of the early year!
Ah! 'twill be long ere thou shalt sing anew,
    And pour thy music on "the Night's dull ear."*
Whether on Spring thy wandering flights await,†   5
    Or whether silent in our groves you dwell,
The pensive Muse shall own thee for her mate,°
    And still protect the song she loves so well.
With cautious step the love-lorn youth shall glide
    Thro' the lone brake that shades thy mossy nest;   10
And shepherd girls from eyes profane shall hide
    The gentle bird, who sings of pity best:
For still thy voice shall soft affections move,
And still be dear to Sorrow, and to Love!

VIII

To spring

Again the wood, and long-withdrawing vale,
    In many a tint of tender green are drest,
Where the young leaves, unfolding, scarce conceal
    Beneath their early shade, the half-form'd nest
Of finch or woodlark; and the primrose pale,   5
    And lavish cowslip, wildly scatter'd round,
Give their sweet spirits to the sighing gale.
    Ah! season of delight!—could aught be found
    To soothe awhile the tortured bosom's pain,

---

* Shakspeare [*Henry V.* Prologue. 11].

† Alludes to the supposed migration of the Nightingale.

° "Whether the Muse or Love call thee his mate. / Both them I serve, and of their train am I." Milton's "First Sonnet" ["O nightingale," lines 13–14].

Of Sorrow's rankling shaft to cure the wound,   10
    And bring life's first delusions once again,
'Twere surely met in thee!—thy prospect fair,
Thy sounds of harmony, thy balmy air,
Have power to cure all sadness—but despair.*

IX

Blest is yon shepherd, on the turf reclined,
    Who on the varied clouds which float above
Lies idly gazing—while his vacant mind
    Pours out some tale antique of rural love!
Ah! *he* has never felt the pangs that move   5
Th' indignant spirit, when with selfish pride,
Friends, on whose faith the trusting heart rely'd,
    Unkindly shun th' imploring eye of woe!
The ills they ought to soothe, with taunts deride,
    And laugh at tears themselves have forced to flow.†   10
Nor *his* rude bosom those fine feelings melt,
    Children of Sentiment and Knowledge born,
Thro' whom each shaft with cruel force is felt,
    Empoison'd by deceit—or barb'd with scorn.

X

To Mrs. G.

Ah! why will Mem'ry with officious care
    The long-lost visions of my days renew?
Why paint the vernal landscape green and fair,
    When Life's gay dawn was opening to my view?

---

* "To the heart inspires / Vernal delight and joy, able to drive / All sadness but despair."
[Milton,] *Paradise Lost,* Fourth Book [IV.154–56].

† "And hard Unkindness' alter'd eye, / That mocks the tear it forced to flow." Thomas Gray
["Ode on a Distant Prospect of Eton College," lines 76–77].

Ah! wherefore bring those moments of delight,   5
    When with my Anna, on the southern shore,
I thought the future, as the present, bright?
    Ye dear delusions!—ye return no more!
Alas! how diff'rent does the truth appear,
    From the warm picture youth's rash hand pourtrays!   10
How fades the scene, as we approach it near,
    And pain and sorrow strike—how many ways!
Yet of that tender heart, ah! still retain
A share for me—and I will not complain.

XI

·

To sleep

Come, balmy Sleep! tired Nature's soft resort!
    On these sad temples all thy poppies shed;
And bid gay dreams, from Morpheus' airy court,
    Float in light vision round my aching head!*
Secure of all thy blessings, partial Power!   5
    On his hard bed the peasant throws him down;
And the poor sea-boy, in the rudest hour,
    Enjoys thee more than he who wears a crown.†
Clasp'd in her faithful shepherd's guardian arms,
    Well may the village-girl sweet slumbers prove;   10

---

* "Float in light vision round the poet's head." Mason [William Mason, "Elegy V. On the Death of a Lady" (1760), line 12].

† "Wilt thou upon the high and giddy mast / Seal up the ship boy's eyes, and rock his brains / In cradle of the rude impetuous surge?" Shakspeare's *Henry IV* [*II Henry IV:* III.i.18–20; "imperious surge" in original].

Sonnet 11. Line 1. **resort:** compare Edward Young's *Night Thoughts*, "Night 1," line 1: "Tir'd Nature's sweet restorer, balmy Sleep!"

Line 3. **Morpheus:** Greek god of sleep.   Line 5. **partial:** friendly; beneficial.

And they, O gentle Sleep! still taste thy charms,
   Who wake to labour, liberty, and love.
But still thy opiate aid dost thou deny
To calm the anxious breast, to close the streaming eye.

XII

Written on the sea shore.—October, 1784

On some rude fragment of the rocky shore,
   Where on the fractured cliff the billows break,
   Musing, my solitary seat I take,
And listen to the deep and solemn roar.

O'er the dark waves the winds tempestuous howl;   5
   The screaming sea-bird quits the troubled sea:
   But the wild gloomy scene has charms for me,
And suits the mournful temper of my soul.*

Already shipwreck'd by the storms of Fate,
   Like the poor mariner, methinks, I stand,   10
   Cast on a rock; who sees the distant land
From whence no succour comes—or comes too late.
Faint and more faint are heard his feeble cries,
'Till in the rising tide the exhausted sufferer dies.

---

* Young [Zanga, the hero of Edward Young's once-popular tragedy, *The Revenge* (1721), begins the play in high-pitched soliloquy: "Rage on, ye winds, burst clouds, and waters roar! / You bear a just resemblance of my fortune, / And suit the gloomy habit of my soul" (I.i.5–7)].

XIII
From Petrarch

Oh! place me where the burning noon*
    Forbids the wither'd flower to blow;
Or place me in the frigid zone,
    On mountains of eternal snow:
Let me pursue the steps of Fame,   5
    Or Poverty's more tranquil road;
Let youth's warm tide my veins inflame,
    Or sixty winters chill my blood:
Tho' my fond soul to heaven were flown,
    Or tho' on earth 'tis doom'd to pine,   10
Prisoner or free—obscure or known,
    My heart, O Laura, still is thine.
Whate'er my destiny may be,
That faithful heart still burns for thee!

XIV
From Petrarch

Loose to the wind her golden tresses stream'd,†
    Forming bright waves with amorous Zephyr's sighs;
    And tho' averted now, her charming eyes
Then with warm love, and melting pity beam'd.
Was I deceived?—Ah! surely, nymph divine!   5
    That fine suffusion on thy cheek was love;
    What wonder then those beauteous tints should move,
Should fire this heart, this tender heart of mine!
Thy soft melodious voice, thy air, thy shape,

---

* "Pommi ove'l Sol, occide i fiori e l'erba." Petrarch, *Sonnetto 112. Parte primo* [Sonnet 145: Smith does borrow Petrarch's underlying conception, but she treats it independently].

† "Erano i capei d'oro all aura [a l'aura] sparsi." *Sonnetto 69. Parte primo* [Sonnet 90].

Were of a goddess—not a mortal maid;   10
    Yet tho' thy charms, thy heavenly charms should fade,
My heart, my tender heart could not escape;
    Nor cure for me in time or change be found:
    The shaft extracted does not cure the wound!

XV

From Petrarch

Where the green leaves exclude the summer beam,*
    And softly bend as balmy breezes blow,
And where, with liquid lapse, the lucid stream
    Across the fretted rock is heard to flow,
Pensive I lay: when she whom earth conceals,   5
    As if still living to my eyes appears,
And pitying Heaven her angel form reveals,
    To say—"Unhappy Petrarch, dry your tears;
Ah! why, sad lover! thus before your time,
    In grief and sadness should your life decay,   10
And like a blighted flower, your manly prime
    In vain and hopeless sorrow fade away?
Ah! yield not thus to culpable despair,
But raise thine eyes to Heaven—and think I wait thee there."

---

* "Se lamentar augelli o verdi fronde." *Sonnetto 21. Parte secondo* [Sonnet 279].

XVI
From Petrarch

Ye vales and woods! fair scenes of happier hours;*
    Ye feather'd people, tenants of the grove;
And you, bright stream! befringed with shrubs and flowers;
    Behold my grief, ye witnesses of love!

For ye beheld my infant passion rise,   5
    And saw thro' years unchang'd my faithful flame;
Now cold, in dust, the beauteous object lies,
    And you, ye conscious scenes, are still the same!

While busy Memory still delights to dwell
    On all the charms these bitter tears deplore,   10
And with a trembling hand describes too well
    The angel form I shall behold no more!
To heaven she's fled! and nought to me remains
But the pale ashes which her urn contains.

XVII
From the thirteenth cantata of Metastasio†

On thy grey bark, in witness of my flame,
    I carve Miranda's cipher—Beauteous tree!
Graced with the lovely letters of her name,
    Henceforth be sacred to my love and me!

---

* "Valle che de lamenti miei se piena." *Sonnetto 33. Parte secondo* [Sonnet 301].

† "Scrivo in te l'amato nome / Di colei, per cui, mi moro." This is not meant as a translation; the original is much longer, and full of images, which could not be introduced in a Sonnet.—And some of them, though very beautiful in the Italian, would not appear to advantage in an English dress.

Sonnet 17. Title. **Metastasio**: Pietro Trapassi, known as Metastasio (1698–1782), was Italy's major poet of the Enlightenment; his thirteenth cantata is entitled "Il Nome" ("The Name"), and the quoted lines read, "I write on you the beloved name of her for whom I die."

Tho' the tall elm, the oak, and darker pine,   5
    With broader arms may noon's fierce ardors break,
To shelter me, and her I love, be thine;
    And thine to see her smile and hear her speak.
No bird, ill-omen'd, round thy graceful head
    Shall clamour harsh, or wave his heavy wing,   10
But fern and flowers arise beneath thy shade,
    Where the wild bees their lullabies shall sing.
And in thy boughs the murmuring ring-dove rest;
And there the nightingale shall build her nest.

XVIII

To the Earl of Egremont

Wyndham! 'tis not thy blood, tho' pure it runs,
    Thro' a long line of glorious ancestry,
Percys and Seymours, Britain's boasted sons,
    Who trust the honors of their race to thee:

'Tis not thy splendid domes, where Science loves   5
    To touch the canvas, and the bust to raise;
Thy rich domains, fair fields, and spreading groves,
    'Tis not all these the Muse delights to praise:

In birth, and wealth, and honors, great thou art!
    But nobler in thy independent mind;   10
And in that liberal hand and feeling heart
    Given thee by Heaven—a blessing to mankind!
Unworthy oft may titled fortune be;
A soul like thine—is true Nobility!

Sonnet 18. Title. **Egremont**: Sir George O'Brien Wyndham, third Earl of Egremont (1751–1837), a Sussex luminary renowned for his charity, his artistic patronage, and his liberal Whig politics. He became a trustee of the Smith inheritance in 1797, but his subsequent blunders greatly taxed and finally embittered the poet. In his later years he gave the painter J. M. W. Turner a studio in his home, Petworth House.

XIX

To Mr. Hayley, on receiving some
elegant lines from him

For me the Muse a simple band design'd
    Of "idle" flowers that bloom the woods among,
Which, with the cypress and the willow join'd,
    A garland form'd as artless as my song.
And little dared I hope its transient hours   5
    So long would last; composed of buds so brief;
'Till Hayley's hand among the vagrant flowers
    Threw from his verdant crown a deathless leaf.
For high in Fame's bright fane has Judgment placed
    The laurel wreath Serena's poet won,   10
Which, woven with myrtles by the hands of Taste,
    The Muse decreed for this her favorite son.
And those immortal leaves his temples shade,
Whose fair, eternal verdure—shall not fade!

XX

To the Countess of A——. Written on the
anniversary of her marriage

On this blest day may no dark cloud, or shower,
    With envious shade the Sun's bright influence hide!
But all his rays illume the favour'd hour,
    That saw thee, Mary!—Henry's lovely bride!

Sonnet 19. Title. **Mr. Hayley:** William Hayley, who helped secure publication for the *Elegiac Sonnets* and to whom Smith dedicated her first two editions.

Line 3. **cypress ... willow:** trees associated with mourning.

Line 10. **Serena's poet:** Serena is the heroine of Hayley's very popular poem about female conduct, *The Triumphs of Temper* (1781). Later editions were illustrated by William Blake.

Sonnet 20. Title. **marriage:** Mary, Lady Abergavenny (1760–1796), married Henry Nevill, Earl of Abergavenny (1755–1843), on 3 October 1781. She was the daughter of John Robinson, Charlotte Smith's brother-in-law through her marriage.

With years revolving may it still arise,   5
    Blest with each good approving Heaven can send!
And still, with ray serene, shall those blue eyes
    Enchant the husband, and attach the friend!

For you fair Friendship's amaranth shall blow,
    And Love's own thornless roses bind your brow;   10
And when—long hence—to happier worlds you go,
    Your beauteous race shall be what you are now!
And future Nevills thro' long ages shine,
With hearts as good, and forms as fair as thine!

XXI
Supposed to be written by Werter

Go, cruel tyrant of the human breast!
    To other hearts thy burning arrows bear;
Go where fond Hope, and fair Illusion rest;
    Ah! why should Love inhabit with Despair!
Like the poor maniac* I linger here,   5
    Still haunt the scene where all my treasure lies;
Still seek for flowers where only thorns appear,
    "And drink delicious poison from her eyes!"†
Tow'rds the deep gulf that opens on my sight
    I hurry forward, Passion's helpless slave!   10

---

* See the "Story of the Lunatic." "Is this the destiny of man? Is he only happy before he possesses his reason, or after he has lost it?—Full of hope you go to gather flowers in Winter, and are grieved not to find any—and do not know why they cannot be found." *Sorrows of Werter. Volume Second.*

† Alexander Pope ["Still on thy breast enamour'd let me lie, / Still drink delicious poison from thy eye, / Pant on thy lip, and to thy heart be presssed." "Eloisa to Abelard," lines 121–23].

Sonnet 20. Line 9. **amaranth ... blow**: the immortal flower of paradise will put forth blossoms.

And scorning Reason's mild and sober light,
    Pursue the path that leads me to the grave!
So round the flame the giddy insect flies,
And courts the fatal fire by which it dies!

XXII

By the same. To solitude

O Solitude! to thy sequester'd vale*
    I come to hide my sorrow and my tears,
And to thy echoes tell the mournful tale
    Which scarce I trust to pitying Friendship's ears!
Amidst thy wild-woods, and untrodden glades,   5
    No sounds but those of melancholy move;
And the low winds that die among thy shades,
    Seem like soft Pity's sighs for hopeless love!
And sure some story of despair and pain,
    In yon deep copse thy murm'ring doves relate;   10
And, hark, methinks in that long plaintive strain,
    Thine own sweet songstress weeps my wayward fate!
Ah, Nymph! that fate assist me to endure,
And bear awhile—what Death alone can cure!

---

* "I climb steep rocks, I break my way through copses, among thorns and briars which tear me to pieces, and I feel a little relief." *Sorrows of Werter. Volume First.*

Sonnet 22. Line 12. **songstress**: the nightingale.

XXIII
By the same. To the North Star

To thy bright beams* I turn my swimming eyes,
    Fair, fav'rite planet! which in happier days
Saw my young hopes, ah! faithless hopes!—arise,
    And on my passion shed propitious rays!
Now nightly wandering 'mid the tempests drear   5
    That howl the woods and rocky steeps among,
I love to see thy sudden light appear
    Thro' the swift clouds—driven by the wind along;
Or in the turbid water, rude and dark,
    O'er whose wild stream the gust of Winter raves,   10
Thy trembling light with pleasure still I mark,
    Gleam in faint radiance on the foaming waves!
So o'er my soul short rays of reason fly,
Then fade:—and leave me to despair, and die!

XXIV
By the same

Make there my tomb, beneath the lime-tree's shade,†
    Where grass and flowers in wild luxuriance wave;
Let no memorial mark where I am laid,
    Or point to common eyes the lover's grave!
But oft at twilight morn, or closing day,   5
    The faithful friend with falt'ring step shall glide,

---

* "The greater Bear, favourite of all the constellations; for when I left you of an evening it used to shine opposite your window." *Sorrows of Werter. Volume Second.*

† "At the corner of the church-yard which looks towards the fields, there are two lime trees—it is there I wish to rest." *Sorrows of Werter. Volume Second.*

Sonnet 23. Title. **North Star**: the fixed point for navigation.

Tributes of fond regret by stealth to pay,
     And sigh o'er the unhappy suicide!
And sometimes, when the sun with parting rays
     Gilds the long grass that hides my silent bed,   10
The tears shall tremble in my CHARLOTTE's eyes;
     Dear, precious drops!—they shall embalm the dead!
Yes—CHARLOTTE o'er the mournful spot shall weep,
Where her poor WERTER—and his sorrows sleep!

XXV

By the same. Just before his death

Why should I wish to hold in this low sphere*
     "A frail and feverish being?" Wherefore try
Poorly from day to day to linger here,
     Against the powerful hand of Destiny?
By those who know the force of hopeless care   5
     On the worn heart—I sure shall be forgiven,
If to elude dark guilt, and dire despair,
     I go uncall'd—to mercy and to heaven!
O thou! to save whose peace I now depart,
     Will thy soft mind thy poor lost friend deplore,   10
When worms shall feed on this devoted heart,
     Where even thy image shall be found no more?†
Yet may thy pity mingle not with pain,
For then thy hapless lover—dies in vain!

---

* "May my death remove every obstacle to your happiness.—Be at peace, I intreat you be at peace." *Sorrows of Werter. Volume Second.*

† From a line in Rousseau's *Eloisa.* [With Goethe's *Werther,* Rousseau's novel *Julie, ou la nouvelle Héloïse* (1761) was a staple of the cult of sensibility in late eighteenth-century Europe.]

XXVI
To the River Arun

On thy wild banks, by frequent torrents worn,
    No glittering fanes, or marble domes appear,
Yet shall the mournful Muse thy course adorn,
    And still to her thy rustic waves be dear.
For with the infant Otway,* lingering here,   5
    Of early woes she bade her votary dream,
While thy low murmurs sooth'd his pensive ear,
    And still the poet—consecrates the stream.
Beneath the oak and birch that fringe thy side,
    The first-born violets of the year shall spring;   10
And in thy hazles, bending o'er the tide,
    The earliest nightingale delight to sing:
While kindred spirits, pitying, shall relate
Thy Otway's sorrows, and lament his fate!

XXVII

Sighing I see yon little troop at play,
    By Sorrow yet untouch'd, unhurt by Care;
While free and sportive they enjoy to-day,
    "Content and careless of to-morrow's fare!"†
O happy age! when Hope's unclouded ray   5
    Lights their green path, and prompts their simple mirth;

---

* Otway was born at Trotten, a village in Sussex. Of Woolbeding, another village on the banks of the Arun (which runs through them both), his father was rector. Here it was, therefore, that he probably passed many of his early years. The Arun is here an inconsiderable stream, winding in a channel deeply worn, among meadow, heath, and wood.

† Thomson [James Thomson, *The Seasons,* "Autumn," line 191].

Sonnet 26. Line 5. **Otway:** Thomas Otway (1652–1685), although a popular playwright and author of the enduring tragedy *Venice Preserved* (1681), lived in extreme poverty in his final years.

Ere yet they feel the thorns that lurking lay
    To wound the wretched pilgrims of the earth;
Making them rue the hour that gave them birth,
    And threw them on a world so full of pain,   10
Where prosperous folly treads on patient worth,
    And, to deaf Pride, Misfortune pleads in vain!
Ah!—for their future fate how many fears
Oppress my heart—and fill mine eyes with tears!

XXVIII
To friendship

O Thou! whose name too often is profaned;
    Whose charms celestial few have hearts to feel!
Unknown to Folly—and by Pride disdained!
    —To thy soft solace may my sorrows steal!
Like the fair moon, thy mild and genuine ray   5
    Thro' Life's long evening shall unclouded last;
While Pleasure's frail attachments fleet away,
    As fades the rainbow from the northern blast!
'Tis thine, O Nymph! with "balmy hands to bind"*
    The wounds inflicted in Misfortune's storm,   10
        And blunt severe Affliction's sharpest dart!
—'Tis thy pure spirit warms my Anna's mind,
    Beams thro' the pensive softness of her form,
        And holds its altar—on her spotless heart!

---

* Collins ["O Thou, the Friend of Man assign'd, / With balmy Hands his Wounds to bind."
William Collins, "Ode to Pity," line 2].

XXIX

To Miss C—on being desired to attempt
writing a comedy

Would'st thou then have *me* tempt the comic scene
   Of gay Thalia? used so long to tread
   The gloomy paths of Sorrow's cypress shade;
And the lorn lay with sighs and tears to stain?
Alas! how much unfit her sprightly vein,   5
   Arduous to try!—and seek the sunny mead,
   And bowers of roses, where she loves to lead
The sportive subjects of her golden reign!
Enough for me, if still to soothe my days,
   Her fair and pensive sister condescend   10
With tearful smile to bless my simple lays;
   Enough, if her soft notes she sometimes lend,
To gain for me of feeling hearts the praise,
   And chiefly thine, my ever partial friend!

Sonnet 29. Title. **comedy**: An anonymous comedy of 1798, *What is She?*, has been attrib-
uted to Smith.

Line 2. **Thalia**: the muse of comedy.   Line 10. **sister**: Erato, the muse of lyric poetry.

XXX
To the River Arun

Be the proud Thames of trade the busy mart!
    Arun! to thee will other praise belong;
Dear to the lover's, and the mourner's heart,
    And ever sacred to the sons of song!

Thy banks romantic hopeless Love shall seek,   5
    Where o'er the rocks the mantling bindwith* flaunts;
And Sorrow's drooping form and faded cheek
    Choose on thy willow'd shore her lonely haunts!

Banks! which inspired thy Otway's plaintive strain!
    Wilds!—whose lorn echoes learn'd the deeper tone   10
Of Collins'† powerful shell! yet once again
    Another poet—Hayley is thine own!
Thy classic stream anew shall hear a lay,
Bright as its waves, and various as its way!

---

* The plant Clematis, Bindwith, Virgin's Bower, or Traveller's Joy, which towards the end of June begins to cover the hedges and sides of rocky hollows with its beautiful foliage, and flowers of a yellowish white of an agreeable fragrance; these are succeeded by seed pods that bear some resemblance to feathers or hair, whence it is sometimes called Old Man's Beard.

† Collins, as well as Otway, was a native of this country, and probably at some period of his life an inhabitant of this neighbourhood, since in his beautiful "Ode on the Death of Colonel Ross," he says, "The Muse shall still, with social aid, [grief] / Her gentlest promise keep; / E'en humble Harting's cottag'd vale / Shall learn the sad repeated tale, / And bid her shepherds weep." And in the "Ode to Pity": "Wild Arun too has heard thy strains, / And Echo, 'midst thy [my] native plains, / Been sooth'd with [by] Pity's lute."

Line 11. **shell**: lyre.

Line 14. **way**: William Collins (1721–59) is buried, near Smith's birthplace, in Chichester Cathedral, where in 1795 he was honored by a memorial tablet designed by John Flaxman with verses inscribed by William Hayley, Smith's patron during the 1780s and 1790s. Smith's tribute is written some eleven years before this memorial to a local luminary was dedicated.

XXXI
Written in Farm Wood, South Downs, in May 1784

Spring's dewy hand on this fair summit weaves
    The downy grass with tufts of Alpine flowers:*
And shades the beechen slopes with tender leaves,
    And leads the shepherd to his upland bowers,
Strewn with wild thyme; while slow-descending showers   5
    Feed the green ear, and nurse the future sheaves!
    —Ah! blest the hind—whom no sad thought bereaves
Of the gay season's pleasures!—All his hours
To wholesome labour given, or thoughtless mirth;
    No pangs of sorrow past, or coming dread,   10
Bend his unconscious spirit down to earth,
    Or chase calm slumbers from his careless head!
Ah! what to me can those dear days restore,
When scenes could charm that now I taste no more!

XXXII
To melancholy. Written on the banks of
the Arun, October 1785

When latest Autumn spreads her evening veil,
    And the grey mists from these dim waves arise,
    I love to listen to the hollow sighs,
Thro' the half-leafless wood that breathes the gale:

---

* An infinite variety of plants are found on these hills, particularly about this spot: many sorts of Orchis and Cistus of singular beauty, with several others.

Sonnet 31. Title. This sonnet is occasioned by Smith's returning to her Sussex environs for a short visit after having spent the previous several months sequestered with her husband and children in the King's Bench prison.

Line 6. **green ear:** corn.

For at such hours the shadowy phantom pale,   5
  Oft seems to fleet before the poet's eyes;
  Strange sounds are heard, and mournful melodies,
As of night-wanderers, who their woes bewail!
Here, by his native stream, at such an hour,
  Pity's own Otway I methinks could meet,   10
  And hear his deep sighs swell the sadden'd wind!
O Melancholy!—such thy magic power,
  That to the soul these dreams are often sweet,
  And soothe the pensive visionary mind!

XXXIII
To the naiad of the Arun

Go, rural Naiad! wind thy stream along
  Thro' woods and wilds: then seek the ocean caves
Where sea-nymphs meet their coral rocks among,
  To boast the various honors of their waves!
'Tis but a little, o'er thy shallow tide,   5
  That toiling trade her burden'd vessel leads;
But laurels grow luxuriant on thy side,
  And letters live along thy classic meads.
Lo! where 'mid British bards thy natives* shine!
  And now another poet helps to raise   10
Thy glory high—the poet of the MINE!
  Whose brilliant talents are his smallest praise:
And who, to all that genius can impart,
Adds the cool head, and the unblemish'd heart!

---

* Otway, Collins, Hayley.

Sonnet 32. Line 10. **Otway:** See Sonnet 26 (page 30).
Sonnet 33. Title. **naiad:** nymph, or local deity; informing principle.
Line 11. **Mine:** John Sargent (d. 1831) published *The Mine* in 1785.

XXXIV
To a friend

Charm'd by thy suffrage, shall I yet aspire
   (All inauspicious as my fate appears,
     By troubles darken'd, that increase with years,)
To guide the crayon, or to touch the lyre?
Ah me!—the sister Muses still require   5
   A spirit free from all intrusive fears,
     Nor will they deign to wipe away the tears
Of vain regret, that dim their sacred fire.
But when thy envied sanction crowns my lays,
   A ray of pleasure lights my languid mind,   10
For well I know the value of thy praise;
     And to how few the flattering meed confin'd,
     That thou,—their highly favour'd brows to bind,
Wilt weave green myrtle and unfading bays!

XXXV
To fortitude

Nymph of the rock! whose dauntless spirit braves
   The beating storm, and bitter winds that howl
Round thy cold breast; and hear'st the bursting waves
   And the deep thunder with unshaken soul;
Oh come!—and shew how vain the cares that press   5
   On my weak bosom—and how little worth
Is the false fleeting meteor, Happiness,
   That still misleads the wanderers of the earth!
Strengthen'd by thee, this heart shall cease to melt
   O'er ills that poor Humanity must bear;   10
Nor friends estranged, or ties dissolved be felt
   To leave regret, and fruitless anguish there:

Sonnet 34. Line 12. **meed:** honor.

And when at length it heaves its latest sigh,
Thou and mild Hope shall teach me how to die!

XXXVI

Should the lone Wanderer, fainting on his way,
    Rest for a moment of the sultry hours,
And tho' his path thro' thorns and roughness lay,
    Pluck the wild rose, or woodbine's gadding flowers,
Weaving gay wreaths beneath some sheltering tree,   5
    The sense of sorrow he awhile may lose;
So have I sought thy flowers, fair Poesy!
    So charm'd my way with Friendship and the Muse.
But darker now grows life's unhappy day,
    Dark with new clouds of evil yet to come,   10
Her pencil sickening Fancy throws away,
    And weary Hope reclines upon the tomb;
And points my wishes to that tranquil shore,
Where the pale spectre Care pursues no more.

XXXVII

Sent to the Honorable Mrs. O'Neill,
with painted flowers

The poet's fancy takes from Flora's realm
    Her buds and leaves to dress fictitious powers,
With the green olive shades Minerva's helm,
    And gives to Beauty's Queen the Queen of flowers.

Sonnet 36. Line 4. **gadding**: growing haphazardly.

Sonnet 37. Title. **Mrs. O'Neill**: Henrietta O'Neill (or O'Neile) (1758–93) of Shane's Castle, Antrim, in Ireland. Her popular "Ode to the Poppy," a tribute to the power of narcotics, was first published by Smith in her novel *Desmond* (1792) and later gathered into the second volume of *Elegiac Sonnets*. It was often reprinted in magazines.

Line 3. **olive**: a traditional emblem of peace; here, perhaps of wisdom too. **Minerva**: classical goddess of wisdom.

But what gay blossoms of luxuriant Spring,   5
 With rose, mimosa, amaranth entwin'd,
Shall fabled Sylphs and fairy people bring,
 As a just emblem of the lovely mind?
In vain the mimic pencil tries to blend
 The glowing dyes that dress the flowery race,   10
  Scented and colour'd by an hand divine!
Ah! not less vainly would the Muse pretend
 On her weak lyre, to sing the native grace
  And native goodness of a soul like thine!

XXXVIII

When welcome slumber sets my spirit free,
 Forth to fictitious happiness it flies,
 And where Elysian bowers of bliss arise,
I seem, my Emmeline—to meet with thee!
Ah! Fancy then, dissolving human ties,   5
 Gives me the wishes of my soul to see;
Tears of fond pity fill thy soften'd eyes:
 In heavenly harmony—our hearts agree.
Alas! these joys are mine in dreams alone,
 When cruel Reason abdicates her throne!   10
  Her harsh return condemns me to complain
Thro' life unpitied, unrelieved, unknown!
  And as the dear delusions leave my brain,
  She bids the truth recur—with aggravated pain!

Sonnet 37. Line 4. **Beauty's ... flowers**: Venus is given roses.

Line 7. **Sylphs**: Pope had popularized the notion of unseen sylphs attending on his heroine Belinda in "The Rape of the Lock."

Sonnets 38 and 39.   These two sonnets come from Smith's *Emmeline: The Orphan of the Castle* (1788), her first novel, where they are penned by Emmeline's lover Godolphin.

XXXIX
To night

I love thee, mournful, sober-suited Night!
   When the faint moon, yet lingering in her wane,
And veil'd in clouds, with pale uncertain light
   Hangs o'er the waters of the restless main.
In deep depression sunk, the enfeebled mind   5
   Will to the deaf cold elements complain,
   And tell the embosom'd grief, however vain,
To sullen surges and the viewless wind.
Tho' no repose on thy dark breast I find,
   I still enjoy thee—cheerless as thou art;   10
   For in thy quiet gloom the exhausted heart
Is calm, tho' wretched; hopeless, yet resign'd.
While to the winds and waves its sorrows given,
May reach—tho' lost on earth—the ear of Heaven!

XL

Far on the sands, the low, retiring tide,
   In distant murmurs hardly seems to flow;
And o'er the world of waters, blue and wide,
   The sighing summer-wind forgets to blow.
As sinks the day-star in the rosy West,   5
   The silent wave, with rich reflection glows:
Alas! can tranquil nature give *me* rest,
   Or scenes of beauty soothe me to repose?
Can the soft lustre of the sleeping main,
   Yon radiant heaven, or all creation's charms,   10

Sonnet 40. This sonnet is written by Lady Adelina Trelawny in Smith's *Emmeline*.

"Erase the written troubles of the brain,"
    Which Memory tortures, and which Guilt alarms?
Or bid a bosom transient quiet prove,
That bleeds with vain remorse and unextinguish'd love!

XLI
To tranquillity

In this tumultuous sphere, for thee unfit,
    How seldom art thou found—Tranquillity!
    Unless 'tis when with mild and downcast eye
By the low cradles thou delight'st to sit
Of sleeping infants—watching the soft breath,   5
    And bidding the sweet slumberers easy lie;
Or sometimes hanging o'er the bed of death,
    Where the poor languid sufferer—hopes to die.
O beauteous sister of the halcyon peace!
    I sure shall find thee in that heavenly scene   10
        Where Care and Anguish shall their power resign;
Where hope alike, and vain regret shall cease,
    And Memory—lost in happiness serene,
        Repeat no more—that misery has been mine!

XLII
Composed during a walk on the Downs,
in November 1787

The dark and pillowy cloud, the sallow trees,
    Seem o'er the ruins of the year to mourn;
And, cold and hollow, the inconstant breeze
    Sobs thro' the falling leaves and wither'd fern.

Sonnet 40. Line 11. **Erase ... brain:** *Macbeth,* V.iii.42.

O'er the tall brow of yonder chalky bourn   5
The evening shades their gather'd darkness fling,
   While, by the lingering light, I scarce discern
The shrieking night-jar sail on heavy wing.*
   Ah! yet a little—and propitious Spring
Crown'd with fresh flowers shall wake the woodland strain;   10
   But no gay change revolving seasons bring
To call forth pleasure from the soul of pain!
Bid Syren Hope resume her long-lost part,
And chase the vulture Care—that feeds upon the heart.

XLIII

The unhappy exile, whom his fates confine
   To the bleak coast of some unfriendly isle,
   Cold, barren, desart, where no harvests smile,
But thirst and hunger on the rocks repine;
When, from some promontory's fearful brow,   5
   Sun after sun he hopeless sees decline
In the broad shipless sea—perhaps may know
   Such heartless pain, such blank despair as mine:
And, if a flattering cloud appears to show
   The fancied semblance of a distant sail,   10
   Then melts away—anew his spirits fail,
While the lost hope but aggravates his woe!
Ah! so for me delusive Fancy toils,
Then, from contrasted truth—my feeble soul recoils.

---

* The night-jar or night-hawk, a dark bird not so big as a rook, which is frequently seen of an evening on the downs. It has a short heavy flight, then rests on the ground, and again, uttering a mournful cry, flits before the traveller, to whom its appearance is supposed by the peasants to portend misfortune. As I have never seen it dead, I know not to what species it belongs.

Sonnet 42. Line 5. **bourn**: outcropping, boundary.

XLIV
Written in the church-yard
at Middleton in Sussex

Press'd by the Moon, mute arbitress of tides,
    While the loud equinox its power combines,
    The sea no more its swelling surge confines,
But o'er the shrinking land sublimely rides.
The wild blast, rising from the Western cave,   5
    Drives the huge billows from their heaving bed;
    Tears from their grassy tombs the village dead,*
And breaks the silent sabbath of the grave!
With shells and sea-weed mingled, on the shore
    Lo! their bones whiten in the frequent wave;   10
    But vain to them the winds and waters rave;
They hear the warring elements no more:
While I am doom'd—by life's long storm opprest,
To gaze with envy on their gloomy rest.

XLV
On leaving a part of Sussex

Farewel, Aruna!—on whose varied shore
    My early vows were paid to Nature's shrine,
    When thoughtless joy, and infant hope were mine,
And whose lorn stream has heard me since deplore
    Too many sorrows! Sighing I resign   5

---

* Middleton is a village on the margin of the sea, in Sussex, containing only two or three houses. There were formerly several acres of ground between its small church and the sea, which now, by its continual encroachments, approaches within a few feet of this half-ruined and humble edifice. The wall, which once surrounded the church-yard, is entirely swept away, many of the graves broken up, and the remains of bodies interred washed into the sea; whence human bones are found among the sand and shingles on the shore.

Thy solitary beauties—and no more
    Or on thy rocks, or in thy woods recline,
Or on the heath, by moonlight lingering, pore
    On air-drawn phantoms[.]—While in Fancy's ear
As in the evening wind thy murmurs swell,   10
    The Enthusiast of the Lyre who wander'd here,*
Seems yet to strike his visionary shell,
    Of power to call forth Pity's tenderest tear,
Or wake wild Phrenzy—from her hideous cell!

XLVI
Written at Penshurst, in autumn 1788

Ye towers sublime! deserted now and drear!
    Ye woods! deep sighing to the hollow blast,
The musing wanderer loves to linger near,
    While History points to all your glories past:
And startling from their haunts the timid deer,   5
    To trace the walks obscured by matted fern,
Which Waller's soothing lyre were wont to hear,
    But where now clamours the discordant hern!†
The spoiling hand of Time may overturn
    These lofty battlements, and quite deface   10
The fading canvas whence we love to learn

---

* Collins [See note to Sonnet 30 (page 33)].

† In the park at Penshurst is an heronry. The house is at present uninhabited, and the windows of the galleries and other rooms, in which there are many invaluable pictures, are never opened but when strangers visit it.

Sonnet 45. Line 12. **shell:** lyre.

Sonnet 46. Title. **Penshurst:** the ancestral home of the Sidneys, celebrated in a famous poem by Ben Jonson ("To Penshurst") as a symbol of enlightened paternalism.

Line 7. **Waller:** Edmund Waller (1606–87) wrote two poems with the title "To Penshurst."

Sydney's* keen look, and Sacharissa's grace;
But fame and beauty still defy decay,
Saved by the historic page—the poet's tender lay!

XLVII

To fancy

Thee, Queen of Shadows!—shall I still invoke,
    Still love the scenes thy sportive pencil drew,
When on mine eyes the early radiance broke
    Which shew'd the beauteous rather than the true!
Alas! long since those glowing tints are dead,   5
    And now 'tis thine in darkest hues to dress
The spot where pale Experience hangs her head
    O'er the sad grave of murder'd Happiness!
Thro' thy false medium, then, no longer view'd,
    May fancied pain and fancied pleasure fly,   10
        And I, as from me all thy dreams depart,
Be to my wayward destiny subdued:
    Nor seek perfection with a poet's eye,
        Nor suffer anguish with a poet's heart!

---

* Algernon Sidney [Algernon Sidney (1622–82), parliamentary leader during the English Commonwealth (1650–60), remained at the center of antimonarchical agitation after the restoration of Charles II. Two decades later, prosecuted for conspiring against the king, he was executed and became a martyr to liberty].

Sonnet 46. Line 12. **Sacharissa:** Lady Dorothea Sidney, to whom Waller wrote amorous verse: their relationship was much romanticized in the eighteenth century.

XLVIII
To Mrs. ****

No more my wearied soul attempts to stray
    From sad reality and vain regret,
Nor courts enchanting Fiction to allay
    Sorrows that Sense refuses to forget:
For of Calamity so long the prey,   5
    Imagination now has lost her powers,
Nor will her fairy loom again essay
    To dress Affliction in a robe of flowers.
But if no more the bowers of Fancy bloom,
    Let one superior scene attract my view,   10
Where Heaven's pure rays the sacred spot illume,
    Let *thy* loved hand with palm and amaranth strew
The mournful path approaching to the tomb,
While Faith's consoling voice endears the friendly gloom.

XLIX
Supposed to have been written in a church-yard, over the grave of a young woman of nineteen

O thou! who sleep'st where hazle-bands entwine
    The vernal grass, with paler violets drest;
I would, sweet maid! thy humble bed were mine,
    And mine thy calm and enviable rest.

Sonnet 48. Line 12. **palm and amaranth**: emblematic, respectively, of triumph and immortality.

Sonnets 49–53 were written for Smith's *Celestina: A Novel,* published in 1791. Here, the heroine Celestina De Mornay, who is herself nineteen, expresses despondency over having lost, as she thinks, the love of George Willoughby.

For never more by human ills opprest   5
   Shall thy soft spirit fruitlessly repine:
   Thou canst not now thy fondest hopes resign
Even in the hour that should have made thee blest.
Light lies the turf upon thy virgin breast;
   And lingering here, to Love and Sorrow true,   10
The youth who once thy simple heart possest
   Shall mingle tears with April's early dew;
While still for him shall faithful Memory save
Thy form and virtues from the silent grave.

L

Farewel, ye lawns!—by fond remembrance blest,
   As witnesses of gay unclouded hours;
Where, to maternal Friendship's bosom prest,
   My happy childhood past amid your bowers.
Ye wood-walks wild!—where leaves and fairy flowers   5
   By Spring's luxuriant hand are strewn anew;
Rocks!—whence with shadowy grace rude Nature lours
   O'er glens and haunted streams!—a long adieu!
And you!—O promised Happiness!—whose voice
   Deluded Fancy heard in every grove,   10
Bidding this tender, trusting heart, rejoice
   In the bright prospect of unfailing love:
Tho' lost to me—still may thy smile serene
Bless the dear lord of this regretted scene.

Sonnet 50. From *Celestina:* Celestina pays a farewell tribute to Alvestone, Willoughby's country seat.

LI
Supposed to have been written in the Hebrides

On this lone island, whose unfruitful breast
    Feeds but the Summer-shepherd's little flock
    With scanty herbage from the half-clothed rock,
Where osprays,* cormorants, and sea-mews rest;
    Even in a scene so desolate and rude   5
I could with *thee* for months and years be blest;
And of thy tenderness and love possest,
    Find all *my* world in this wild solitude!
When summer suns these northern seas illume,
    With thee admire the light's reflected charms,   10
And when drear Winter spreads his cheerless gloom,
    Still find Elysium in thy shelt'ring arms:
For thou to me canst sovereign bliss impart,
Thy mind my empire—and my throne thy heart.

LII
The pilgrim

Faltering and sad the unhappy Pilgrim roves,
    Who, on the eve of bleak December's night,
Divided far from all he fondly loves,
    Journeys alone, along the giddy height
Of these steep cliffs; and as the sun's last ray   5
    Fades in the west, sees, from the rocky verge,
Dark tempest scowling o'er the shortened day,
    And hears, with ear appall'd, the impetuous surge

---

* The sea-eagle.

Sonnet 51. From *Celestina:* separated from her friends during an exploring party, Celestina once more reverts to thoughts of Willoughby.

Sonnet 52. From *Celestina:* composed by Celestina in late November among the Hebrides.

Beneath him thunder!—So, with heart oppress'd,
   Alone, reluctant, desolate, and slow,   10
By Friendship's cheering radiance *now* unblest,
   Along Life's rudest path I seem to go;
Nor see where yet the anxious heart may rest,
   That, trembling at the past—recoils from future woe.

LIII

The Laplander

The shivering native who, by Tenglio's side,
   Beholds with fond regret the parting light
Sink far away, beneath the darkening tide,
   And leave him to long months of dreary night,
Yet knows, that springing from the eastern wave   5
   The sun's glad beams shall re-illume his way,
And from the snows secured—within his cave
   He waits in patient hope—returning day.
Not so the sufferer feels, who, o'er the waste
   Of joyless life, is destin'd to deplore   10
Fond love forgotten, tender friendship past,
   Which, once extinguish'd, can revive no more!
O'er the blank void he looks with hopeless pain;
For him those beams of heaven shall never shine again.

Sonnet 53. From *Celestina:* Celestina's final poetic effusion from the isolated Hebrides.

Line 1. **Tenglio's side:** perhaps the Arctic river, called in Norwegian the Tana and in Finnish the Tena, that forms the boundary between the two countries, or the Tana Fjord into which it empties.

LIV
The sleeping woodman. Written in April 1790

Ye copses wild, where April bids arise
    The vernal grasses, and the early flowers;
My soul depress'd—from human converse flies
    To the lone shelter of your pathless bowers.

Lo!—where the Woodman, with his toil oppress'd,   5
    His careless head on bark and moss reclined,
    Lull'd by the song of birds, the murmuring wind,
Has sunk to calm tho' momentary rest.

Ah! would 'twere mine in Spring's green lap to find
    Such transient respite from the ills I bear!   10
Would I could taste, like this unthinking hind,
    A sweet forgetfulness of human care,*
Till the last sleep these weary eyes shall close,
And Death receive me to his long repose.

LV
The return of the nightingale. Written in May 1791

Borne on the warm wing of the western gale,
    How tremulously low is heard to float
Thro' the green budding thorns that fringe the vale,
    The early Nightingale's prelusive note.

'Tis Hope's instinctive power that thro' the grove   5
    Tells how benignant Heaven revives the earth;
'Tis the soft voice of young and timid Love
    That calls these melting sounds of sweetness forth.

---

* Pope ["Divine Oblivion of low-thoughted care," "Eloisa to Abelard," line 298].

With transport, once, sweet bird! I hail'd thy lay,
   And bade thee welcome to our shades again,   10
To charm the wandering poet's pensive way
   And soothe the solitary lover's pain;
But now!—such evils in my lot combine,
As shut my languid sense—to Hope's dear voice and thine!

LVI
The captive escaped in the wilds of America.
Addressed to the Hon. Mrs. O'Neill

If, by his torturing, savage foes untraced,
   The breathless Captive gain some trackless glade,
Yet hears the war-whoop howl along the waste,
   And dreads the reptile-monsters of the shade;
The giant reeds that murmur round the flood,   5
   Seem to conceal some hideous form beneath;
And every hollow blast that shakes the wood,
   Speaks to his trembling heart of woe and death.
With horror fraught, and desolate dismay,
   On such a wanderer falls the starless night;   10
But if, far streaming, a propitious ray
   Leads to some amicable fort his sight,
He hails the beam benign that guides his way,
   As I, my Harriet, bless thy friendship's cheering light.

Sonnet 55. Line 12. **pain**: The earlier sonnets on the nightingale, 3 (page 14) and 7 (page 17), express sentiments exactly opposite those recollected here.

Sonnet 56. Title. **O'Neill**: addressed, like Sonnet 37 (page 37), to Smith's friend Henrietta O'Neill.

LVII
To dependence

Dependence! heavy, heavy are thy chains,
    And happier they who from the dangerous sea,
Or the dark mine, procure with ceaseless pains
    An hard-earn'd pittance—than who trust to thee!
More blest the hind, who from his bed of flock   5
    Starts—when the birds of morn their summons give,
And waken'd by the lark—"the shepherd's clock,"*
    Lives but to labour—labouring but to live.
More noble than the sycophant, whose art
    Must heap with taudry flowers thy hated shrine;   10
I envy not the meed thou canst impart
    To crown *his* service—while, tho' Pride combine
With Fraud to crush me—my unfetter'd heart
    Still to the Mountain Nymph† may offer mine.

LVIII
The glow-worm

When on some balmy-breathing night of Spring
    The happy child, to whom the world is new,
Pursues the evening moth, of mealy wing,
    Or from the heath-bell beats the sparkling dew;

---

* Shakspeare ["And merry larks are ploughman's clocks" (*Love's Labour's Lost*, V.ii.901)].
† The mountain goddess, Liberty. Milton [*L'Allegro*, line 36].

Sonnet 57. Title. Although this sonnet appears to refer to the chronic problem artists face of securing patronage without sacrificing freedom, Smith also seems to intrude on her forceful denunciation the particular indignities suffered by a woman. Lines 12–13 refer specifically to the protracted legal suit over her father-in-law's estate in which a woman litigant could not be admitted, perhaps as well to the legal rights over her earnings held by her estranged husband.

He sees before his inexperienced eyes   5
   The brilliant Glow-worm, like a meteor, shine
On the turf-bank;—amazed, and pleased, he cries,
   "Star of the dewy grass!*—I make thee mine!"—
Then, ere he sleep, collects "the moisten'd" flower,[†]
   And bids soft leaves his glittering prize enfold   10
And dreams that Fairy-lamps illume his bower:
   Yet with the morning shudders to behold
His lucid treasure, rayless as the dust!
—So turn the world's bright joys to cold and blank disgust.

LIX
Written September 1791, during a remarkable thunder storm, in which the moon was perfectly clear, while the tempest gathered in various directions near the earth

What awful pageants crowd the evening sky!
   The low horizon gathering vapours shroud;
   Sudden, from many a deep-embattled cloud
Terrific thunders burst, and lightnings fly—
While in serenest azure, beaming high,   5
   Night's regent, of her calm pavilion proud,
Gilds the dark shadows that beneath her lie,
   Unvex'd by all their conflicts fierce and loud.

---

* "Star of the earth." Dr. Darwin [Erasmus Darwin, *Economy of Vegetation,* I.196].

† "The moisten'd blade—" Walcot's beautiful "Ode to the Glow-worm" ["Hanging thy lamp upon the moisten'd blade," line 9; Smith quotes this ephemeral poem in full in her *Rural Walks* (London: Cadell and Davies, 1795), I, 172–74].

Sonnet 58. Line 6. **meteor:** not an asteroid, but a will-o'-the wisp or ignis fatuus, the phosphorescent light emitted by marsh gas.

Sonnet 59. Line 6. **Night's regent:** the moon.

—So, in unsullied dignity elate,
    A spirit conscious of superior worth,   10
In placid elevation firmly great,
    Scorns the vain cares that give Contention birth;
And blest with peace above the shocks of Fate,
    Smiles at the tumult of the troubled earth.

LX

To an amiable girl

Miranda! mark where shrinking from the gale,
    Its silken leaves yet moist with early dew,
That fair faint flower, the Lily of the Vale,
    Droops its meek head, and looks, methinks, like you!
Wrapp'd in a shadowy veil of tender green,   5
    Its snowy bells a soft perfume dispense,
And bending as reluctant to be seen,
    In simple loveliness it soothes the sense.
With bosom bared to meet the garish day,
    The glaring Tulip, gaudy, undismay'd,   10
Offends the eye of taste; that turns away
    To seek the Lily in her fragrant shade.
With such unconscious beauty, pensive, mild,
Miranda charms—Nature's soft modest child.

Sonnet 60. This sonnet was written for *Rural Walks*, the first of Smith's educational books for children on natural subjects, a context that determines its tone and import.

LXI
Supposed to have been written in America

Ill–omen'd bird!* whose cries portentous float
    O'er yon savannah with the mournful wind;
While, as the Indian hears your piercing note,
    Dark dread of future evil fills his mind;
Wherefore with early lamentation break   5
    The dear delusive visions of repose?
Why from so short felicity awake
    My wounded senses to substantial woes?
O'er my sick soul thus rous'd from transient rest,
    Pale Superstition sheds her influence drear,   10
And to my shuddering fancy would suggest
    Thou com'st to speak of every woe I fear.
Ah! Reason little o'er the soul prevails,
When, from ideal ill, the enfeebled spirit fails!

---

* This Sonnet, first inserted in the Novel called the *Old Manor House*, is founded on a superstition attributed *(vide* Bertram's *Travels in America)* [William Bartram, *Travels through North and South Carolina, Georgia, East and West Florida...* (1791)] to the Indians, who believe that the cry of this night-hawk *(Caprimulgus Americanus)* portends some evil, and when they are at war, assert that it is never heard near their tents or habitations but to announce the death of some brave warrior of their tribe, or some other calamity.

Title. This sonnet, from Smith's *The Old Manor House: A Novel* (1793), is penned by Orlando Somerive in the midst of a cypress swamp, which, through imaginative geography, is located in the Canadian wilderness on the banks of the St. Lawrence River.

Line 2. **savannah:** flat grassland.

LXII

Written on passing by moon-light through a village, while the ground was covered with snow

While thus I wander, cheerless and unblest,
    And find in change of place but change of pain;
In tranquil sleep the village labourers rest,
    And taste that quiet I pursue in vain!
Hush'd is the hamlet now, and faintly gleam   5
    The dying embers, from the casement low
Of the thatch'd cottage; while the Moon's wan beam
    Lends a new lustre to the dazzling snow.
O'er the cold waste, amid the freezing night,
    Scarce heeding whither, desolate I stray;   10
For me, pale Eye of Evening, thy soft light
    Leads to no happy home; *my* weary way
Ends but in sad vicissitudes of care:
I only fly from doubt—to meet despair!

LXIII

The gossamer

O'er faded heath-flowers spun, or thorny furze,*
    The filmy Gossamer is lightly spread;
Waving in every sighing air that stirs,
    As Fairy fingers had entwined the thread:
A thousand trembling orbs of lucid dew   5
    Spangle the texture of the fairy loom,

---

* The web, charged with innumerable globules of bright dew, that is frequently on heaths and commons in autumnal mornings, can hardly have escaped the observation of any lover of nature—The slender web of the field spider is again alluded to in Sonnet 77 [page 66].

Sonnet 62. Another effusion of Orlando Somerive's in *The Old Manor House*.

As if soft Sylphs, lamenting as they flew,
    Had wept departed Summer's transient bloom:
But the wind rises, and the turf receives
    The glittering web:—So, evanescent, fade   10
Bright views that Youth with sanguine heart believes:
    So vanish schemes of bliss, by Fancy made;
Which, fragile as the fleeting dews of morn,
Leave but the wither'd heath, and barren thorn!

LXIV
Written at Bristol in the summer of 1794

Here from the restless bed of lingering pain
    The languid sufferer seeks the tepid wave,
And feels returning health and hope again
    Disperse "the gathering shadows of the grave!"
And here romantic rocks that boldly swell,   5
    Fringed with green woods, or stain'd with veins of ore,
Call'd native Genius forth, whose Heav'n-taught skill
    Charm'd the deep echos of the rifted shore.
But tepid waves, wild scenes, or summer air,
    Restore they palsied Fancy, woe-deprest?   10
Check they the torpid influence of Despair,
    Or bid warm Health re-animate the breast;
Where Hope's soft visions have no longer part,
And whose sad inmate is—a broken heart?

Sonnet 64. From *The Banished Man: A Novel* (1794), where it is addressed by Smith's proto-
type, Mrs. Denzil, to her friend Mrs. Armitage and entitled "Sonnet written at Bristol Hot-
well, in answer to a friend, who recommended a residence there to the author."

Line 4. **grave**: Hayley, "Epistle to a Friend on the Death of John Thornton" (1780), line 190.

Line 7. **call'd ... forth**: According to a note in *The Banished Man,* this phrase refers to Tho-
mas Chatterton, who died a suicide in 1770, and Smith's contemporary Ann Yearsley,
known as the Milkwoman of Clifton, near Bristol. Both were celebrated as plebeian
geniuses who wrote poetry without the advantages of formal schooling.

LXV*

To Dr. Parry of Bath, with some botanic drawings which had been made some years

In happier hours, ere yet so keenly blew
   Adversity's cold blight, and bitter storms,
   Luxuriant Summer's evanescent forms,
And Spring's soft blooms with pencil light I drew:
But as the lovely family of flowers   5
   Shrink from the bleakness of the Northern blast,
   So fail from present care and sorrow past
The slight botanic pencil's mimic powers—
Nor will kind Fancy even by Memory's aid,
   Her visionary garlands now entwine;   10
Yet while the wreaths of Hope and Pleasure fade,
   Still is one flower of deathless blossom mine,
That dares the lapse of Time, and Tempest rude,
The unfading Amaranth of Gratitude.

---

* To the excellent friend and Physician to whom these lines are addressed, I was obliged for the kindest attention, and for the recovery from one dangerous illness of that beloved child whom a few months afterwards his skill and most unremitted and disinterested exertions could not save! [Smith refers to the devastating blow she suffered when her favorite daughter, Anna Augusta de Foville, died in childbirth in the spring of 1795. Her death is alluded to, as well, in Sonnets 74, 78, 89, 90, and 91, and is the subject of "April" and the "Ode to Death," poems included in the second volume of *Elegiac Sonnets*.]

Title. **Dr. Parry**: Dr. Caleb Hillier Parry (1755–1822) became a local institution, enjoying distinguished social connections and high professional repute, after he made Bath his residence in 1789. His treatise on angina pectoris, published in 1799, is considered a groundbreaking study of heart disease.

Line 14. **Amaranth**: the immortal flower of paradise.

LXVI
Written in a tempestuous night,
on the coast of Sussex

The night-flood rakes upon the stony shore;
    Along the rugged cliffs and chalky caves
Mourns the hoarse Ocean, seeming to deplore
    All that are buried in his restless waves[.]—
Mined by corrosive tides, the hollow rock   5
    Falls prone, and rushing from its turfy height,
Shakes the broad beach with long-resounding shock,
    Loud thundering on the ear of sullen Night;
Above the desolate and stormy deep,
    Gleams the wan Moon, by floating mist opprest;   10
Yet here while youth, and health, and labour sleep,
    Alone I wander[.] —Calm untroubled rest,
    "Nature's soft nurse," deserts the sigh-swoln breast,
And shuns the eyes, that only wake to weep!

Title. Originally published in Smith's *Montalbert: A Novel* (1795), where it is penned by the melancholy hero Sommers Walsingham. It was, however, Smith noted in a footnote in *Elegiac Sonnets*, "written on the coast of Sussex during very tempestuous weather in December 1791."

Line 5. **Mined:** undermined.

Line 13. **Nature's soft nurse:** *2 Henry IV*, III.i.6.

LXVII

On passing over a dreary tract of country, and near the ruins of a deserted chapel, during a tempest

Swift fleet the billowy clouds along the sky,
    Earth seems to shudder at the storm aghast;
While only beings as forlorn as I,
    Court the chill horrors of the howling blast.
Even round yon crumbling walls, in search of food,   5
    The ravenous Owl foregoes his evening flight,
And in his cave, within the deepest wood,
    The Fox eludes the tempest of the night.
But to *my* heart congenial is the gloom
    Which hides me from a World I wish to shun;   10
That scene where Ruin saps the mouldering tomb,
    Suits with the sadness of a wretch undone.
Nor is the deepest shade, the keenest air,
Black as my fate, or cold as my despair.

LXVIII

Written at Exmouth, midsummer, 1795

Fall, dews of Heaven, upon my burning breast,
    Bathe with cool drops these ever-streaming eyes;
Ye gentle Winds, that fan the balmy West,
    With the soft rippling tide of morning rise,
And calm my bursting heart, as here I keep   5
    The vigil of the wretched!—Now away
Fade the pale stars, as wavering o'er the deep
    Soft rosy tints announce another day,

Sonnet 67. Another sonnet written by Sommers Walsingham in Smith's *Montalbert.*

The day of Middle Summer!—Ah! in vain
 To those who mourn like me, does radiant June   10
Lead on her fragrant hours; for hopeless pain
 Darkens with sullen clouds the Sun of Noon,
And veil'd in shadows Nature's face appears
To hearts o'erwhelm'd with grief, to eyes suffused with tears.

LXIX

Written at the same place, on seeing a seaman return who had been imprisoned at Rochfort

Clouds, gold and purple, o'er the westering ray
 Threw a bright veil, and catching lights between,
 Fell on the glancing sail, that we had seen
With soft, but adverse winds, throughout the day
Contending vainly: as the vessel nears,   5
 Encreasing numbers hail it from the shore;
Lo! on the deck a pallid form appears,
 Half wondering to behold himself once more
Approach his home[.]—And now he can discern
 His cottage thatch amid surrounding trees;   10
 Yet, trembling, dreads lest sorrow or disease
Await him there, embittering his return:
But all he loves are safe; with heart elate,
Tho' poor and plunder'd, he absolves his fate!

Sonnet 69. Title. **Rochfort**: the French naval prison during the Napoleonic Wars, located north of Bordeaux. Release came through an organized exchange of prisoners between the countries or, as the last line of this sonnet might suggest, ransom.

LXX
On being cautioned against walking on an headland overlooking the sea, because it was frequented by a lunatic

Is there a solitary wretch who hies
　　To the tall cliff, with starting pace or slow,
And, measuring, views with wild and hollow eyes
　　Its distance from the waves that chide below;
Who, as the sea-born gale with frequent sighs   5
　　Chills his cold bed upon the mountain turf,
With hoarse, half-utter'd lamentation, lies
　　Murmuring responses to the dashing surf?
In moody sadness, on the giddy brink,
　　I see him more with envy than with fear;   10
He has no *nice felicities* that shrink*
　　From giant horrors; wildly wandering here,
He seems (uncursed with reason) not to know
The depth or the duration of his woe.

LXXI
Written at Weymouth in winter

The chill waves whiten in the sharp North-east;
　　Cold, cold the night-blast comes, with sullen sound;
And black and gloomy, like my cheerless breast,
　　Frowns the dark pier and lonely sea-view round.
Yet a few months—and on the peopled strand   5
　　Pleasure shall all her varied forms display;

---

* "'Tis delicate felicity that shrinks / When rocking winds are loud." Walpole [untraced; these lines are not included in the modern, definitive edition of Horace Walpole's writings].

Sonnet 71. Title. **Weymouth:** Weymouth, a south-coast port in Dorset, became a fashionable summer bathing resort after George III began periodic visits in 1789.

Nymphs lightly tread the bright reflecting sand,
   And proud sails whiten all the summer bay:
Then, for these winds that whistle keen and bleak,
   Music's delightful melodies shall float   10
O'er the blue waters; but 'tis mine to seek
   Rather, some unfrequented shade, remote
From sights and sounds of gaiety[.]—I mourn
All that gave *me* delight—Ah! never to return!

LXXII
To the morning star. Written near the sea

Thee! lucid arbiter 'twixt day and night,*
   The Seaman greets, as on the Ocean stream
Reflected, thy precursive friendly beam
Points out the long-sought haven to his sight.

Watching for thee, the lover's ardent eyes   5
   Turn to the eastern hills; and as above
Thy brilliance trembles, hails the lights that rise
   To guide his footsteps to expecting love!

I mark thee too, as night's dark clouds retire,
   And thy bright radiance glances on the sea;   10
But never more shall thy heraldic fire
   Speak of approaching morn with joy to me!
Quench'd in the gloom of death that heavenly ray
Once lent to light me on my thorny way!

---

* Milton ["The sun was sunk, and after him the star / Of Hesperus, whose office is to bring / Twilight upon the Earth, short arbiter / 'Twixt day and night." *Paradise Lost*, IX.48–51].

Sonnet 71. Line 7. **Nymphs**: young women of fashion.

LXXIII

To a querulous acquaintance

Thou! whom Prosperity has always led
    O'er level paths, with moss and flow'rets strewn;
For whom she still prepares a downy bed
    With roses scatter'd, and to thorns unknown,
Wilt thou yet murmur at a mis-placed leaf?*   5
    Think, ere thy irritable nerves repine,
    How many, born with feelings keen as thine,
Taste all the sad vicissitudes of grief;
How many steep in tears their scanty bread;
    Or, lost to reason, Sorrow's victims! rave: 10
How many know not where to lay their head;
    While some are driven by anguish to the grave!
Think; nor impatient at a feather's weight,
Mar the uncommon blessings of thy fate!

LXXIV

The winter night

"Sleep, that knits up the ravell'd sleeve of care,"†
    Forsakes me, while the chill and sullen blast,
    As my sad soul recalls its sorrows past,
Seems like a summons, bidding me prepare

---

* From a story (I know not where told) of a fastidious being, who on a bed of rose leaves complained that his or her rest was destroyed because one of those leaves was doubled.

† Shakspeare [*Macbeth*, II.ii.36].

Sonnet 73. Line 6. **irritable nerves**: Excessive or misplaced sensibility is a frequent object of attack in later eighteenth-century moral writings. As a weakness particularly associated with self-indulgent, manipulative women, it is roundly condemned by Mary Wollstonecraft and other feminists. Here Smith accentuates upper-class indulgence.

For the last sleep of death[.]—Murmuring I hear   5
   The hollow wind around the ancient towers,*
While night and silence reign; and cold and drear
   The darkest gloom of Middle Winter lours;
But wherefore fear existence such as mine,
   To change for long and undisturb'd repose?   10
Ah! when this suffering being I resign,
   And o'er my miseries the tomb shall close,
By her, whose loss in anguish I deplore,
I shall be laid, and feel that loss no more!

LXXV

Where the wild woods and pathless forests frown,
   The darkling Pilgrim seeks his unknown way,
Till on the grass he throws him weary down,
   To wait in broken sleep the dawn of day:
Thro' boughs just waving in the silent air,   5
   With pale capricious light the Summer Moon
Chequers his humid couch; while Fancy there,
   That loves to wanton in the Night's deep noon,
Calls from the mossy roots and fountain edge
   Fair visionary Nymphs that haunt the shade,   10
Or Naiads rising from the whispering sedge;
   And, 'mid the beauteous group, his dear loved maid
Seems beckoning him with smiles to join the train:
Then, starting from his dream, he feels his woes again!

---

*These lines were written in a residence among ancient public buildings.

Sonnet 74. Line 13. **her**: her daughter Anna Augusta who died in 1795: see Sonnet 65 (page 57).

Sonnet 75. Line 2. **darkling**: in the night; after dark.

Line 8. **Night's ... noon**: midnight.

Lines 10–11. **Nymphs ... Naiads**: spirits informing, respectively, trees and streams.

LXXVI
To a young man entering the world

Go now, ingenuous Youth!—The trying hour
  Is come: The World demands that thou shouldst go
To active life: There titles, wealth and power
  May all be purchas'd—Yet I joy to know
Thou wilt not pay their price. The base controul   5
  Of petty despots in their pedant reign
  Already hast thou felt;*—and high disdain
Of Tyrants is imprinted on thy soul[.]—
  Not, where mistaken Glory, in the field
Rears her red banner, be thou ever found;   10
  But, against proud Oppression raise the shield
Of Patriot daring—So shalt thou renown'd
  For the best virtues *live;* or that denied
  May'st die, as Hampden or as Sydney died!

---

* This was not addressed to my son, who suffered with many others in an event which will long be remembered by those parents who had sons at a certain public school, in 1793, but to another young man, not *compelled* as he was, in consequence of that dismission, to abandon the fairest prospects of his future life. [Smith's son Lionel, a principal in a schoolboys' rebellion at Winchester College, was forced to step down.]

Sonnet 76. From Smith's *Marchmont: A Novel* (1796) where it is discovered in a notebook left behind by the hero Edward-Armyn Marchmont.

Line 14. **Hampden … Sydney**: John Hampden, champion of the Commonwealth, and Algernon Sydney, executed for his vocal opposition to Charles II, were heroes of Whig legend, celebrated for their commitment to the liberties of the English people.

LXXVII
To the insect of the gossamer

Small, viewless Æronaut, that by the line*
Of Gossamer suspended, in mid air
Float'st on a sun beam—Living Atom, where
Ends thy breeze-guided voyage;—with what design

---

* The almost imperceptible threads floating in the air, towards the end of Summer or Autumn, in a still evening, sometimes are so numerous as to be felt on the face and hands. It is on these that a minute species of spider convey themselves from place to place; sometimes rising with the wind to a great height in the air. Dr. Lister, among other naturalists, remarked these insects. "To fly they cannot strictly be said, they being carried into the air by external force; but they can, in case the wind suffer them, steer their course, perhaps mount and descend at pleasure: and to the purpose of rowing themselves along in the air, it is observable that they ever take their flight backwards, that is, their head looking a contrary way like a sculler upon the Thames. It is scarcely credible to what height they will mount; which is yet precisely true, and a thing easily to be observed by one that shall fix his eye some time on any part of the heavens, the white web, at a vast distance, very distinctly appearing from the azure sky—But this is in Autumn only, and that in very fair and calm weather." From the Encyclop. Brit.

Dr. Darwin, whose imagination so happily applies every object of Natural History to the purposes of Poetry, makes the Goddess of Botany thus direct her Sylphs—"Thin clouds of Gossamer in air display, / And hide the vale's chaste lily from the ray" [*Economy of Vegetation*, IV. 561–62].

These filmy threads form a part of the equipage of Mab: "Her waggon spokes are made of spiders legs, / The cover of the wings of grasshoppers, / The traces of the smallest spider's web" [*Romeo and Juliet*, I.iv.59–61].

Juliet, too, in anxiously waiting for the silent arrival of her lover, exclaims, "—Oh! so light of [a] foot / Will ne'er wear out the everlasting flint; / A lover may bestride the Gossamer / That idles in the wanton Summer air, / And yet not fall—" [*Ibid.* II.vi.16–20. The speaker is actually Friar Laurence describing Juliet's arrival at his cell.]

Line 1. **viewless**: so small as to be inaccessible to sight.

Line 2. **gossamer**: When this sonnet first appeared in *Conversations Introducing Poetry* (1804), Charlotte Smith appended this further note: "Gossamer is the web of a very small spider. In that entertaining and instructive book, [Gilbert] White's *History of Selborne* [1789], is an account of a wonderful shower of gossamer which fell in and about that village, on the 21st of September, 1741. The letter containing the history of this phenomenon concludes thus–'Every day in fine weather, in Autumn chiefly, do I see those spiders shooting out their webs and mounting aloft. They will go off from your finger if you will take them in your hand. Last Summer one alighted on my book as I was reading in the parlour; and running to the top of the page, and shooting out a web, took off with considerable velocity, in a place where no air was stirring; and I am sure I did not assist it with my breath; so that these little crawlers seem to have, while mounting, some loco-motive power, without the use of wings, and to move in the air faster than the air itself.' White's *History of Selborne*, 192."

In Æther dost thou launch thy form minute,   5
Mocking the eye?—Alas! before the veil
    Of denser clouds shall hide thee, the pursuit
Of the keen Swift may end thy fairy sail!—
    Thus on the golden thread that Fancy weaves
Buoyant, as Hope's illusive flattery breathes,   10
    The young and visionary Poet leaves
Life's dull realities, while sevenfold wreaths
    Of rainbow-light around his head revolve.
Ah! soon at Sorrow's touch the radiant dreams dissolve!

LXXVIII
Snowdrops

Wan Heralds of the Sun and Summer gale!
    That seem just fallen from infant Zephyrs' wing;
Not now, as once, with heart revived I hail
    Your modest buds, that for the brow of Spring
Form the first simple garland[.] —Now no more   5
    Escaping for a moment all my cares,
Shall I, with pensive, silent step, explore
    The woods yet leafless; where to chilling airs
Your green and pencil'd blossoms, trembling, wave.
    Ah! ye soft, transient children of the ground,   10
More fair was she on whose untimely grave
    Flow my unceasing tears! Their varied round
The Seasons go; while I through all repine:
For fixt regret, and hopeless grief are mine.

Sonnet 77. Line 8. **Swift**: a kind of swallow that feeds on insects.

Sonnet 78. Line 11. **she**: another reference to Smith's daughter Anna Augusta. See the earlier Sonnets 65 (page 57) and 74 (page 63).

LXXIX

To the goddess of botany*

Of Folly weary, shrinking from the view
Of Violence and Fraud, allow'd to take
All peace from humble life; I would forsake
Their haunts for ever, and, sweet Nymph! with you
Find shelter; where my tired, and tear-swoln eyes,   5
Among your silent shades of soothing hue,

---

* "Rightly to spell," as Milton wishes, in *Il Penseroso,* "Of every herb that sips the dew,"
[ll.170–72] seems to be a resource for the sick at heart—for those who from sorrow or dis-
gust may without affectation say "Society is nothing to one not sociable!" ["society is no
comfort / To one not sociable," Shakespeare, *Cymbeline,* IV.ii.12–13] and whose wearied
eyes and languid spirits find relief and repose amid the shades of vegetable nature.—*I* can-
not now turn to any other pursuit that for a moment soothes my wounded mind.

"Je pris gout a cette récreation des yeux, qui dans l'infortune, repose, amuse, distrait
l'esprit, et suspend le sentiment des peines" [I took a liking to this recreation of the eyes,
which in misfortune rests, amuses, distracts the spirit and suspends the feelings of pain].
Thus speaks the singular, the unhappy Rousseau, when in his "Promenades" [*Reveries du
Promenade Solitaire,* Book 7] he enumerates the causes that drove him from the society of
men, and occasioned his pursuing with renewed avidity the study of Botany. "I was," says
he, "Forcé de m'abstenir de penser, de peur de penser a mes malheurs malgré moi; forcé de
contenir les restes d'une imagination riante, mais languissante, que tant d'angoisses pour-
roient effaroucher a la fin—" ["I was forced to keep myself from thinking, to fear thinking
about my misfortunes despite myself, was forced to repress the remnants of a cheerful but
stagnant imagination which so much distress could startle to its end"].

Without any pretensions to those talents which were in him so heavily taxed with that
excessive irritability, too often if not always the attendant on genius, it has been my misfor-
tune to have endured real calamities that have disqualified me for finding any enjoyment in
the pleasures and pursuits which occupy the generality of the world. I have been engaged in
contending with persons whose cruelty has left so painful an impression on my mind, that I
may well say, "Brillantes fleurs, émail des prés[,] ombrages frais, [ruisseaux,] bosquets, ver-
dure, venez purifier mon imagination de tous [salie par tous] ces hideux objets!" ["Brilliant
flowers, adornment of meadows, cool shades, [streams,] arbors, foliage, come purify my
imagination sullied by all these hideous objects."]

Perhaps, if any situation is more pitiable than that which compels us to wish to escape
from the common business and forms of life, it is that where the sentiment is forcibly felt,
while it cannot be indulged; and where the sufferer, chained down to the discharge of duties
from which the wearied spirit recoils, feels like the wretched Lear, when Shakspeare makes
him exclaim "Oh! I am bound upon a wheel of fire, / Which my own tears do scald like
melted lead" [*King Lear,* IV.vii.47–48].

Your "bells and florets of unnumber'd dyes"
    Might rest—And learn the bright varieties
That from your lovely hands are fed with dew;
    And every veined leaf, that trembling sighs   10
In mead or woodland; or in wilds remote,
    Or lurk with mosses in the humid caves,
    Mantle the cliffs, on dimpling rivers float,
    Or stream from coral rocks beneath the Ocean waves.

LXXX

To the invisible moon*

Dark and conceal'd art thou, soft Evening's Queen,
    And Melancholy's votaries that delight
To watch thee, gliding thro' the blue serene,
    Now vainly seek thee on the brow of night [.] —
Mild Sorrow, such as Hope has not forsook,   5
    May love to muse beneath thy silent reign;
But *I* prefer from some steep rock to look
    On the obscure and fluctuating main,
What time the martial star with lurid glare,
    Portentous, gleams above the troubled deep;   10
Or the red comet shakes his blazing hair;
    Or on the fire-ting'd waves the lightnings leap;
While thy fair beams illume another sky,
And shine for beings less accurst than I.

---

* I know not whether this is correctly expressed —I suspect that it is not —What I mean, however, will surely be understood —I address the Moon when not visible at night in our hemisphere. "The Sun to me is dark, / And silent as the Moon / When she deserts the night, / Hid in her secret interlunar cave." Milton. *Samson Agonistes* [lines 86–89].

Sonnet 79. Line 7. **bells ... dyes**: "bells and flowerets of a thousand hues," Milton, *Lycidas*, line 135.

Sonnet 80. Line 9. **martial star**: named for Mars, the classical god of war.

LXXXI

He may be envied, who with tranquil breast
    Can wander in the wild and woodland scene,
When Summer's glowing hands have newly drest
    The shadowy forests, and the copses green;
Who, unpursued by care, can pass his hours   5
    Where briony and woodbine fringe the trees,*
On thymy banks reposing, while the bees
Murmur "their fairy tunes in praise of flowers;"†
    Or on the rock with ivy clad, and fern
That overhangs the osier-whispering bed   10
    Of some clear current, bid his wishes turn
From this bad world; and by calm reason led,
    Knows, in refined retirement, to possess
    By friendship hallow'd—rural happiness!

---

* Briony, *Bryonia dioica, foliis palmatis,* &c. White Briony, growing plentifully in woods and hedges, and twisting around taller plants.

† A line taken, *I believe,* from a Poem called "Vacuna," printed in Dodsley's collection ["Vacuna" by Dr. D— (1739), printed in *A Collection of Poems* (London: J. Dodsley, 1770), V, 97, contains the following lines: "By vale or brook to loiter not displeas'd: / Hear the stream's pebbled roar, and the sweet bee / Humming her fairy tunes, in praise of flowers…"].

Sonnet 81. This sonnet was originally printed in *Rambles Farther* (1796), a sequel to Smith's educational book for children *Rural Walks*.

LXXXII
To the shade of Burns*

Mute is thy wild harp, now, O Bard sublime!
  Who, amid Scotia's mountain solitude,
Great Nature taught to "build the lofty rhyme,"
  And even beneath the daily pressure, rude,
Of labouring Poverty, thy generous blood,   5
Fired with the love of freedom[.] —Not subdued
  Wert thou by thy low fortune: But a time
  Like this we live in, when the abject chime
Of echoing Parasite is best approved,
  Was not for thee [.] —Indignantly is fled   10
Thy noble Spirit; and no longer moved
  By all the ills o'er which thine heart has bled,
  Associate worthy of the illustrious dead,
Enjoys with them "the Liberty it loved." †

---

* Whoever has tasted the charm of original genius so evident in the composition of this genuine Poet, a Poet "of nature's own creation," [James Thomson, *Coriolanus,* III.iii] cannot surely fail to lament his unhappy life, (latterly passed, as I have understood, in an employment to which such a mind as his must have been averse,) nor his premature death. For one, herself made the object of *subscription,* is it proper to add, that whoever *has* thus been delighted with the wild notes of the Scottish bard, must have a melancholy pleasure in relieving by their benevolence the unfortunate family he has left? [This sonnet, with the attached note, was first printed in the second volume of *Elegiac Sonnets* (1797), which was published by subscription.]

† Pope ["Such this Man was, who now, from earth remov'd, / At length enjoys that Liberty he lov'd." "Epitaph on Sir William Trumbull," lines 11–12].

Line 1. **Bard sublime:** The sonnet is written on the occasion of the Scots poet Robert Burns's death in 1796.

Line 3. **build the lofty rhyme:** Milton, *Lycidas,* line 11.

LXXXIII*
The sea view

The upland Shepherd, as reclined he lies
   On the soft turf that clothes the mountain brow,
Marks the bright Sea-line mingling with the skies;
   Or from his course celestial, sinking slow,
   The Summer-Sun in purple radiance low,   5
Blaze on the western waters; the wide scene
   Magnificent, and tranquil, seems to spread
Even o'er the Rustic's breast a joy serene,
   When, like dark plague-spots by the Demons shed,
Charged deep with death, upon the waves, far seen,   10
   Move the war-freighted ships; and fierce and red,
   Flash their destructive fire [.]—The mangled dead
And dying victims then pollute the flood.
Ah! thus man spoils Heaven's glorious works with blood!

LXXXIV
To the Muse

Wilt thou forsake me who in life's bright May
   Lent warmer lustre to the radiant morn;
   And even o'er Summer scenes by tempests torn,
Shed with illusive light the dewy ray
Of pensive pleasure?—Wilt thou, while the day   5
   Of saddening Autumn closes, as I mourn

---

* Suggested by the recollection of having seen, some years since, on a beautiful evening of Summer, an engagement between two armed ships, from the high down called the Beacon Hill, near Brighthelmstone [modern Brighton].

Sonnet 84. This was the final sonnet, and thus the final statement in the series of *Elegiac Sonnets*, in the second volume of poems added in 1797.

In languid, hopeless sorrow, far away
  Bend thy soft step, and never more return?—
Crush'd to the earth, by bitterest anguish prest,
  From my faint eyes thy graceful form recedes;   10
  Thou canst not heal an heart like mine that bleeds;
But, when in quiet earth that heart shall rest,
  Haply may'st thou one sorrowing vigil keep,
  Where Pity and Remembrance bend and weep!*

LXXXV

The fairest flowers are gone! for tempests fell,
  And with wild wing swept some unblown away,
While on the upland lawn or rocky dell
  More faded in the day-star's ardent ray;
And scarce the copse, or hedge-row shade beneath,   5
  Or by the runnel's grassy course, appear
  Some lingering blossoms of the earlier year,
Mingling bright florets, in the yellow wreath
That Autumn with his poppies and his corn
  Binds on his tawny temples[.]—So the schemes   10
Rais'd by fond Hope in youth's unclouded morn,
  While sanguine youth enjoys delusive dreams,
Experience withers; till scarce one remains
Flattering the languid heart, where only Reason reigns!

---

* "Where melancholy friendship bends and weeps."   Thomas Gray ["Epitaph on Sir William Williams," line 12].

Sonnet 85. Printed in Smith's *The Young Philosopher: A Novel* (1798), where it is written by Mrs. Glenmorris to accompany the botanical drawings of her daughter Medora.

Line 1. **fell:** the sense requires this be construed as a verb.

Line 2. **unblown:** buds not yet in bloom.   Line 4. **day-star:** the sun.

LXXXVI

Written near a port on a dark evening

Huge vapours brood above the clifted shore,
   Night on the Ocean settles, dark and mute,
Save where is heard the repercussive roar
   Of drowsy billows, on the rugged foot
Of rocks remote; or still more distant tone   5
   Of seamen in the anchor'd bark that tell
The watch reliev'd; or one deep voice alone
   Singing the hour, and bidding "Strike the bell."
All is black shadow, but the lucid line
   Mark'd by the light surf on the level sand,   10
Or where afar the ship-lights faintly shine
   Like wandering fairy fires, that oft on land
Mislead the Pilgrim[.]—Such the dubious ray
That wavering Reason lends, in life's long darkling way.

LXXXVII

Written in October

The blasts of Autumn as they scatter round
   The faded foliage of another year,
And muttering many a sad and solemn sound,
   Drive the pale fragments o'er the stubble sere,
Are well attuned to my dejected mood;   5
   (Ah! better far than airs that breathe of Spring!)
   While the high rooks, that hoarsely clamouring
Seek in black phalanx the half-leafless wood,

Sonnet 86. Printed originally in *The Young Philosopher;* written by Delmont to his mother-in-law Mrs. Glenmorris as he awaits favorable winds for crossing from Wales to Ireland.

Line 12. **fairy fires**: the ignis fatuus or will-o'-the-wisp.

Sonnet 87. From *The Young Philosopher,* an effusion left among the papers of the young suicide Elizabeth Lisburne.

I rather hear, than that enraptured lay
Harmonious, and of Love and Pleasure born,　　　　　　10
　Which from the golden furze, or flowering thorn
　Awakes the Shepherd in the ides of May;
Nature delights *me* most when most she mourns,
For never more to me the Spring of Hope returns!

LXXXVIII
Nepenthe*

Oh! for imperial Polydamna's art,
　Which to bright Helen was in Egypt taught,
　To mix with magic power the oblivious draught
Of force to staunch the bleeding of the heart,

---

* Of what nature this Nepenthe was, has ever been a matter of doubt and dispute. See Wakefield's note to Pope's *Odyssey,* Book iv, verse 302 [1796 edition].
　But the passage here alluded to runs thus:

　　"Meanwhile with genial joy to warm the soul
　　Bright Helen mix'd a mirth-inspiring bowl,
　　Temper'd with drugs, of sovereign use t'assuage
　　The boiling bosom of tumultuous rage;
　　To clear the cloudy front of wrinkled care,
　　And dry the tearful sluices of despair;
　　Charm'd with that virtuous draught, th' exalted mind
　　All sense of woe delivers to the wind.
　　Tho' on the blazing pile his father lay,
　　Or a loved brother groan'd his life away,
　　Or darling son, oppress'd by ruffian force,
　　Fell breathless at his feet a mangled corse,
　　From morn to eve, impassive and serene,
　　The man entranced would view the deathful scene:
　　These drugs so friendly to the joys of life,
　　Bright Helen learn'd from Thone's imperial wife."

Milton thus speaks of it in Comus:

　　"Behold this cordial julep here,
　　That flames and dances in his crystal bounds!
　　Not that Nepenthe, which the wife of Thone
　　In Egypt gave to Jove-born Helena,
　　Is of such power as this to stir up joy,
　　To life so friendly, or so cool to thirst." [*Comus,* lines 672–78, with liberties]

And to Care's wan and hollow cheek impart   5
    The smile of happy youth, uncursed with thought.
Potent indeed the charm that could appease
    Affection's ceaseless anguish, doom'd to weep
O'er the cold grave; or yield even transient ease
    By soothing busy Memory to sleep!   10
—Around me those who surely must have tried
    Some charm of equal power, I daily see,
But still to *me* Oblivion is denied,
    There's no Nepenthe, now, on earth for me.

LXXXIX*
To the sun

Whether awaken'd from unquiet rest
    I watch "the opening eyelids of the Morn,"
When thou, O Sun! from Ocean's silver'd breast
    Emerging, bidst another day be born—
Or whether in thy path of cloudless blue,   5
    Thy noontide fires I mark with dazzled eyes;
Or to the West thy radiant course pursue,
    Veil'd in the gorgeous broidery of the skies,
Celestial lamp! thy influence bright and warm
    That renovates the world with life and light   10
Shines not for me—for never more the form
    I loved—so fondly loved, shall bless my sight;
And nought thy rays illumine, *now* can charm
    My misery, or to day convert my night!

---

* "I woke, she fled, and day brought back my night." Milton [Sonnet 23, line 14].

Sonnet 89. Line 2. **Morn**: Milton, *Lycidas,* line 26.
Line 11. **form**: Smith's late daughter: see Sonnet 65 (page 57).

XC
To oblivion

Forgetfulness! I would thy hand could close
   These eyes that turn reluctant from the day;
   So might this painful consciousness decay,
And, with my memory, end my cureless woes.
   Sister of Chaos and eternal Night!   5
Oblivion! take me to thy quiet reign,
   Since robb'd of all that gave my soul delight,
I only ask exemption from the pain
   Of knowing "such things were"—and are no more;
Of dwelling on the hours for ever fled,   10
   And heartless, helpless, hopeless to deplore
"Pale misery living, joy and pleasure dead:"*
While dragging thus unwish'd a length of days,
"Death seems prepared to strike, yet still delays."†

XCI
Reflections on some drawings of plants

I can in groups these mimic flowers compose,
   These bells and golden eyes, embathed in dew;
Catch the soft blush that warms the early Rose,
   Or the pale Iris cloud with veins of blue;
Copy the scallop'd leaves, and downy stems,   5

---

* "See misery living, hope and pleasure dead." Sir Brook Boothby [Sonnet 13, line 6, from *Sorrows. Sacred to the Memory of Penelope* (London: Cadell and Davies, 1796), 19].

† "Death seems prepared, yet still delays to strike." Thomas Warton ["Ode I. To Sleep," line 16: "Death stands prepar'd, but still delays, to strike"].

Sonnet 90. Line 9. **such ... were**: an allusion to Macduff's inability to remain stoic after the murder of his wife and children: "I cannot but remember that such things were, / That were most precious to me" *(Macbeth*, IV.ii.222–23). The referent once more seems to be Smith's late daughter.

And bid the pencil's varied shades arrest
Spring's humid buds, and Summer's musky gems:
    But, save the portrait on my bleeding breast,
I have no semblance of that form adored,
        That form, expressive of a soul divine,   10
        So early blighted; and while life is mine,
With fond regret, and ceaseless grief deplored—
        That grief, my angel! with too faithful art
Enshrines thy image in thy Mother's heart.

XCII
Written at Bignor Park in Sussex, in August, 1799

Low murmurs creep along the woody vale,
    The tremulous Aspens shudder in the breeze,
Slow o'er the downs the leaden vapours sail,
    While I, beneath these old paternal trees,
Mark the dark shadows of the threaten'd storm,   5
    As gathering clouds o'erveil the morning sun;
They pass!—But oh! ye visions bright and warm
    With which even here my sanguine youth begun,
Ye are obscured for ever!—And too late
    The poor Slave shakes the unworthy bonds away   10
    Which crush'd her!—Lo! the radiant star of day
Lights up this lovely scene anew[.] —My fate
    Nor hope nor joy illumines—Nor for me
    Return those rosy hours which here I used to see!

Sonnet 91. Line 9. **form adored**: a further tribute to her daughter.

Sonnet 92. Title. **Bignor Park**: Bignor Park was the home in which Charlotte Smith was raised, and in later life, it served as a reminder of the placid genteel existence once promised but then denied her.

Line 4. **paternal**: descending through a family; reminders of her father.

Lines 10–11. **The ... her**: Although the estate of her father-in-law is at last sufficiently settled that the trusts left to her children can be activated, her freedom comes too late to liberate her mind. In fact, this settlement proved illusive and litigation continued.

Ode to despair

Thou spectre of terrific mien!
   Lord of the hopeless heart and hollow eye,
In whose fierce train each form is seen
   That drives sick Reason to insanity!
I woo thee with unusual prayer,   5
"Grim-visaged, comfortless Despair!"
Approach—in me a willing victim find,
Who seeks thine iron sway—and calls thee kind!

Ah! hide for ever from my sight
   The faithless flatterer Hope—whose pencil gay,   10
Pourtrays some vision of delight,
   Then bids the fairy tablet fade away;
While in dire contrast to mine eyes
Thy phantoms, yet more hideous, rise,
And Memory draws from Pleasure's wither'd flower,   15
Corrosives for the heart—of fatal power!

I bid the traitor Love adieu!
   Who to this fond believing bosom came,
A guest insidious and untrue,
   With Pity's soothing voice—in Friendship's name;   20
The wounds *he* gave, nor Time shall cure,
Nor Reason teach me to endure.
And to that breast mild Patience pleads in vain,
Which feels the curse—of meriting its pain.

Yet not to me, tremendous Power!   25
   Thy worst of spirit-wounding pangs impart,

Ode to Despair. From Smith's *Emmeline* (1788), where it is authored by Lady Adelina Trelawny.

Line 6. **Grim ... Despair**: Thomas Gray, "Ode on a Distant Prospect of Eton College," line 69.

With which, in dark conviction's hour,
    Thou strikest the guilty unrepentant heart;
But of Illusion long the sport,
That dreary, tranquil gloom I court,   30
Where my past errors I may still deplore,
And dream of long-lost happiness no more!

To thee I give this tortured breast,
    Where Hope arises but to foster Pain;
Ah! lull its agonies to rest!   35
    Ah! let me never be deceived again!
But callous, in thy deep repose,
Behold, in long array, the woes
Of the dread future, calm and undismay'd,
Till I may claim the hope—that shall not fade!   40

Elegy *

"Dark gathering clouds involve the threatening skies,
    The sea heaves conscious of the impending gloom,
Deep, hollow murmurs from the cliffs arise;
    They come—the Spirits of the Tempest come!

Oh, may such terrors mark the approaching night   5
    As reign'd on that these streaming eyes deplore!
Flash, ye red fires of heaven! with fatal light,
    And with conflicting winds, ye waters! roar.

---

* This elegy is written on the supposition that an indigent young woman had been addressed by the son of a wealthy yeoman, who resenting his attachment, had driven him from home, and compelled him to have recourse for subsistence to the occupation of a pilot, in which, in attempting to save a vessel in distress, he perished.

    The father dying, a tomb is supposed to be erected to his memory in the church-yard mentioned in Sonnet the 44th [page 42]. And while a tempest is gathering, the unfortunate young woman comes thither; and courting the same death as had robbed her of her lover, she awaits its violence, and is at length overwhelmed by the waves.

Loud and more loud, ye foaming billows! burst;
    Ye warring elements! more fiercely rave,   10
Till the wide waves o'erwhelm the spot accurst
    Where ruthless Avarice finds a quiet grave!"

Thus with clasp'd hands, wild looks, and streaming hair,
    While shrieks of horror broke her trembling speech,
A wretched maid—the victim of Despair,   15
    Survey'd the threatening storm and desart beech:

Then to the tomb where now the father slept
    Whose rugged nature bade her sorrows flow,
Frantic she turn'd—and beat her breast and wept,
    Invoking vengeance on the dust below.   20

"Lo! rising there above each humbler heap,
    Yon cipher'd stones *his* name and wealth relate,
Who gave his son—remorseless—to the deep,
    While I, his living victim, curse my fate.

Oh! my lost love! no tomb is placed for thee,   25
    That may to strangers' eyes thy worth impart;
Thou hast no grave but in the stormy sea!
    And no memorial but this breaking heart!

Forth to the world, a widow'd wanderer driven,
    I pour to winds and waves the unheeded tear,   30
Try with vain effort to submit to Heaven,
    And fruitless call on him—'who cannot hear.' *

---

* 'I fruitless mourn to him who [that] cannot hear, / And weep the more because I weep in vain.' Gray's exquisite Sonnet; in reading which it is impossible not to regret that he wrote only one [Thomas Gray, "On the Death of Richard West," lines 13–14].

Oh! might I fondly clasp him once again,
    While o'er my head the infuriate billows pour,
Forget in death this agonizing pain,   35
    And feel his father's cruelty no more!

Part, raging waters! part, and shew beneath,
    In your dread caves, his pale and mangled form;
Now, while the Demons of Despair and Death
    Ride on the blast, and urge the howling storm!   40

Lo! by the lightning's momentary blaze,
    I see him rise the whitening waves above,
No longer such as when in happier days
    He gave the enchanted hours—to me and love.

Such, as when daring the enchafed sea,   45
    And courting dangerous toil, he often said
That every peril, one soft smile from me,
    One sigh of speechless tenderness o'erpaid.

But dead, disfigured, while between the roar
    Of the loud waves his accents pierce mine ear,   50
And seem to say—Ah, wretch! delay no more,
    But come, unhappy mourner—meet me here.

Yet, powerful Fancy! bid the phantom stay,
    Still let me hear him!—'Tis already past!
Along the waves his shadow glides away,   55
    I lose his voice amid the deafening blast!

Line 45. **enchafed sea**: "the enchafed flood" (*Othello*, II.i.17).

Ah! wild Illusion, born of frantic Pain!
    He hears not, comes not from his watery bed!
My tears, my anguish, my despair are vain,
    The insatiate ocean gives not up its dead.   60

'Tis not his voice! Hark! the deep thunders roll!
    Upheaves the ground; the rocky barriers fail!
Approach, ye horrors that delight my soul!
    Despair, and Death, and Desolation, hail!"

The Ocean hears—The embodied waters come—   65
    Rise o'er the land, and with resistless sweep
Tear from its base the proud aggressor's tomb,
    And bear the injured to eternal sleep!

Song
From the French of Cardinal Bernis

Fruit of Aurora's tears, fair Rose,
   On whose soft leaves fond Zephyrs play,
O queen of flowers! thy buds disclose,
   And give thy fragrance to the day;
Unveil thy transient charms:—ah, no!   5
   A little be thy bloom delay'd,
Since the same hour that bids thee blow,
   Shall see thee droop thy languid head.

But go! and on Themira's breast
   Find, happy flower! thy throne and tomb!   10
While, jealous of a fate so blest,
   How shall I envy thee thy doom!
Should some rude hand approach thee there,

Title. **Bernis:** Cardinal François Joachim de Pierre de Bernis (1715–94) was, as well as a churchman, a major politician, whose career was promoted by Madame de Pompadour, and a diplomat, serving as French ambassador to Rome from 1769 to 1794. When originally published in 1784, the "Song" was preceded by its French original:

I.

Tendre fruit des pleurs de l'Aurore,
Objet des baisers du Zephir,
Reine de l'empire de Flore,
Hate toi de t'epanouir,
Que dis je?—Helas! crains de paraître,
Differe un moment de t'ouvrir;
L'instant qui doit te faire naître
Est celui qui doit te fletrir.

II.

Va meurs sur le sein de Themire,
Qu'il soit ton trône, et ton tombeau;
Jaloux de ton sort, je n'aspire
Qu'au bonheur d'un trepas si beau.

Si quelque main a l'imprudence,
D'y venir troubler ton repos;
Tu porte avec toi ta defence,
Garde une epine à mes rivaux.

III.

L'Amour aura soin de t'instruire
De quel côté tu dois pancher,
Eclate à ses yeux sans me nuire,
Pare son sein, sans le cacher.
Qu'enfin elle rende les armes
Au Dieu qui doit former nos liens,
Et qu'en voyant fletrir tes charmes,
Elle apprend à jouir des siens.

Line 1. **Aurora's tears:** morning dew.   Line 7. **blow:** bloom.

Guard the sweet shrine thou wilt adorn;
Ah! punish those who rashly dare, 15
And for my rivals keep thy thorn.

Love shall himself thy boughs compose,
And bid thy wanton leaves divide;
He'll shew thee how, my lovely Rose,
To deck her bosom, not to hide: 20
And thou shalt tell the cruel maid
How frail are Youth and Beauty's charms,
And teach her, ere her own shall fade,
To give them to her lover's arms.

The origin of flattery *

When Jove, in anger to the sons of Earth,
Bid artful Vulcan give Pandora birth,
And sent the fatal gift which spread below
O'er all the wretched race contagious woe,
Unhappy man, by Vice and Folly tost, 5
Found in the storms of life his quiet lost,
While Envy, Avarice, and Ambition, hurl'd
Discord and death around the warring world;
Then the blest peasant left his fields and fold,

* This little poem was written almost extempore on occasion of a conversation where many
pleasant things were said on the subject of flattery; and some French gentlemen who were of
the party enquired for a synonime in English to the French word fleurette. The poem was
inserted in the two first editions, and having been asked for by very respectable subscribers
to the present [the fifth, 1789], it is reprinted. The sonnets have been thought too gloomy;
and the author has been advised to insert some of a more cheerful cast. This poem may by
others be thought too gay, and is indeed so little in unison with the present sentiments and
feelings of its author, that it had been wholly omitted but for the respectable approbation of
those to whose judgment she owed implicit deference.

The origin of flattery. Line 3. **gift**: Pandora's box, the receptacle of human vices and of
hope.

And barter'd love and peace for power and gold;   10
Left his calm cottage and his native plain,
In search of wealth to tempt the faithless main;
Or, braving danger, in the battle stood,
And bathed his savage hands in human blood!
No longer then, his woodland walks among,   15
The shepherd-lad his genuine passion sung,
Or sought at early morn his soul's delight,
Or graved her name upon the bark at night;
To deck her flowing hair no more he wove
The simple wreath, or with ambitious love   20
Bound his own brow with myrtle or with bay,
But broke his pipe, or threw his crook away.
The nymphs forsaken other pleasures sought;
Then first for gold their venal hearts were bought,
And Nature's blush to sickly Art gave place,   25
And Affectation seized the seat of Grace:
No more Simplicity by Sense refined,
Or generous Sentiment, possess'd the mind;
No more they felt each other's joy and woe,
And Cupid fled and hid his useless bow.   30
But with deep grief propitious Venus pined,
To see the ills which threaten'd womankind;
Ills that she knew her empire would disarm,
And rob her subjects of their sweetest charm:
Good humour's potent influence destroy,   35
And change for lowering frowns the smile of joy.
Then deeply sighing at the mournful view,
She try'd at length what heavenly art could do
To bring back Pleasure to her pensive train,
And vindicate the glories of her reign.   40
A thousand little loves attend the task,
And bear from Mars's head his radiant casque,
The fair enchantress on its silver bound

Line 42. **radiant casque**: the red war-helmet of Mars.

Weaved with soft spells her magic cestus round.
Then shaking from her hair ambrosial dew,   45
Infused fair hope, and expectation new,
And stifled wishes, and persuasive sighs,
And fond belief, and "eloquence of eyes,"
And falt'ring accents, which explain so well
What studied speeches vainly try to tell;   50
And more pathetic silence, which imparts
Infectious tenderness to feeling hearts;
Soft tones of pity; fascinating smiles;
And Maia's son assisted her with wiles,
And brought gay dreams, fantastic visions brought,   55
And waved his wand o'er the seducing draught.
Then Zephyr came; to him the goddess cry'd,
"Go fetch from Flora all her flowery pride
To fill my charm, each scented bud that blows,
And bind my myrtles with her thornless rose;   60
Then speed thy flight to Gallia's smiling plain,
Where rolls the Loire, the Garonne, and the Seine;
Dip in their waters thy celestial wing,
And the soft dew to fill my chalice bring;
But chiefly tell thy Flora, that to me   65
She send a bouquet of her fleurs de lys;
That poignant spirit will complete my spell."

Line 44. **magic cestus**: the girdle of Venus, which awakens love in all who behold it.

Line 48. **eloquence ... eyes**: a direct allusion to Pope's description of the qualities inherent in the cestus of Venus: "Fond Love, the gentle Vow, the gay Desire, / The kind Deceit, the still-reviving Fire, / Persuasive Speech, and more persuasive Sighs, / Silence that Spoke, and Eloquence of Eyes" *(Iliad,* xIV.249–52).

Line 54. **Maia's son**: Mercury, messenger of the gods, often associated with duplicity.

Line 57. **Zephyr**: the west wind, here associated with spring fertility.

Line 60. **myrtles ... rose**: the myrtle is associated with love; a thornless rose, symbol of nature's perfection, would render love painless.

Line 61. **Gallia's ... plain**: France, to the British a country of social polish, artifice, and licentiousness.

Line 66. **fleurs de lys**: irises: the national flower of France, symbol of its refined court.

—'Tis done: the lovely sorceress says 'tis well.
And now Apollo lends a ray of fire,
The cauldron bubbles, and the flames aspire;   70
The watchful Graces round the circle dance,
With arms entwined to mark the work's advance;
And with full quiver sportive Cupid came,
Temp'ring his favorite arrows in the flame.
Then Venus speaks; the wavering flames retire,   75
And Zephyr's breath extinguishes the fire.
At length the goddess in the helmet's round
A sweet and subtil spirit duly found,
More soft than oil, than æther more refined,
Of power to cure the woes of womankind,   80
And call'd it Flattery!—balm of female life,
It charms alike the widow, maid, and wife;
Clears the sad brow of virgins in despair,
And smooths the cruel traces left by care;
Bids palsied age with youthful spirit glow,   85
And hangs May's garlands on December's snow.
Delicious essence! howsoe'er apply'd,
By what rude nature is thy charm deny'd?
Some form seducing still thy whisper wears,
Stern Wisdom turns to thee her willing ears,   90
And Prudery listens and forgets her fears.
The rustic nymph whom rigid aunts restrain,
Condemn'd to dress, and practise airs in vain,
At thy first summons finds her bosom swell,
And bids her crabbed gouvernantes farewel;   95
While, fired by thee with spirit not her own,
She grows a toast, and rises into *ton*.

Line 79. **æther**: the fifth essence or quint-essence, an invisible substance through which the likes of heat and light were transmitted; from the Middle Ages into the Enlightenment the term was much discussed and seldom carefully defined.

Line 95. **gouvernantes**: chaperones.

Line 97. **She ... ton**: She is toasted by many would-be lovers and begins to circulate in high society.

The faded beauty who with secret pain
Sees younger charms usurp her envied reign,
By thee assisted, can with smiles behold   100
The record where her conquests are enroll'd;
And dwelling yet on scenes by memory nursed,
When George the Second reign'd, or George the First;
She sees the shades of ancient beaux arise,
Who swear her eyes exceeded modern eyes,   105
When poets sung for her, and lovers bled,
And giddy fashion follow'd as she led.
Departed modes appear in long array,
The flowers and flounces of her happier day;
Again her locks the decent fillets bind,   110
The waving lappet flutters in the wind,
And then comparing with a proud disdain
The more fantastic tastes that now obtain,
She deems ungraceful, trifling and absurd,
The gayer world that moves round George the Third.   115
Nor thy soft influence will the train refuse,
Who court in distant shades the modest Muse,
Tho' in a form more pure and more refined,
Thy soothing spirit meets the letter'd mind.
Not Death itself thine empire can destroy;   120
Tow'rds thee, even then, we turn the languid eye;
Still trust in thee to bid our memory bloom,
And scatter roses round the silent tomb.

Line 102. **scenes ... nursed**: Since this poem dates from 1783 or earlier, the "faded beauty" is remembering conquests from a quarter century before (George II died in 1760) and even perhaps as far back as 1727, the last year of George I's reign.

Line 108. **modes**: fashions.

Line 111. **lappet**: a flounce or loose fold of fabric on headgear or dress.

Lines 116–17. **Nor ... Muse**: The final section is a gentle self-satire on a writer's pretensions to lasting fame.

The peasant of the Alps

Where cliffs arise by winter crown'd,
  And thro' dark groves of pine around,
Down the deep chasms the snow-fed torrents foam,
Within some hollow, shelter'd from the storms,
The PEASANT of the ALPS his cottage forms,   5
And builds his humble, happy home.

Unenvied is the rich domain,
  That far beneath him on the plain
Waves its wide harvests and its olive groves;
More dear to him his hut with plantain thatch'd,   10
Where long his unambitious heart attach'd,
Finds all he wishes, all he loves.

There dwells the mistress of his heart,
  And *Love,* who teaches every art,
Has bid him dress the spot with fondest care;   15
When borrowing from the vale its fertile soil,
He climbs the precipice with patient toil,
To plant her favorite flowrets there.

With native shrubs, a hardy race,
  There the green myrtle finds a place,   20
And roses there the dewy leaves decline;
While from the craggs abrupt, and tangled steeps,
With bloom and fruit the Alpine-berry peeps,
And, blushing, mingles with the vine.

The peasant of the Alps. This poem is the response of the despondent title figure in Smith's
novel *Celestina* to reading of an Alpine cottage destroyed by an avalanche.

Line 10. **plantain**: a common weed with broad leaves.

His garden's simple produce stored, 25
   Prepared for him by hands adored,
Is all the little luxury he knows:
And by the same dear hands are softly spread,
The chamois' velvet spoil that forms the bed,
Where in her arms he finds repose. 30

But absent from the calm abode,
   Dark thunder gathers round his road;
Wild raves the wind, the arrowy lightnings flash,
Returning quick the murmuring rocks among,
His faint heart trembling as he winds along; 35
Alarm'd—he listens to the crash

Of rifted ice!—O man of woe!
   O'er his dear cot—a mass of snow,
By the storm sever'd from the cliff above,
Has fallen—and buried in its marble breast, 40
All that for him—lost wretch!—the world possest,
His home, his happiness, his love!

Aghast the heart-struck mourner stands,
   Glazed are his eyes—convulsed his hands,
O'erwhelming anguish checks his labouring breath; 45
Crush'd by despair's intolerable weight,
Frantic he seeks the mountain's giddiest height,
And headlong seeks relief in death!

A fate too similar is mine,
   But I—in lingering pain repine, 50
And still my lost felicity deplore!
Cold, cold to me is that dear breast become
Where this poor heart had fondly fix'd its home,
And love and happiness are mine no more!

Song

Does Pity give, tho' Fate denies,
   And to my wounds her balm impart?
O speak—with those expressive eyes!
   Let one low sigh escape thine heart.

The gazing crowd shall never guess   5
   What anxious, watchful Love can see;
Nor know what those soft looks express,
   Nor dream that sigh is meant for me.

Ah! words are useless, words are vain,
   Thy generous sympathy to prove;   10
And well that sigh, those looks explain,
   That Clara mourns my hapless love.

Thirty-eight
Addressed to Mrs. H– – – –Y

In early youth's unclouded scene,
The brilliant morning of eighteen,
With health and sprightly joy elate
   We gazed on life's enchanting spring,
   Nor thought how quickly time would bring   5
The mournful period——Thirty-eight.

Then the starch maid, or matron sage,
Already of that sober age,

Thirty-eight. Title. **Mrs. H – – – –Y:** Eliza Hayley, wife of the poet William Hayley, whom she married in 1769 at the age of 19. Twenty years later in 1789, shortly after this poem was written, she and her husband effected a permanent separation. Smith was a year her elder.

Line 7. **starch:** stiff, inflexible.

We view'd with mingled scorn and hate;
  In whose sharp words, or sharper face,
  With thoughtless mirth we loved to trace
The sad effects of——Thirty-eight.

Till saddening, sickening at the view,
We learn'd to dread what Time might do;
And then preferr'd a prayer to Fate
  To end our days ere that arrived;
  When (power and pleasure long survived)
We met neglect and——Thirty-eight.

But Time, in spite of wishes, flies,
And Fate our simple prayer denies,
And bids us Death's own hour await:
  The auburn locks are mix'd with grey,
  The transient roses fade away,
But Reason comes at——Thirty-eight.

Her voice the anguish contradicts
That dying vanity inflicts;
Her hand new pleasures can create,
  For us she opens to the view
  Prospects less bright—but far more true,
And bids us smile at——Thirty-eight.

No more shall *Scandal's* breath destroy
The social converse we enjoy
With bard or critic tête à tête;—
  O'er Youth's bright blooms her blights shall pour,
  But spare the improving friendly hour
That Science gives to——Thirty-eight.

Line 32. **social converse**: conversation free from amorous intent.

Line 36. **Science**: knowledge, learning.

Stripp'd of their gaudy hues by Truth,
We view the glitt'ring toys of youth,
And blush to think how poor the bait
   For which to public scenes we ran,   40
   And scorn'd of sober Sense the plan,
Which gives content at——Thirty-eight.

Tho' Time's inexorable sway
Has torn the myrtle bands away,
For other wreaths 'tis not too late,   45
   The amaranth's purple glow survives,
   And still Minerva's olive lives
On the calm brow of——Thirty-eight.

With eye more steady we engage
To contemplate approaching age,   50
And life more justly estimate;
   With firmer souls, and stronger powers,
   With reason, faith, and friendship ours,
   We'll not regret the stealing hours
That lead from Thirty——even to Forty-eight.   55

Line 44. **myrtle bands:** flowers associated with young love.

Line 46. **amaranth's ... glow:** the amaranth is the immortal flower of paradise.

Line 47. **Minerva's olive:** peace, wisdom.

Verses intended to have been prefixed to the novel of Emmeline, but then suppressed

O'erwhelm'd with sorrow, and sustaining long
"The proud man's contumely, th' oppressor's wrong,"
Languid despondency, and vain regret,
Must my exhausted spirit struggle yet?
Yes!—Robb'd myself of all that fortune gave,   5
Even of all hope—but shelter in the grave,
Still shall the plaintive lyre essay its powers
To dress the cave of Care with Fancy's flowers,
Maternal Love the fiend Despair withstand,
Still animate the heart and guide the hand.   10
—May you, dear objects of my anxious care,
Escape the evils I was born to bear!
Round *my* devoted head while tempests roll,
Yet there, where I have treasured up my soul,
May the soft rays of dawning hope impart   15
Reviving Patience to my fainting heart;—
And when its sharp solicitudes shall cease,
May I be conscious in the realms of peace
That every tear which swells my children's eyes,
From sorrows past, not present ills arise.   20
Then, with some friend who loves to share your pain,
For 'tis my boast that *some* such friends remain,
By filial grief, and fond remembrance prest,
You'll seek the spot where all my sorrows rest;
Recal my hapless days in sad review,   25
The long calamities I bore for you,
And—with an happier fate—resolve to prove
How well you merited—your mother's love.

Title. Originally entitled "To my children." Printed as the final poem of the first volume of *Elegiac Sonnets*, it stands as a summary statement about Smith's tribulations and endurance.
Line 2. **The...wrong**: *Hamlet*, III.i.71.   Line 7. **plaintive lyre**: i.e. elegiac sonnets.
Line 14. **where...soul**: see Matt. 6:19–21.

The dead beggar
An elegy, addressed to a lady, who was affected at seeing the funeral of a nameless pauper, buried at the expence of the parish, in the church-yard at Brighthelmstone, in November 1792*

> Swells then thy feeling heart, and streams thine eye
>   O'er the deserted being, poor and old,
> Whom cold, reluctant, Parish Charity
>   Consigns to mingle with his kindred mold?
>
> Mourn'st thou, that *here* the time-worn sufferer ends   5
>   Those evil days still threatening woes to come;
> Here, where the friendless feel no want of friends,
>   Where even the houseless wanderer finds an home?
>
> What tho' no kindred croud in sable forth,
>   And sigh, or seem to sigh, around his bier;   10
> Tho' o'er his coffin with the humid earth
>   No children drop the unavailing tear?

---

* I have been told that I have incurred blame for having used in this short composition, terms that have become obnoxious to certain persons [a reference to line 20, "rights of Man," a term that in 1792 indicated sympathy with the French Revolution]. Such remarks are hardly worth notice; and it is very little my ambition to obtain the suffrage of those who suffer party prejudice to influence their taste; or of those who desire that because they have themselves done it, every one else should be willing to sell their best birth-rights, the liberty of thought, and of expressing thought, for the *promise* of a mess of pottage [a reference to Esau's selling his patrimony as first-born to his brother Jacob; see Gen. 25:27–34].

  It is surely not too much to say, that in a country like ours, where such immense sums are annually raised for the poor, there ought to be some regulation which should prevent any miserable deserted being from perishing through want, as too often happens to such objects as that on whose interment these stanzas were written.

  It is somewhat remarkable that a circumstance exactly similar is the subject of a short poem called the Pauper's Funeral, in a volume lately published by Mr. Southey [*Poems* (1797), I, 47–48].

Title. **Brighthelmstone:** modern Brighton.

Line 3. **Parish Charity:** The Poor Laws gave each parish, that is, district church, responsibility for the indigent resident within its precincts.

Line 9. **in sable:** in the black clothes reserved for mourning.

Rather rejoice that *here* his sorrows cease,
    Whom sickness, age, and poverty oppress'd;
Where Death, the Leveller, restores to peace   15
    The wretch who living knew not where to rest.

Rejoice, that tho' an outcast spurn'd by Fate,
    Thro' penury's rugged path his race he ran;
In earth's cold bosom, equall'd with the great,
    Death vindicates the insulted rights of Man.   20

Rejoice, that tho' severe his earthly doom,
    And rude, and sown with thorns the way he trod,
Now, (where unfeeling Fortune cannot come)
    He rests upon the mercies of his GOD.

The female exile. Written at Brighthelmstone in November 1792*

November's chill blast on the rough beach is howling,
    The surge breaks afar, and then foams to the shore,
Dark clouds o'er the sea gather heavy and scowling,
    And the white cliffs re-echo the wild wintry roar.

Beneath that chalk rock, a fair stranger reclining,   5
    Has found on damp sea-weed a cold lonely seat;
Her eyes fill'd with tears, and her heart with repining,
    She starts at the billows that burst at her feet.

---

* This little Poem, of which a sketch first appeared in blank verse in a Poem called "The Emigrants" ["The Emigrants," pages 142–43, lines 200 ff.], was suggested by the sight of the group it attempts to describe—a French lady and her children.

Title. **Brighthelmstone:** modern Brighton.

There, day after day, with an anxious heart heaving,
    She watches the waves where they mingle with air;   10
For the sail which, alas! all her fond hopes deceiving,
    May bring only tidings to add to her care.

Loose stream to wild winds those fair flowing tresses,
    Once woven with garlands of gay Summer flowers;
Her dress unregarded, bespeaks her distresses,   15
    And beauty is blighted by grief's heavy hours.

Her innocent children, unconscious of sorrow,
    To seek the gloss'd shell, or the crimson weed stray;
Amused with the present, they heed not to-morrow,
    Nor think of the storm that is gathering to day.   20

The gilt, fairy ship, with its ribbon-sail spreading,
    They launch on the salt pool the tide left behind;
Ah! victims—for whom *their* sad mother is dreading
    The multiplied miseries that wait on mankind!

To fair fortune born, she beholds them with anguish,   25
    Now wanderers with her on a once hostile soil,
Perhaps doom'd for life in chill penury to languish,
    Or abject dependance, or soul-crushing toil.

But the sea-boat, her hopes and her terrors renewing,
    O'er the dim grey horizon now faintly appears;   30
She flies to the quay, dreading tidings of ruin,
    All breathless with haste, half expiring with fears.

Poor mourner!—I would that my fortune had left me
    The means to alleviate the woes I deplore;
But like thine my hard fate has of affluence bereft me,   35
    I can warm the cold heart of the wretched no more!

Written for the benefit of a distressed player, detained at Brighthelmstone for debt, November 1792

When in a thousand swarms, the Summer o'er,
The birds of passage quit our English shore,
By various routs the feather'd myriad moves;
The *Becca-fica* seeks Italian groves,
No more a *Wheat-ear;** while the soaring files   5
Of sea-fowl gather round the Hebrid-isles.

But if by bird-lime touch'd, unplum'd, confined,
Some poor ill-fated straggler stays behind,
Driven from his transient perch, beneath your eaves
On his unshelter'd head the tempest raves,   10
While drooping round, redoubling every pain,
His *Mate* and Nestlings ask his help in vain.

So we, the buskin and the sock who wear,
And "strut and fret," our little season here,
Dismiss'd at length, as Fortune bids divide—   15
Some (lucky rogues!) sit down on Thames's side;
Others to Liffy's western banks proceed,

---

* From an idea that the Wheat-ear is the Becca-fica of Italy, which I doubt. [The birds come from different families, the wheat-ear being a warbler and the beccafica a thrush.]

Title. **Brighthelmstone:** modern Brighton.

Line 2. **birds of passage:** migratory birds.   Line 3. **routs:** routes.

Line 7. **bird-lime:** a sticky substance used to ensnare small birds.   **unplum'd:** defeathered; with wings clipped.

Line 13. **buskin ... sock:** buskins were boots donned to give stature to actors in classical tragedy; socks were light shoes worn in classical comedies: so, players of tragedy and comedy.

Line 14. **strut and fret:** "Life's but a walking shadow, a poor player / That struts and frets his time upon the stage / And then is heard no more" (*Macbeth*, V.v.24–26).

Line 16. **Thames's side:** the London theatrical scene.

Line 17. **Liffy's ... banks:** in Dublin, capitol of Ireland, furthest west of the British Isles.

And some—driven far a-field, across the Tweed:
But pinion'd here, alas! I cannot fly:
The *hapless, unplumed,* lingering straggler I!   20
Unless the healing pity you bestow,
Shall imp my shatter'd wings—and let me go.

  Hard is *his* fate, whom evil stars have led
To seek in scenic art *precarious* bread,
While still, thro' wild vicissitudes afloat,   25
An Hero now, and now a *Sans Culotte!**
That eleemosinary bread he gains
Mingling—with real distresses—mimic pains.

  See in our group, a pale, lank Falstaff stare!
Much needs he stuffing:—while young Ammon there   30
Rehearses—in a garret—ten feet square!
And as his soft *Statira* sighs consent,
Roxana comes not—but a dun for rent!
Here shivering Edgar, in his blanket roll'd,
Exclaims—with too much reason, "Tom's a-cold!"   35

---

* At that time little else was talked of.

Line 18. **across ... Tweed:** into Scotland, specifically Edinburgh.

Line 22. **imp:** a term from falconry, meaning to graft new feathers to a damaged wing.

Line 26. **Sans Culotte:** "without breeches": the extreme radicals of the early years of the French Revolution. Two months after this poem was written the French guillotined Louis XVI and Britain declared war on the revolutionary government.

Line 27. **eleemosinary:** eleemosynary: charitable.

Line 29. **pale ... Falstaff:** Falstaff is renowned for his girth.

Line 30. **Ammon:** Alexander the Great, visiting the temple of Jupiter Ammon in Libya, was greeted by the priests as the son of the god and thus is sometimes styled Ammon. He is greeted in this manner on his entrance in Nathaniel Lee's historic tragedy, *The Rival Queens* (1677), the drama referred to here.

Line 32. **Statira:** Statira and Roxana are the rival queens of Lee's play.

Line 34. **Edgar:** The Duke of Gloucester's legitimate heir in *King Lear.*

Line 35. **Tom's a-cold!:** The cry of Tom o-Bedlam, the "unaccommodated man" Edgar impersonates when Lear encounters him on the heath during a violent storm.

And vainly tries his sorrows to divert,
While *Goneril* or *Regan* —wash his shirt!

Lo! fresh from Calais, Edward! mighty king!
Revolves—a mutton chop upon a string!
And Hotspur, plucking "honour from the moon,"   40
Feeds a *sick infant* with a pewter spoon!

More blest the Fisher, who undaunted braves
In his small bark, the impetuous winds and waves;
For though he plough the sea when others sleep,
He draws, like Glendower, spirits from the deep!*   45
And while the storm howls round, amidst his trouble,
Bright *moonshine* still illuminates the cobble!
Pale with her fears for him, some fair *Poissarde,*

---

* *Glen.* "I can call spirits from the vasty deep." / *Hotsp.* "But will they come when you do call for them?" Shakspeare [*1 Henry IV,* III.i.52, 54].

    The *spirits* that animate the night voyages of the Sussex fishermen are often sunk in their kegs on any alarm from the Custom-House officers; and being attached to a buoy, the adventurers go out when the danger of detection is over, and draw them up. A coarse sort of white brandy which they call *moonshine*, is a principal article of this illegal commerce.

Line 37. **Goneril ... Regan**: Lear's cruel daughters who connive to deprive Edgar of his father's love and his right of inheritance.

Line 38. **Edward**: This is Edward III (reign 1327–77) who started the Hundred Years' War to enforce his claim to the French throne and, after the French king was taken prisoner at the Battle of Poitiers, signed the Treaty of Calais in 1360. The king was not a popular subject for drama, but his son (who actually won the famous battle) is the histrionic title figure of William Shirley's *Edward the Black Prince*, which was introduced to the stage by Garrick in 1750 and became a staple of nationalistic theater as tensions rose with revolutionary France. This is probably the play invoked here.

Line 39. **Revolves**: suspends over an open fire.

Line 40. **Hotspur ... moon**: "To pluck bright honour from the pale-faced moon" *1 Henry IV,* I.iii.202.

Line 45. **Glendower**: Owen Glendower, the Welsh Lord with whom Hotspur leagues in revolt against Henry IV.   **spirits**: a pun on contraband liquor.

Line 47. **moonshine**: a clear and potent eau-de-vie.

Line 48. **Poissarde**: fish-wife; here, probably a light-hearted pun on a notorious event of the recent past, when an amazonian army of *poissardes* walked from Paris to Versailles on 5 October 1789 to demand the army's return to the capital to defend the revolution.

Watches his nearing boat; with fond regard
Smiles when she sees his little canvas handing,   50
And clasps her dripping lover on his landing.

More blest the *Peasant*, who, with nervous toil
Hews the rough oak, or breaks the stubborn soil:
Weary, indeed, he sees the evening come,
But then, the rude, yet tranquil hut, his home,   55
Receives its rustic inmate; then are his,
Secure repose, and dear domestic bliss!
The orchard's blushing fruit, the garden's store,
The pendant hop, that mantles round the door,
Are his:—and while the cheerful faggots burn,   60
"His lisping children hail their sire's return!"*

But wandering Players, "unhousel'd, unanneal'd,"
And unappointed, scour life's common field,
A flying squadron!—disappointments cross 'em,
And the campaign concludes, perhaps, at Horsham!†   65

Oh! ye, whose timely bounty deigns to shed
Compassion's balm upon my luckless head,
Benevolence, with warm and glowing breast,
And soft, celestial mercy, doubly blest!°
Smile on the generous act!—where means are given,   70
To aid the wretched is—to merit Heaven.

---

* "No children run to lisp their sire's return." Gray ["Elegy Written in a Country Church-yard," line 23].

† At Horsham is the county jail.

° "It is twice blessed, / It blesseth him that gives and him that takes." Shakspeare ["It" refers to "the quality of mercy." *Merchant of Venice*, IV.i.185–86].

Line 59. **hop:** hops, a necessary ingredient in beer, are a principal crop of southeastern England.

Line 62. **unhousel'd, unanneal'd:** "Unhouseled, disappointed, unanealed"—the ghost of Hamlet's father describes his murder (*Hamlet*, I.v.77).

Inscription

On a stone, in the church-yard at Boreham, in Essex;
raised by the Honourable Elizabeth Olmius, to the
memory of Ann Gardner, who died at New Hall,
after a faithful service of forty years

Whate'er of praise, and of regret attend
The grateful Servant, and the humble friend,
Where strict integrity and worth unite
To raise the lowly in their Maker's sight,
Are her's; whose faithful service, long approved,   5
Wept by the Mistress whom thro' life she loved.
Here ends her earthly task; in joyful trust
To share the eternal triumph of the Just.

A descriptive ode,

Supposed to have been written under the ruins of
Rufus's Castle, among the remains of the
ancient Church on the Isle of Portland*

Chaotic pile of barren stone,
That Nature's hurrying hand has thrown,
   Half-finish'd, from the troubled waves;
On whose rude brow the rifted tower

---

* The singular scenery here attempted to be described, is almost the only part of this rock of stones worth seeing. On an high broken cliff hang the ruins of some very ancient building, which the people of the island call Bow and Arrow Castle, or Rufus' Castle. Beneath, but still high above the sea, are the half-fallen arches and pillars of an old church, and around are scattered the remains of tomb-stones, and almost obliterated memorials of the dead. These verses were written for, and first inserted in, a Novel, called Marchmont; and the close alludes to the circumstance of the story related in the Novel. [Written by the title figure of the novel, Edward-Armyn Marchmont, the original title is "Descriptive Ode, Written among the Ruins of the Old Church, on the West Side of Portland; above which are Ruins called Bow-and-Arrow, or Rufus's Castle." Although called an island, Portland is actually a long peninsula jutting into the ocean south of Weymouth in Dorset.]

Has frown'd, thro' many a stormy hour,   5
   On this drear site of tempest-beaten graves.

Sure Desolation loves to shroud
His giant form within the cloud
   That hovers round thy rugged head;
And as thro' broken vaults beneath,   10
The future storms low-muttering breathe,
   Hears the complaining voices of the dead.

Here marks the Fiend with eager eyes,
Far out at sea the fogs arise
   That dimly shade the beacon'd strand,   15
And listens the portentous roar
Of sullen waves, as on the shore,
   Monotonous, they burst, and tell the storm at hand.

Northward the Demon's eyes are cast
O'er yonder bare and sterile waste,   20
   Where, born to hew and heave the block,
Man, lost in ignorance and toil,
Becomes associate to the soil,
   And his heart hardens like his native rock.

On the bleak hills, with flint o'erspread,   25
No blossoms rear the purple head;
   No shrub perfumes the Zephyrs' breath,
But o'er the cold and cheerless down
Grim Desolation seems to frown,
   Blasting the ungrateful soil with partial death.   30

Here the scathed trees with leaves half-drest,
Shade no soft songster's secret nest,

Line 13. **Fiend:** i.e. desolation—also, the "Demon" (line 19) and "Spirit" (line 49).
Line 15. **beacon'd strand:** At the southern tip of the Isle of Portland is a lighthouse.

Whose spring-notes soothe the pensive ear;
But high the croaking cormorant flies,
And mews and awks with clamorous cries   35
   Tire the lone echoes of these caverns drear.

Perchance among the ruins grey
Some widow'd mourner loves to stray,
   Marking the melancholy main
Where once, afar she could discern   40
O'er the white waves *his* sail return
   Who never, never now, returns again!

On these lone tombs, by storms up-torn,
The hopeless wretch may lingering mourn,
   Till from the ocean, rising red,   45
The misty Moon with lurid ray
Lights her, reluctant, on her way,
   To steep in tears her solitary bed.

Hence the dire Spirit oft surveys
The ship, that to the western bays   50
   With favouring gales pursues its course;
Then calls the vapour dark that blinds
The pilot—calls the felon winds
   That heave the billows with resistless force.

Commixing with the blotted skies,   55
High and more high the wild waves rise,
   Till, as impetuous torrents urge,
Driven on yon fatal bank accurst,
The vessel's massy timbers burst,
   And the crew sinks beneath the infuriate surge. 60

Line 35. **mews and awks**: sea-birds.

There find the weak an early grave,
While youthful strength the whelming wave
    Repels; and labouring for the land,
With shorten'd breath and upturn'd eyes,
Sees the rough shore above him rise,   65
    Nor dreams that rapine meets him on the strand.

And are there then in human form
Monsters more savage than the storm,
    Who from the gasping sufferer tear
The dripping weed?—who dare to reap   70
The inhuman harvest of the deep,
    From half-drown'd victims whom the tempests spare?

Ah! yes! by avarice once possest,
No pity moves the rustic breast;
    Callous he proves—as those who haply wait   75
Till I (a pilgrim weary worn)
To my own native land return,
    With legal toils to drag me to my fate!

Verses supposed to have been written in the New Forest, in early spring

As in the woods, where leathery lichen weaves
Its wint'ry web among the sallow leaves,*
Which (thro' cold months in whirling eddies blown)
Decay beneath the branches once their own,
From the brown shelter of their foliage sear,   5
Spring the young blooms that lead the floral year:
When, waked by vernal suns, the Pilewort dares
Expand her spotted leaves, and shining stars;
And (veins empurpling all her tassels pale)
Bends the soft Wind-flower in the tepid gale;   10
Uncultured bells of azure Jacinths blow,†
And the breeze-scenting Violet lurks below;°
So views the wanderer, with delighted eyes,
Reviving hopes from black despondence rise,
When, blighted by Adversity's chill breath,   15

---

* Mosses and lichens are the first efforts of Nature to clothe the earth: as they decay, they form an earth that affords nourishment to the larger and more succulent vegetables: several species of lichen are found in the woods, springing up among the dead leaves, under the drip of forest trees: these, and the withered foliage of preceding years, afford shelter to the earliest wild flowers about the skirts of woods, and in hedge-rows and copses.

The Pile-wort (*Ranuncula Ficaria*) and the Wood Anemone (*Anemone Nemerosa*) or Wind-flower, blow in the woods and copses. Of this latter beautiful species there is in Oxfordshire a blue one, growing wild, (*Anemone pratensis pedunculo involucrato, petalis apice reflexis foliis bipinnatis*—Lin. Sp. Pl. 760.) It is found in Whichwood Forest, near Cornbury quarry. (*Vide Flora Oxoniensis* [by John Sibthorp, 1794]). I do not mention this by way of exhibiting botanical knowledge (so easy to possess in appearance) but because I never saw the Blue Anemone wild in any other place, and it is a flower of singular beauty and elegance.

† *Hyacinthus non scriptus.* Hare-bell.

° To the Violet there needs no note, it being like the Nightingale and the Rose, in *constant requisition* by the poets.

Title. The New Forest is a tract of woodland near Southampton set aside as a timber reserve for the nearby shipyards of the Royal Navy. This poem from Smith's *Marchmont* is written by the title character under the assumption (which proves erroneous) that his many afflictions are over.

Line 5. **sear**: sere, dry.

Those hopes had felt a temporary death;
Then with gay heart he looks to future hours,
When Love shall dress for him the Summer bowers!
And, as delicious dreams enchant his mind,
Forgets his sorrows past, or gives them to the wind.   20

Song from the French*

"Ah! say," the fair Louisa cried,
    "Say where the abode of Love is found?"
Pervading Nature, I replied,
    His influence spreads the world around.
When Morning's arrowy beams arise,   5
    He sparkles in the enlivening ray,
And blushes in the glowing skies
    When rosy Evening fades away.

The Summer winds that gently blow,
    The flocks that bleat along the glades,   10
The nightingale, that soft and low,
    With music fills the listening shades:
The murmurs of the silver surf
    All echo Love's enchanting notes,
From Violets lurking in the turf,   15
    His balmy breath thro' æther floats.

From perfumed flowers and dewy leaves
    Delicious scents he bids exhale,
He smiles amid Autumnal sheaves,
    And clothes with green the grassy vale;   20

---

* A free translation of a favourite French song. "Un jour me demandoit Hortense, / Ou se trouve le tendre amour?" ["One day Hortense asked me where tender love is to be found."]

Song from the French. Line 16. **æther**: the stream of air.

But when that throne the God assumes
   Where his most powerful influence lies,
'Tis on Louisa's cheek he blooms,
   And lightens from her radiant eyes!

Apostrophe to an old tree*

Where thy broad branches brave the bitter North,
Like rugged, indigent, unheeded, worth,
Lo! Vegetation's guardian hands emboss
Each giant limb with fronds of studded moss,†
Clothing the bark with many a fringed fold   5
Begemm'd with scarlet shields and cups of gold,
Which, to the wildest winds their webs oppose,
And mock the arrowy sleet, or weltering snows.
—But to the warmer *West* the Woodbine° fair
With tassels that perfumed the Summer air,   10
The mantling Clematis, whose feathery bowers
Waved in festoons with Nightshade's‡ purple flowers,
The silver weed,• whose corded fillets wove

---

* The philosophy [botanical knowledge] of these few lines may not be very correct, since mosses are known to injure the stems and branches of trees to which they adhere; but the images of Poetry cannot always be exactly adjusted to objects of Natural History.

† The foliage, if it may be so called, of this race of plants, is termed fronds; and their flowers, or fructification, assume the shapes of cups and shields; of those of this description, more particularly adhering to trees, is *Lichen Pulmonarius*, Lungwort Lichen, with *shields;* the *Lichen Caperatus*, with red cups; and many others which it would look like pedantry to enumerate.

° The Woodbine and the Clematis are well known plants, ornamenting our hedge-rows in Summer with fragrant flowers.

‡ Nightshade, (*Solanum Lignosum*) Woody Nightshade, is one of the most beautiful of its tribe.

• The silver weed, *Convolvulus Major* (Raii Syn. 275) or greater Bind-weed, which, however the beauty of the flowers may enliven the garden or the wilds, is so prejudicial to the gardener and farmer, that it is seen by them with dislike equal to the difficulty of extirpating it from the soil. Its cord-like stalks, plaited together, can hardly be forced from the branches round which they have twined themselves.

Round thy pale rind, even as deceitful love
Of mercenary beauty would engage   15
The dotard fondness of decrepit age;
All these, that during Summer's halcyon days
With their green canopies conceal'd thy sprays,
Are gone for ever; or disfigured, trail
Their sallow relics in the Autumnal gale;   20
Or o'er thy roots, in faded fragments tost,
But tell of happier hours, and sweetness lost!
—Thus in Fate's trying hour, when furious storms
Strip social life of Pleasure's fragile forms,
And aweful *Justice*, as his rightful prey   25
Tears Luxury's silk, and jewel'd robe, away,
While reads *Adversity* her lesson stern,
And *Fortune's* minions tremble as they learn;
The crouds around her gilded car that hung,
Bent the lithe knee, and troul'd the honey'd tongue,   30
Desponding fall, or fly in pale despair;
And *Scorn* alone remembers that they were.
Not so *Integrity;* unchanged he lives
In the rude armour conscious Honor gives,
And dares with hardy front the troubled sky,   35
In Honesty's uninjured panoply.
Ne'er on Prosperity's enfeebling bed
Or rosy pillows, he reposed his head,
But given to useful arts, his ardent mind
Has sought the general welfare of mankind;   40
To mitigate *their* ills his greatest bliss,
While studying *them*, has taught him *what he is;*
He, when the human tempest rages worst,
And the earth shudders as the thunders burst,
Firm, as thy northern branch, is rooted fast,   45
And if he can't *avert*, endures the blast.

Line 25. **aweful**: compelling awe.

Line 30. **troul'd**: trolled; moved the tongue nimbly or volubly.

The forest boy*

The trees have now hid at the edge of the hurst
    The spot where the ruins decay
Of the cottage, where Will of the Woodlands was nursed
And lived so beloved, till the moment accurst
    When he went from the woodland away.   5

---

* Late circumstances have given rise to many mournful histories like this, which may well be said to be founded in truth!—*I*, who have been so sad a sufferer in this miserable contest [her third son Charles lost a leg at Dunkirk in 1793], may well *endeavour* to associate myself with those who apply what powers they have to deprecate the horrors of war. Gracious God! will mankind never be reasonable enough to understand that all the miseries which our condition subjects us to, are light in comparison of what we bring upon ourselves by indulging the folly and wickedness of those who make nations destroy each other for *their* diversion, or to administer to their senseless ambition.

    —If the stroke of war
Fell certain on the guilty head, none else—
If they that make the cause might taste th' effect,
And drink themselves the bitter cup they mix;
Then might the Bard (the child of peace) delight
To twine fresh wreaths around the conqueror's brow;
Or haply strike his high-toned harp, to swell
The trumpet's martial sound, and bid them on
When *Justice* arms for vengeance; but, alas!
That undistinguishing and deathful storm
Beats heaviest on the exposed and innocent;
And they that stir its fury, while it raves,
Safe and at distance send their mandates forth
Unto the mortal ministers that wait
To do their bidding!—— CROWE.

I have in these stanzas, entitled the Forest Boy, attempted the measure so successfully adopted in one of the poems of a popular novel, and so happily imitated by Mr. Southey in "Poor Mary" [Robert Southey's "Mary, the Maid of the Inn" was included in his *Poems* of 1797].

Crowe: William Crowe, 1745–1829, was best known for *Lewesdon Hill* (1788), a loco-descriptive poem containing strong pacifist sentiments similar to those quoted by Smith. These lines were printed without attribution in the *European Magazine*, 27 (June 1795), 418–19, and reprinted by Coleridge in *The Watchman*, 5 (2 April 1796), 144–45, introduced by him as "admirable lines, written by MR. CROWE, the public Orator of the University of Oxford: they were intended to have been spoken by an Under-Graduate at the Installation of the Duke of Portland; but were rejected by the Vice-Chancellor, on account of the *too free* sentiments which they conveyed." The full text can be found in *British War Poetry of the Romantic Age, 1793–1815*, ed. Betty T. Bennett (New York: Garland, 1973), 174–75.

Line 1. **hurst**: a wooded eminence.

Among all the lads of the plough or the fold,
    Best esteem'd by the sober and good,
Was Will of the Woodlands; and often the old
Would tell of his frolics, for active and bold
    Was William the Boy of the wood.   10

Yet gentle was he, as the breath of the May,
    And when sick and declining was laid
The Woodman his father, young William away
Would go to the forest to labour all day,
    And perform his hard task in his stead.   15

And when his poor father the forester died,
    And his mother was sad, and alone,
He toil'd from the dawn, and at evening he hied
In storm or in snow, or whate'er might betide,
    To supply all her wants from the town.   20

One neighbour they had on the heath to the west,
    And no other the cottage was near,
But she would send Phoebe, the child she loved best,
To stay with the widow, thus sad and distrest,
    Her hours of dejection to cheer.   25

As the buds of wild roses, the cheeks of the maid
    Were just tinted with youth's lovely hue,
Her form like the aspen, soft graces display'd,
And the eyes, over which her luxuriant locks stray'd,
    As the skies of the Summer were blue!   30

Still labouring to live, yet reflecting the while,
    Young William consider'd his lot;
'Twas hard, yet 'twas honest; and one tender smile

Line 31. **labouring**: working industriously.

From Phoebe at night overpaid ev'ry toil,
    And then all his fatigues were forgot.   35

By the brook where it glides thro' the copse of Arbeal,
    When to eat his cold fare he reclined,
Then soft from her home his sweet Phoebe would steal
And bring him wood-strawberries to finish his meal,
    And would sit by his side while he dined.   40

And tho' when employ'd in the deep forest glade,
    His days have seem'd slowly to move,
Yet Phoebe going home, thro' the wood-walk has stray'd
To bid him good night!—and whatever she said
    Was more sweet than the voice of the dove.   45

Fair Hope, that the lover so fondly believes,
    Then repeated each soul-soothing speech,
And touch'd with illusion, that often deceives
The future with light; as the sun thro' the leaves
    Illumines the boughs of the beech.   50

But once more the tempests of chill Winter blow,
    To depress and disfigure the earth;
And now ere the dawn, the young Woodman must go
To his work in the forest, half buried in snow,
    And at night bring home wood for the hearth.   55

The bridge on the heath by the flood was wash'd down,
    And fast, fast fell the sleet and the rain,
The stream to a wild rapid river was grown,
And long might the widow sit sighing alone
    Ere sweet Phoebe could see her again.   60

At the town was a market—and now for supplies
    Such as needed their humble abode,
Young William went forth; and his mother with sighs

Watch'd long at the window, with tears in her eyes,
  Till he turn'd thro' the fields, to the road.   65

Then darkness came on; and she heard with affright
  The wind rise every moment more high;
She look'd from the door; not a star lent its light,
But the tempest redoubled the gloom of the night,
  And the rain fell in floods from the sky.   70

The clock in her cottage now mournfully told
  The hours that went heavily on;
'Twas midnight; her spirits sunk hopeless and cold,
For the wind seem'd to say as in loud gusts it roll'd,
  That long, long would her William be gone.   75

Then heart-sick and faint to her sad bed she crept,
  Yet first made up the fire in the room
To guide his dark steps; but she listen'd and wept,
Or if for a moment forgetful she slept,
  She soon started!—and thought he was come.   80

'Twas morn; and the wind with an hoarse sullen moan
  Now seem'd dying away in the wood,
When the poor wretched mother still drooping, alone,
Beheld on the threshold a figure unknown,
  In gorgeous apparel who stood.   85

"Your son is a soldier," abruptly cried he,
  "And a place in our corps has obtain'd,
Nay, be not cast down; you perhaps may soon see
Your William a captain! he now sends by me
  The purse he already has gain'd."   90

So William entrapp'd 'twixt persuasion and force,
    Is embark'd for the isles of the West,
But he seem'd to begin with ill omens his course,
And felt recollection, regret, and remorse
    Continually weigh on his breast.   95

With useless repentance he eagerly eyed
    The high coast as it faded from view,
And saw the green hills, on whose northernmost side
Was his own sylvan home: and he falter'd and cried
    "Adieu! ah! for ever adieu!   100

Who now, my poor mother, thy life shall sustain,
    Since thy son has thus left thee forlorn?
Ah! canst thou forgive me? And not in the pain
Of this cruel desertion, of William complain,
    And lament that he ever was born?   105

Sweet Phoebe!—if ever thy lover was dear,
    Now forsake not the cottage of woe,
But comfort my mother; and quiet her fear,
And help her to dry up the vain fruitless tear
    That too long for my absence will flow.   110

Yet what if my Phoebe another should wed,
    And lament her lost William no more?"
The thought was too cruel; and anguish soon sped
The dart of disease—With the brave numerous dead
    He has fall'n on the plague-tainted shore.   115

Line 91. **entrapp'd**: Press gangs were notorious for using force to secure sufficient sailors to man the ships of the Royal Navy.

Line 92. **isles ... West**: the West Indies, where the institution of slavery was upheld by British arms.

In the lone village church-yard, the chancel-wall near,
   The high grass now waves over the spot
Where the mother of William, unable to bear
His loss, who to her widow'd heart was so dear,
   Has both him and her sorrows forgot.   120

By the brook where it winds thro' the wood of Arbeal,
   Or amid the deep forest, to moan,
The poor wandering Phoebe will silently steal;
The pain of her bosom no reason can heal,
   And she loves to indulge it alone.   125

Her senses are injured; her eyes dim with tears;
   By the river she ponders; and weaves
Reed garlands, against her dear William appears,
Then breathlessly listens, and fancies she hears
   His light step in the half-wither'd leaves.   130

Ah! such are the miseries to which ye give birth,
   Ye cold statesmen! unknowing a scar;
Who from pictured saloon, or the bright sculptured hearth,
Disperse desolation and death thro' the earth,
   When ye let loose the demons of war.   135

Line 128. **against … appears**: in anticipation of his return.

Line 133. **pictured saloon**: elegant reception room. **sculptured hearth**: elaborately carved fireplace mantel.

Verses, on the death of [Henrietta O'Neill], written in September, 1794

Like a poor ghost the night I seek;
    Its hollow winds repeat my sighs;
The cold dews mingle on my cheek
    With tears that wander from mine eyes.

The thorns that still my couch molest,   5
    Have robb'd these heavy eyes of sleep;
But tho' deprived of tranquil rest,
    I here at least am free to weep.

Twelve times the moon, that rises red
    O'er yon tall wood of shadowy pine,   10
Has fill'd her orb, since low was laid
    My Harriet! that sweet form of thine!

While each sad month, as slow it past,
    Brought some new sorrow to deplore;
Some grief more poignant than the last,   15
    But thou canst calm those griefs no more.

Title. **September, 1794**: This memorial poem to the close friend also addressed in Sonnet 37 was first published in *The Banished Man* (1794), as the production of Charlotte Denzil, a fictionalized self-portrait of Smith. In *Elegiac Sonnets*, Volume 2, it followed two interpolated and anonymous poems by Mrs. O'Neill: her popular "Ode to the poppy," originally inserted by Smith in *Desmond*, and a piece entitled "Written by the same lady on seeing her two sons at play." There they were accompanied by the following note: "This and the following Poem were written (the first of them at my request, for a Novel) by a lady whose death in her thirty-sixth year was a subject of the deepest concern to all who knew her. Would to God the last line which *my* regret on that loss drew from me, had been prophetic—and that *my* heart had indeed been cold, instead of having suffered within the next twelve months after that line was written, a deprivation which has rendered *my* life a living death." The second occasion for Smith's grief is, once again, the death of her daughter Anna Augusta during the spring of 1795.

No more thy friendship soothes to rest
   This wearied spirit tempest-tost;
The cares that weigh upon my breast
   Are doubly felt since thou art lost.   20

Bright visions of ideal grace
   That the young poet's dreams inflame,
Were not more lovely than thy face;
   Were not more perfect than thy frame.

Wit, that no sufferings could impair,   25
   Was thine, and thine those mental powers
Of force to chase the fiends that tear
   From Fancy's hands her budding flowers.

O'er what, my angel friend, thou wert,
   Dejected Memory loves to mourn;   30
Regretting still that tender heart,
   Now withering in a distant urn!

But ere that wood of shadowy pine
   Twelve times shall yon full orb behold,
This sickening heart, that bleeds for thine,   35
   My Harriet!—may like thine be cold!

April

Green o'er the copses Spring's soft hues are spreading,
    High wave the Reeds in the transparent floods,
The Oak its sear and sallow foliage shedding,
    From their moss'd cradles start its infant buds.*

Pale as the tranquil tide of Summer's ocean,   5
    The Willow now its slender leaf unveils;
And thro' the sky with swiftly fleeting motion,
    Driven by the wind, the rack of April sails.

Then, as the gust declines, the stealing showers
    Fall fresh and noiseless; while at closing day   10
The low Sun gleams on moist and half-blown flowers
    That promise garlands for approaching May.

Blest are yon peasant children, simply singing,
    Who thro' the new-sprung grass rejoicing rove;

---

* The Oak, and, in sheltered situations, the Beech, retain the leaves of the preceding year till the new foliage appears.
    The return of the Spring, which awakens many to new sentiments of pleasure, now serves only to remind *me* of past misery. This sensation is common to the wretched—and too many Poets have felt it in all its force. "Zefiro torno [torna], e'l bel tempo rimena, / E i fiori, e l'erbe, sua dolce famiglia; &c. &c. / —Ma per me lasso!"—Petrarch on the Death of Laura [Sonnet 310. lines 1–2, 9: "The west wind returns and once more brings lovely weather, and flowers and grass, its sweet family, but for me only lassitude."]
    And these lines of Guarini have always been celebrated. "O primavera gioventù dell' anno, / Bella madre di fiori / D'erbe novelle e di novelli amori; / Tu torni ben, ma teco / Non tornano i sereni / E fortunati di, delle mie gioje; / Tu torni ben, tu torni, / Ma teco altro non torna / Che del perduto mio caro tesoro, / La rimembranza misera e dolente." [*Il Pastor Fido*, III.i.1–10. "O Spring, youth of the world, lovely mother of flowers, of new grass, and of new loves: you return surely, but with you do not return my serene and lucky days of joy; you return, you return, but with you nothing returns of my dear lost treasure except the sad and wretched memory."]

Line 3. **sear and sallow**: sere (dry) and pale yellow.   Line 8. **rack**: broken clouds.
Line 11. **half-blown**: barely blooming.

More blest! to whom the *Time*, fond thought is bringing,   15
  Of friends expected, or returning love.

The pensive wanderer blest, to whom reflection
  Points out some future views that sooth his mind;
Me how unlike!—whom cruel recollection
  But tells of comfort I shall never find!   20

Hope, that on Nature's youth is still attending,
  No more to me her syren song shall sing;
Never to *me* her influence extending,
  Shall I again enjoy the days of Spring!

Yet, how I loved them once these scenes remind me,   25
  When light of heart, in childhood's thoughtless mirth,
I reck'd not that the cruel lot assign'd me
  Should make me curse the hour that gave me birth!

Then, from thy wild-wood banks, Aruna! roving,
  Thy thymy downs with sportive steps I sought,   30
And Nature's charms, with artless transport loving,
  Sung like the birds, unheeded and untaught.

But now the Springtide's pleasant hours returning,
  Serve to awaken me to sharper pain;
Recalling scenes of agony and mourning,   35
  Of baffled hope and prayers preferr'd in vain.

Thus shone the Sun, his vernal rays displaying,
  Thus did the woods in early verdure wave,
While dire Disease on all I loved was preying,
  And flowers seem'd rising but to strew her grave!   40

Line 29. **Aruna:** The river Arun in Sussex, a frequent subject of the *Elegiac Sonnets*: see Sonnets 26 (page 30), 30 (page 33), 32 (page 34), 33 (page 35), 45 (page 42).

Line 40. **grave:** Smith's daughter Anna Augusta died in the spring of 1795: see Sonnet 65 (page 57).

Now, 'mid reviving blooms, I coldly languish,
    Spring seems devoid of joy to me alone;
Each sound of pleasure aggravates my anguish,
    And speaks of beauty, youth, and sweetness gone!

Yet, as stern Duty bids, with faint endeavour   45
    I drag on life, contending with my woe,
Tho' conscious Misery still repeats, that never
    My soul one pleasureable hour shall know.

Lost in the tomb, when Hope no more appeases
    The fester'd wounds that prompt the eternal sigh,   50
Grief, the most fatal of the heart's diseases,
    Soon teaches, whom it fastens on, to die.

The wretch undone, for pain alone existing,
    The abject dread of Death shall sure subdue,
And far from his decisive hand resisting,   55
    Rejoice to bid a world like this adieu!

Ode to death*

Friend of the wretched! wherefore should the eye
    Of blank Despair, whence tears have ceased to flow,
Be turn'd from thee?—Ah! wherefore fears to die
    He, who compell'd each poignant grief to know,
    Drains to its lowest dregs the cup of woe?   5

---

* From the following sentence in Lord Bacon's Essays. "Death is no such formidable enemy,
since a man has so many champions about him that can win the combat of him—Revenge
triumphs over Death; Love slights it; Honour courts it; Dread of Disgrace chooses it; Grief
flies to it; Fear anticipates it." [The edition Smith used has not been traced; the original is
in many respects different. "Of Death," No. 2 of *The Essayes or Counsels, Civill and Morall*
(1612) reads: "And therefore Death, is no such terrible Enemie, when a man hath so many
Attendants, about him, that can winne the combat of him. *Revenge* triumphs over *Death*;
Love slights it; *Honour* aspireth to it; delivery from *Ignominy* chuseth it; *Griefe* flieth to it;
Feare pre-occupateth it…"]

Would Cowardice postpone thy calm embrace,
  To linger out long years in torturing pain?
Or not prefer thee to the ills that chase
  Him, who too much impoverish'd to obtain
  From BRITISH THEMIS *right*, implores her aid in vain!   10

Sharp goading Indigence who would not fly,
  That urges toil the exhausted strength above?
Or shun the *once* fond friend's *averted* eye?
  Or who to *thy* asylum not remove,
  To lose the wasting pain of unrequited love?   15

Can then the wounded wretch who must deplore
  What most she loved, to thy cold arms consign'd,
Who hears the voice that sooth'd her soul no more,
  Fear *thee*, O Death!—Or hug the chains that bind
  To joyless, cheerless life, her sick, reluctant mind?   20

Oh! Misery's Cure; who e'er in pale dismay
  Has watch'd the angel form they could not save,
And seen their dearest blessing torn away,
  May well the terrors of *thy* triumph brave,
  Nor pause in fearful dread before the opening grave!   25

Stanzas

Ah! think'st thou, Laura, then, that wealth
Should make me thus my youth, and health,
  And freedom and repose resign?—

Line 10. **BRITISH THEMIS**: the British judicial system.

Line 17. **What ... loved**: Smith's daughter Anna Augusta.

Stanzas. Initially published in Smith's *The Young Philosopher: A Novel* (1798), these are impromptu verses written by Glenmorris to his future wife Laura.

Ah, no!—I toil to gain by stealth
  One look, one tender glance of thine.   5

Born where huge hills on hills are piled,
In Caledonia's distant wild,
  Unbounded Liberty was mine:
But thou upon my hopes hast smiled,
  And bade me be a slave of thine!   10

Amid these gloomy haunts of gain,
Of weary hours I not complain,
  While Hope forbids me to repine,
And whispering tells me I obtain
  Pity from that soft heart of thine.   15

Tho' far capricious Fortune flies,
Yet Love will bless the sacrifice,
  And all his purer joys combine;
While I my little world comprise
  In that fair form, and fairer soul of thine.   20

To the winds

Ye vagrant Winds! yon clouds that bear
Thro' the blue desart of the air,
  Soft sailing in the Summer sky,
Do e'er your wandering breezes meet
A wretch in misery so complete,   5
                      So lost as I?

Stanzas. Line 7. **Caledonia's ... wild**: the Scottish Highlands.   Line 11. **gain**: commerce.
To the winds. From *The Young Philosopher;* like Sonnet 87, an effusion by the youthful sui-
cide Elizabeth Lisburne.
Line 2. **desart**: emptiness.

And yet, where'er your pinions wave
O'er some lost friend's—some lover's grave,
   Surviving sufferers still complain;
Some parent of his hopes deprived,   10
Some wretch who has himself survived,
           Lament in vain.

Blow where ye list on this sad earth,
Some soul-corroding care has birth,
   And Grief in all her accents speaks;   15
Here dark Dejection groans, and there
Wild Phrenzy, daughter of Despair,
          Unconscious shrieks.

Ah! were it Death had torn apart
The tie that bound him to my heart,   20
   Tho' fatal still the pang would prove;
Yet had it soothed this bleeding breast
To know, I had till then possest
          Hillario's love.

And where his dear, dear ashes slept,   25
Long nights and days I then had wept,
   Till by slow-mining Grief opprest
As Memory fail'd, its vital heat
This wayward heart had lost, and beat
          Itself to rest.   30

But still Hillario lives, to prove
To some more happy maid his love!
   Hillario at her feet I see!

Line 18. **Unconscious:** unaware of her actions.

Line 27. **slow-mining:** slowly undermining.

His voice still murmurs fond desire,
Still beam his eyes with lambent fire,   35
   But not for me!

Ah! words, my bosom's peace that stole,
Ah! looks, that won my melting soul;
  Who dares your dear delusion try,
In dreams may all Elysium see,   40
Then undeceiv'd, awake, like me,
   Awake and die.

Like me, who now abandon'd, lost,
Roam wildly on the rocky coast,
  With eager eyes the sea explore;   45
But hopeless watch and vainly rave,
Hillario o'er the western wave
   Returns no more!

Yet, go forgiven, Hillario go,
Such anguish may you never know   50
  As that which checks my labouring breath;
Pain so severe not long endures,
And I have still my choice of cures,
   Madness or death.

To Vesper

Thou! who behold'st with dewy eye
  The sleeping leaves and folded flowers,
And hear'st the night-wind lingering sigh
  Thro' shadowy woods and twilight bowers;

To Vesper. Also from the pen of Elizabeth Lisburne in *The Young Philosopher*, an intimation of her suicide by drowning. Vesper is the evening star.

Thou wast the signal once that seem'd to say,   5
Hillario's beating heart reproved my long delay.

I see thy emerald lustre stream
    O'er these rude cliffs and cavern'd shore;
But here, orisons to thy beam
    The woodland chantress pours no more;   10
Nor I, as once, thy lamp propitious hail,
Seen indistinct thro' tears; confus'd, and dim, and pale.

Soon shall thy arrowy radiance shine
    On the broad ocean's restless wave,
Where this poor cold swoln form of mine   15
    Shall shelter in its billowy grave,
Safe from the scorn the World's sad outcasts prove,
Unconscious of the pain of ill-requited Love.

Lydia

O'er the high down the night-wind blew,
    And as it chill and howling past,
The Juniper and scathed Yew*
    Shrunk from the bitter blast.

Yet on the sea-mark's chalky height,   5
    The rude memorial of the Dane,

---

* The Juniper and the Yew are almost the only trees that grow spontaneously on the highest
chalky hills, and they are often ragged and stunted by the violence of the wind.
    Some of the most elevated mounds of earth on these hills are sea-marks, and have for-
merly surrounded beacons; others are considered as memorials of the dead, and are called
Saxon, Danish, or Roman, according to the systems of different observers.

To Vesper. Line 10. **woodland chantress**: a bird, probably the nightingale.
Lydia. Line 1. **high down**: the Sussex uplands.

Thro' many a drear and stormy night
Had hapless Lydia lain.

When I a lonely wanderer too,
Who loved to climb and gaze around, 10
Even as the Autumnal Sun withdrew,
The poor forlorn one found.

"Ah! wherefore, maiden, sit you so,
The cold wind raving round your breast,
While in the villages below 15
All are retired to rest?

The fires are out, no lights appear
But the red flames of burning lime,*
None but the Horseman's ghost is here†
At this pale evening time." 20

With wild yet vacant eye, the maid
Gazed on me, and a mournful smile
On her wan sunken features play'd
As thus she spoke the while:

"Yes, to their beds my friends are gone, 25
They have no grief; they slumber soon;
But 'tis for me to wait alone
To meet the midnight Moon.

---

* From eminences in those countries where lime is burnt as a manure, a chain of lime kilns for many miles may be sometimes seen, which blazing amid the doubtful darkness of an extensive landscape, have a fine effect.

† Some years ago a strange notion prevailed among the people occasionally passing over one of the highest of the South Downs, that a man on horseback was often seen coming towards those who were returning from market on Saturday evening. This appearance, the noise of whose horse's feet they distinctly heard, vanished as soon as it came within an hundred yards of the passengers who often tried to meet it. At other times it was seen following them. They have stopped to let it approach, but it always melted into air. I have been present when a farmer not otherwise particularly weak or ignorant, said, that he had seen it, and distinctly heard the horse galloping towards him.

The Moon will rise anon, and trace
    Her silver pathway on the sea;*   30
I saw it from this very place,
    When Edward went from me.

Tho' like a mist the Horseman's ghost
    From yon deep dell I often see,
Glide o'er the mountain to the coast,   35
    It gives no fear to me.

I rather dread the clouds that rise
    Like towers and turrets from afar,
And swelling high, obscure the skies,
    And every shining star.   40

For then I can no longer trace
    That long bright pathway in the sea,
Where Edward bade me mark the place
    When last he went from me!

'Twas here, when loth to go, he gave   45
    To his poor Girl his last adieu;
He mark'd the moonlight on the wave,
    And bade me mark it too.

And, Lydia!—then he sighing cried,
    When the tenth time that light so clear   50
Shine on the Sea—whate'er betide,
    Thy Edward will be here.

Since then I watch with eager eyes,
    (Nor feel I cold, or wind or rain,)

---

* The bright lustre of the moon reflected from the sea, is almost as distinctly visible from the Downs as the moon itself; forming a long line of radiance from the horizon to the shore.

Till the tenth blessed moon arise,   55
    And Edward comes again."

"Ah, wretched Girl!" I would have cried,
    But why awaken her to pain?
"Long since thy wandering Lover died,
    The moon returns in vain!   60

Tho' with her wane, thy visions fade,
    Yet hopest thou, till again she shine?"
—The hopes of half the World, poor Maid!
    Are not more rational than thine!

Line 61. **her wane:** the dark of the moon.

The Emigrants

{ 1793 }

The Emigrants: As the Revolution unfolded in France, a great many who had enjoyed power and privilege under the *ancien regime* sought refuge in England. Their ranks were of such dimensions that from among the men could be assembled a counter-revolutionary army which then invaded France in a disastrous chivalric gesture, suffering wholesale military defeat. Thus, to the numbers of unprotected women who had been sent abroad with their children for safety were added others whose husbands had emigrated with them but had then returned to France to fight and die, leaving unprovided widows to their fate in a strange land. The extent to which the rules made by men at once keep women dependent and leave them no recourse when left alone links these distressed emigrants and the poet who observes them.

TO *WILLIAM COWPER, ESQ.*

Dear Sir,

There is, I hope, some propriety in my addressing a Composition to you, which would never perhaps have existed, had I not, amid the heavy pressure of many sorrows, derived infinite consolation from your Poetry, and some degree of animation and of confidence from your esteem.

The following performance is far from aspiring to be considered as an imitation of your inimitable Poem, The Task; I am perfectly sensible, that it belongs not to a feeble and feminine hand to draw the Bow of Ulysses.

The force, clearness, and sublimity of your admirable Poem; the 10 felicity, almost peculiar to your genius, of giving to the most familiar objects dignity and effect, I could never hope to reach; yet, having read The Task almost incessantly from its first publication to the present time, I felt that kind of enchantment described by Milton, when he says,

> The Angel ended, and in Adam's ear
> So charming left his voice, that he awhile
> Thought him still speaking.—   *[Paradise Lost*, VIII. 1–3]

And from the force of this impression, I was gradually led to attempt, in Blank Verse, a delineation of those interesting objects which 20 happened to excite my attention, and which even pressed upon an heart, that has learned, perhaps from its own sufferings, to feel with acute, though unavailing compassion, the calamity of others.

A Dedication usually consists of praises and of apologies; *my* praise can add nothing to the unanimous and loud applause of your country.

Line 7. The Task: Cowper's long meditative poem in blank verse was a major influence on a characteristic mode of Romantic poetry, usually exemplified by Wordsworth's epic of self-development, *The Prelude.* The first work actually to establish this vein of self-conscious filtering of reality in a conversational style is Smith's *Emigrants.*

Lines 8–9. **Bow of Ulysses:** In the *Odyssey* none of Penelope's suitors had the strength to draw this bow and prove himself the match of her husband. As Smith knows well, it is the beggar at the door shunned by the famous and proud, the disguised Odysseus, who finally draws the bow and silences the pretenders to his position.

She regards you with pride, as one of the few, who, at the present period, rescue her from the imputation of having degenerated in Poetical talents; but in the form of Apology, I should have much to say, if I again dared to plead the pressure of evils, aggravated by their long continuance, as an excuse for the defects of this attempt.   30

Whatever may be the faults of its execution, let me vindicate myself from those, that may be imputed to the design.—In speaking of the Emigrant Clergy, I beg to be understood as feeling the utmost respect for the integrity of their principles; and it is with pleasure I add my suffrage to that of those, who have had a similar opportunity of witnessing the conduct of the Emigrants of all descriptions during their exile in England; which has been such as does honour to *their* nation, and ought to secure to them in ours the esteem of every liberal mind.

Your philanthropy, dear Sir, will induce you, I am persuaded, to join with me in hoping, that this painful exile may finally lead to the extirpation of that reciprocal hatred so unworthy of great and enlightened   40
nations; that it may tend to humanize both countries, by convincing each, that good qualities exist in the other; and at length annihilate the prejudices that have so long existed to the injury of both.

Yet it is unfortunately but too true, that with the body of the English, this national aversion has acquired new force by the dreadful scenes which have been acted in France during the last summer—even those who are the victims of the Revolution, have not escaped the odium, which the undistinguishing multitude annex to all the natives of a country where such horrors have been acted: nor is this the worst   50
effect those events have had on the minds of the English; by confounding the original cause with the wretched catastrophes that have followed

---

Line 33. **Emigrant Clergy**: priests who fled when the new Republic abolished the state religion and largely confiscated the extensive church holdings. Most of Smith's readers would have shared a distrust of Catholicism fostered in England since the days of Henry VIII.

Line 47. **scenes ... summer**: Smith refers to the storming of the Tuileries in August 1792, when the king was deposed and imprisoned with his family, and to the reaction against the subsequent invasion by Austro-Prussian forces, which resulted in the September Massacres (2–4 September 1792) of hundreds of Royalist sympathizers in Paris. Smith dates her dedication in the midst of the Terror, when the internal struggles between radical Jacobins and moderate Girondists resulted in the execution of many of the latter. The English sympathizers with the Revolution tended to favor the Girondists.

its ill management; the attempts of public virtue, with the outrages that
guilt and folly have committed in its disguise, the very name of Liberty
has not only lost the charm it used to have in British ears, but many,
who have written, or spoken, in its defence, have been stigmatized as
promoters of Anarchy, and enemies to the prosperity of their country.
Perhaps even the Author of THE TASK, with all his goodness and tender-
ness of heart, is in the catalogue of those, who are reckoned to have
been too warm in a cause, which it was once the glory of Englishmen to   60
avow and defend—The exquisite Poem, indeed, in which you have
honoured Liberty, by a tribute highly gratifying to her sincerest friends,
was published some years before the demolition of regal despotism in
France, which, in the fifth book, it seems to foretell—All the truth and
energy of the passage to which I allude, must have been strongly felt,
when, in the Parliament of England, the greatest Orator of our time
quoted the sublimest of our Poets—when the eloquence of Fox did jus-
tice to the genius of Cowper.

    I am, dear SIR, with the most perfect esteem, your obliged and obe-
dient servant,   70

                                                            CHARLOTTE SMITH.
Brighthelmstone, May 10, 1793.

Line 66. **greatest Orator**: Charles James Fox, "the man of the People," who as leader of the
Whig minority in the House of Commons supported moderation in both France and
England and opposed the counter-revolutionary war. The conclusion to Smith's dedication
has decided political overtones.

THE EMIGRANTS

BOOK THE FIRST

Book I

SCENE, *on the Cliffs to the Eastward of the Town of*
Brighthelmstone in Sussex.

TIME, *a Morning in November, 1792.*

Slow in the Wintry Morn, the struggling light
Throws a faint gleam upon the troubled waves;
Their foaming tops, as they approach the shore
And the broad surf that never ceasing breaks
On the innumerous pebbles, catch the beams   5
Of the pale Sun, that with reluctance gives
To this cold northern Isle, its shorten'd day.
Alas! how few the morning wakes to joy!
How many murmur at oblivious night
For leaving them so soon; for bearing thus   10
Their fancied bliss (the only bliss they taste!),
On her black wings away!—Changing the dreams
That sooth'd their sorrows, for calamities
(And every day brings its own sad proportion)
For doubts, diseases, abject dread of Death,   15
And faithless friends, and fame and fortune lost;
Fancied or real wants; and wounded pride,
That views the day star, but to curse his beams.

Brighthelmstone: modern Brighton, located across the English Channel from France.

November, 1792: On September 22nd, two weeks after the Massacres, France had declared itself a Republic. By November Robespierre had gained complete control over the French Convention, which on the 19th of that month affirmed its support for all revolutionary movements in Europe, posing a threat of insurrection to the British government.

Line 18. **day star:** the sun.

Yet He, whose Spirit into being call'd
This wond'rous World of Waters; He who bids   20
The wild wind lift them till they dash the clouds,
And speaks to them in thunder; or whose breath,
Low murmuring o'er the gently heaving tides,
When the fair Moon, in summer night serene,
Irradiates with long trembling lines of light   25
Their undulating surface; that great Power,
Who, governing the Planets, also knows
If but a Sea-Mew falls, whose nest is hid
In these incumbent cliffs; He surely means
To us, his reasoning Creatures, whom He bids   30
Acknowledge and revere his awful hand,
Nothing but good: Yet Man, misguided Man,
Mars the fair work that he was bid enjoy,
And makes himself the evil he deplores.
How often, when my weary soul recoils   35
From proud oppression, and from legal crimes
(For such are in this Land, where the vain boast
Of equal Law is mockery, while the cost
Of seeking for redress is sure to plunge
Th' already injur'd to more certain ruin   40
And the wretch starves, before his Counsel pleads)
How often do I half abjure Society,
And sigh for some lone Cottage, deep embower'd
In the green woods, that these steep chalky Hills
Guard from the strong South West; where round their
        base   45
The Beach wide flourishes, and the light Ash
With slender leaf half hides the thymy turf!—

Line 31. **awful**: commanding awe.

Lines 36–41. **legal crimes … pleads**: a reflection of Smith's frustration at her inability to gain control over the trust established by her father-in-law for support of her children.

Line 45. **the strong South West**: winds off the Atlantic Ocean.

Line 46. **Beach**: the context suggests the beech tree.

There do I wish to hide me; well content
If on the short grass, strewn with fairy flowers,
I might repose thus shelter'd; or when Eve 50
In Orient crimson lingers in the west,
Gain the high mound, and mark these waves remote
(Lucid tho' distant), blushing with the rays
Of the far-flaming Orb, that sinks beneath them;
For I have thought, that I should then behold 55
The beauteous works of God, unspoil'd by Man
And less affected then, by human woes
I witness'd not; might better learn to bear
Those that injustice, and duplicity
And faithlessness and folly, fix on me: 60
For never yet could I derive relief,
When my swol'n heart was bursting with its sorrows,
From the sad thought, that others like myself
Live but to swell affliction's countless tribes!
—Tranquil seclusion I have vainly sought; 65
Peace, who delights in solitary shade,
No more will spread for me her downy wings,
But, like the fabled Danaïds—or the wretch,
Who ceaseless, up the steep acclivity,
Was doom'd to heave the still rebounding rock, 70
Onward I labour; as the baffled wave,
Which yon rough beach repulses, that returns
With the next breath of wind, to fail again.—
Ah! Mourner—cease these wailings: cease and learn,
That not the Cot sequester'd, where the briar 75
And wood-bine wild, embrace the mossy thatch,
(Scarce seen amid the forest gloom obscure!)
Or more substantial farm, well fenced and warm,

Line 68. **the fabled Danaïds**: The fifty daughters of Danaüs, who had murdered their husbands on their wedding night, were condemned in Tartarus to an eternity of trying to draw water in a sieve.   **the wretch**: Sisyphus, who eternally rolls his stone to the the top of a hill, whence it falls back to the base.

Where the full barn, and cattle fodder'd round
Speak rustic plenty; nor the statelier dome   80
By dark firs shaded, or the aspiring pine,
Close by the village Church (with care conceal'd
By verdant foliage, lest the poor man's grave
Should mar the smiling prospect of his Lord),
Where offices well rang'd, or dove-cote stock'd,   85
Declare manorial residence; not these
Or any of the buildings, new and trim
With windows circling towards the restless Sea,
Which ranged in rows, now terminate my walk,
Can shut out for an hour the spectre Care,   90
That from the dawn of reason, follows still
Unhappy Mortals, 'till the friendly grave
(Our sole secure asylum) "ends the chace."*
    Behold, in witness of this mournful truth,
A group approach me, whose dejected looks,   95
Sad Heralds of distress! proclaim them Men
Banish'd for ever and for conscience sake
From their distracted Country, whence the name
Of Freedom misapplied, and much abus'd
By lawless Anarchy, has driven them far   100
To wander; with the prejudice they learn'd
From Bigotry (the Tut'ress of the blind),
Thro' the wide World unshelter'd; their sole hope,

---

* I have a confused notion, that this expression, with nearly the same application, is to be found in Young: but I cannot refer to it. [The phrase remains unidentified.]

Line 85. **offices well rang'd**: extensive outbuildings (kitchens, dairy, stables, etc.) attached to a manor-house.

Lines 87–89. **buildings ... rows**: In the mid 1780s the Prince of Wales established his principal residence at Brighton, and it quickly became the center of a high-living, spendthrift society symbolized by the ornate Royal Pavilion that took 35 years to attain its full opulence. Smith ignores the royal presence, concentrating instead on the signs of nouveau riche real-estate speculation.

Line 95. **A group**: members of various Catholic religious orders.

That German spoilers, thro' that pleasant land
May carry wide the desolating scourge 105
Of War and Vengeance; yet unhappy Men,
Whate'er your errors, I lament your fate:
And, as disconsolate and sad ye hang
Upon the barrier of the rock, and seem
To murmur your despondence, waiting long 110
Some fortunate reverse that never comes;
Methinks in each expressive face, I see
Discriminated anguish; there droops one,
Who in a moping cloister long consum'd
This life inactive, to obtain a better, 115
And thought that meagre abstinence, to wake
From his hard pallet with the midnight bell,
To live on eleemosynary bread,
And to renounce God's works, would please that God.
And now the poor pale wretch receives, amaz'd, 120
The pity, strangers give to his distress,
Because these strangers are, by his dark creed,
Condemn'd as Heretics—and with sick heart
Regrets his pious prison, and his beads.*—
Another, of more haughty port, declines 125
The aid he needs not; while in mute despair
His high indignant thoughts go back to France,

---

* Lest the same attempts at misrepresentation should now be made, as have been made on former occasions, it is necessary to repeat, that nothing is farther from my thoughts, than to reflect invidiously on the Emigrant clergy, whose steadiness of principle excites veneration, as much as their sufferings compassion. Adversity has now taught them the charity and humility they perhaps wanted, when they made it a part of their faith, that salvation could be obtained in no other religion than their own.

Line 104. **German spoilers**: The Austro-Prussian army that invaded France in August 1792 was driven back, but continued to threaten the security of the new republic.

Line 118. **eleemosynary bread**: alms.   Line 124. **Regrets**: remembers with regret.

Dwelling on all he lost—the Gothic dome,
That vied with splendid palaces;* the beds
Of silk and down, the silver chalices,   130
Vestments with gold enwrought for blazing altars;
Where, amid clouds of incense, he held forth
To kneeling crowds the imaginary bones
Of Saints suppos'd, in pearl and gold enchas'd,
And still with more than living Monarchs' pomp   135
Surrounded; was believ'd by mumbling bigots
To hold the keys of Heaven, and to admit
Whom he thought good to share it—Now alas!
He, to whose daring soul and high ambition
The World seem'd circumscrib'd; who, wont to dream   140
Of Fleuri, Richelieu, Alberoni, men
Who trod on Empire, and whose politics
Were not beyond the grasp of his vast mind,
Is, in a Land once hostile, still prophan'd
By disbelief, and rites un-orthodox,   145
The object of compassion[.]—At his side,
Lighter of heart than these, but heavier far
Than he was wont, another victim comes,
An Abbé—who with less contracted brow

---

* Let it not be considered as an insult to men in fallen fortune, if these luxuries (undoubt-edly inconsistent with their profession) be here enumerated—France is not the only coun-try, where the splendour and indulgences of the higher, and the poverty and depression of the inferior Clergy, have alike proved injurious to the cause of Religion. [The ambiguity of Smith's prose seems meant to imply that such inequality exists as well within the Anglican establishment.]

Lines 128–36. **Gothic ... Surrounded**: The splendor in which the higher orders of the Church indulged themselves was publicized as justifying the revolutionary government in confiscating the vast ecclesiastical holdings in France.

Line 141. **Fleuri, Richelieu, Alberoni**: three cardinals who held powerful political offices. Cardinal André Hercule de Fleury (1653–1743), once tutor to Louis XV, became de facto prime minister of France from 1726 to 1743. A century earlier Armand Jean du Plessis, Duc de Richelieu (1585–1643), as principal minister to Louis XIII over a period of eighteen years, oversaw France's transition to a modern state. Cardinal Giulio Alberoni (1664–1752), though Italian, was the de facto prime minister of Spain from 1716 to 1719.

Still smiles and flatters, and still talks of Hope;   150
Which, sanguine as he is, he does not feel,
And so he cheats the sad and weighty pressure
Of evils present;—Still, as Men misled
By early prejudice (so hard to break),
I mourn your sorrows; for I too have known   155
Involuntary exile; and while yet
England had charms for me, have felt how sad
It is to look across the dim cold sea,
That melancholy rolls its refluent tides
Between us and the dear regretted land   160
We call our own—as now ye pensive wait
On this bleak morning, gazing on the waves
That seem to leave your shore; from whence the wind
Is loaded to your ears, with the deep groans
Of martyr'd Saints and suffering Royalty,   165
While to your eyes the avenging power of Heaven
Appears in aweful anger to prepare
The storm of vengeance, fraught with plagues and death.
Even he of milder heart, who was indeed
The simple shepherd in a rustic scene,   170
And, 'mid the vine-clad hills of Languedoc,
Taught to the bare-foot peasant, whose hard hands
Produc'd* the nectar he could seldom taste,
Submission to the Lord for whom he toil'd;

---

* See the finely descriptive Verses written at Montauban in France in 1750, by Dr. Joseph Warton. Printed in Dodsley's *Miscellanies*, Vol. IV. page 203. [The poem begins: Tarn, how delightful wind thy willow'd waves, / But ah! they fructify a land of slaves! / In vain thy bare-foot, sun-burnt peasants hide / With luscious grapes yon hill's romantic side; / No cups nectareous shall their toils repay, / The priest's, the soldier's, and the fermier's prey...]

Line 156. **Involuntary exile**: a reference to Smith's residence in Normandy from fall 1784 to spring 1785, the result of her husband's insolvency.

Line 165. **suffering Royalty**: Louis XVI, Marie Antoinette, and other members of the French royal family had been consigned to prison in August 1792; many royalists had perished in the September Massacres two months before.

Line 167. **aweful**: awesome.   Line 173. **nectar**: wine.

He, or his brethren, who to Neustria's son   175
Enforc'd religious patience, when, at times,
On their indignant hearts Power's iron hand
Too strongly struck; eliciting some sparks
Of the bold spirit of their native North;
Even these Parochial Priests, these humbled men,   180
Whose lowly undistinguish'd cottages
Witness'd a life of purest piety,
While the meek tenants were, perhaps, unknown
Each to the haughty Lord of his domain,
Who mark'd them not; the Noble scorning still   185
The poor and pious Priest, as with slow pace
He glided thro' the dim arch'd avenue
Which to the Castle led; hoping to cheer
The last sad hour of some laborious life
That hasten'd to its close—even such a Man   190
Becomes an exile; staying not to try
By temperate zeal to check his madd'ning flock,
Who, at the novel sound of Liberty
(Ah! most intoxicating sound to slaves!),
Start into licence[.]—Lo! dejected now,   195
The wandering Pastor mourns, with bleeding heart,
His erring people, weeps and prays for them,
And trembles for the account that he must give
To Heaven for souls entrusted to his care.—
Where the cliff, hollow'd by the wintry storm,   200
Affords a seat with matted sea-weed strewn,
A softer form reclines; around her run,
On the rough shingles, or the chalky bourn,
Her gay unconscious children, soon amus'd;
Who pick the fretted stone, or glossy shell,   205
Or crimson plant marine: or they contrive

Line 175. **Neustria's sons**: inhabitants of Normandy.

Line 200. Compare "The female exile" (pages 97–98).

Line 203. **chalky bourn**: an outcropping.

The fairy vessel, with its ribband sail
And gilded paper pennant: in the pool,
Left by the salt wave on the yielding sands,
They launch the mimic navy—Happy age!   210
Unmindful of the miseries of Man!—
Alas! too long a victim to distress,
Their Mother, lost in melancholy thought,
Lull'd for a moment by the murmurs low
Of sullen billows, wearied by the task   215
Of having here, with swol'n and aching eyes
Fix'd on the grey horizon, since the dawn
Solicitously watch'd the weekly sail
From her dear native land, now yields awhile
To kind forgetfulness, while Fancy brings,   220
In waking dreams, that native land again!
Versailles appears—its painted galleries,
And rooms of regal splendour; rich with gold,
Where, by long mirrors multiply'd, the crowd
Paid willing homage—and, united there,   225
Beauty gave charms to empire—Ah! too soon
From the gay visionary pageant rous'd,
See the sad mourner start!—and, drooping, look
With tearful eyes and heaving bosom round
On drear reality—where dark'ning waves,   230
Urg'd by the rising wind, unheeded foam
Near her cold rugged seat:—To call her thence
A fellow-sufferer comes: dejection deep
Checks, but conceals not quite, the martial air,
And that high consciousness of noble blood,   235
Which he has learn'd from infancy to think
Exalts him o'er the race of common men:
Nurs'd in the velvet lap of luxury,
And fed by adulation—could *he* learn,
That worth alone is true Nobility?   240
And that *the peasant* who, "amid the sons
Of Reason, Valour, Liberty, and Virtue,

Displays distinguish'd merit, is a Noble
Of Nature's own creation!"*—If even here,
If in this land of highly vaunted Freedom,   245
Even Britons controvert the unwelcome truth,
Can it be relish'd by the sons of France?
Men, who derive their boasted ancestry
From the fierce leaders of religious wars,
The first in Chivalry's emblazon'd page;   250
Who reckon Gueslin, Bayard, or De Foix,
Among their brave Progenitors? *Their* eyes,
Accustom'd to regard the splendid trophies
Of Heraldry (that with fantastic hand
Mingles, like images in feverish dreams,   255
"Gorgons and Hydras, and Chimeras dire,"
With painted puns, and visionary shapes;),
See not the simple dignity of Virtue,
But hold all base, whom honours such as these
Exalt not from the crowd†—As one, who long   260
Has dwelt amid the artificial scenes

---

* These lines are Thomson's [from James Thomson's adaption of *Coriolanus*, III.iii., spoken by Posthumous Cominius], and are among those sentiments which are now called (when used by living writers), not common-place declamation, but sentiments of dangerous tendency.

† It has been said, and with great appearance of truth, that the contempt in which the Nobility of France held the common people, was remembered, and with all that vindictive asperity which long endurance of oppression naturally excites, when, by a wonderful concurrence of circumstances, the people acquired the power of retaliation. Yet let me here add, what seems to be in some degree inconsistent with the former charge, that the French are good masters to their servants, and that in their treatment of their Negro slaves, they are allowed to be more mild and merciful than other Europeans. [Since the only "other Europeans" with extensive slave-holding colonies were the British, Smith's innuendo should not be lost.]

Line 251. **Gueslin, Bayard, or De Foix**: famous French warriors. Bertrand De Guesclin (c. 1323–80) was named Constable of France; Pierre Bayard (c. 1473–1524), known as an exemplary knight, fought at the side of his countryman Gaston de Foix (1489–1512) at the Battle of Ravenna (1512).

Line 254. **Heraldry**: noble family's coat of arms; armorial bearings.

Line 256. **Gorgons … dire**: Milton, *Paradise Lost*, I.628.

Of populous City, deems that splendid shows,
The Theatre, and pageant pomp of Courts,
Are only worth regard; forgets all taste
For Nature's genuine beauty; in the lapse   265
Of gushing waters hears no soothing sound,
Nor listens with delight to sighing winds,
That, on their fragrant pinions, waft the notes
Of birds rejoicing in the trangled copse;
Nor gazes pleas'd on Ocean's silver breast,   270
While lightly o'er it sails the summer clouds
Reflected in the wave, that, hardly heard,
Flows on the yellow sands: so to *his* mind,
That long has liv'd where Despotism hides
His features harsh, beneath the diadem   275
Of worldly grandeur, abject Slavery seems,
If by that power impos'd, slavery no more:
For luxury wreathes with silk the iron bonds,
And hides the ugly rivets with her flowers,
Till the degenerate triflers, while they love   280
The glitter of the chains, forget their weight.
But more the Men, whose ill acquir'd wealth*
Was wrung from plunder'd myriads, by the means
Too often legaliz'd by power abus'd,
Feel all the horrors of the fatal change,   285
When their ephemeral greatness, marr'd at once
(As a vain toy that Fortune's childish hand
Equally joy'd to fashion or to crush),

---

* The Financiers and Fermiers Generaux are here intended. In the present moment of clamour against all those who have spoken or written in favour of the first Revolution of France, the declaimers seem to have forgotten, that under the reign of a mild and easy tempered Monarch, in the most voluptuous Court in the world, the abuses by which men of this description were enriched, had arisen to such height, that their prodigality exhausted the immense resources of France: and, unable to supply the exigencies of Government, the Ministry were compelled to call Le Tiers Etat; a meeting that gave birth to the Revolution, which has since been so ruinously conducted.

Line 269. **trangled**: probably a misprint for tangled.

Leaves them expos'd to universal scorn
For having nothing else; not even the claim   290
To honour, which respect for Heroes past
Allows to ancient titles; Men, like these,
Sink even beneath the level, whence base arts
Alone had rais'd them;—unlamented sink,
And know that they deserve the woes they feel.   295
   Poor wand'ring wretches! whosoe'er ye are,
That hopeless, houseless, friendless, travel wide
O'er these bleak russet downs; where, dimly seen,
The solitary Shepherd shiv'ring tends
His dun discolour'd flock (Shepherd, unlike   300
Him, whom in song the Poet's fancy crowns
With garlands, and his crook with vi'lets binds);
Poor vagrant wretches! outcasts of the world!
Whom no abode receives, no parish owns;
Roving, like Nature's commoners, the land   305
That boasts such general plenty: if the sight
Of wide-extended misery softens yours
Awhile, suspend your murmurs!—here behold
The strange vicissitudes of fate—while thus
The exil'd Nobles, from their country driven,   310
Whose richest luxuries were their's, must feel
More poignant anguish, than the lowest poor,
Who, born to indigence, have learn'd to brave
Rigid Adversity's depressing breath!—
Ah! rather Fortune's worthless favourites!   315
Who feed on England's vitals—Pensioners
Of base corruption, who, in quick ascent
To opulence unmerited, become
Giddy with pride, and as ye rise, forgetting
The dust ye lately left, with scorn look down   320

Lines 299–302. **The solitary Shepherd ... binds**: The shepherd of pastoral tradition contrasts with this living figure who ekes out his bare subsistence, as the past elegance of the French aristocrat contrasts with his present indigence.

On those beneath ye (tho' your *equals* once
In fortune, and *in worth superior still,*
They view the eminence, on which ye stand,
With wonder, not with envy; for they know
The means, by which ye reach'd it, have been such   325
As, in all honest eyes, degrade ye far
Beneath the poor dependent, whose sad heart
Reluctant pleads for what your pride denies);
Ye venal, worthless hirelings of a Court!
Ye pamper'd Parasites! whom Britons pay   330
For forging fetters for them; rather here
Study a lesson that concerns ye much;
And, trembling, learn, that if oppress'd too long,
The raging multitude, to madness stung,
Will turn on their oppressors; and, no more   335
By sounding titles and parading forms
Bound like tame victims, will redress themselves!
Then swept away by the resistless torrent,
Not only all your pomp may disappear,
But, in the tempest lost, fair Order sink   340
Her decent head, and lawless Anarchy
O'erturn celestial Freedom's radiant throne;—
As now in Gallia; where Confusion, born
Of party rage and selfish love of rule,
Sully the noblest cause that ever warm'd   345
The heart of Patriot Virtue[.]*—There arise
The infernal passions; Vengeance, seeking blood,
And Avarice; and Envy's harpy fangs
Pollute the immortal shrine of Liberty,
Dismay her votaries, and disgrace her name.   350
Respect is due to principle; and they,
Who suffer for their conscience, have a claim,
Whate'er that principle may be, to praise.

---

* This sentiment will probably *renew* against me the indignation of those, who have an
interest in asserting that no such virtue any where exists.

These ill-starr'd Exiles then, who, bound by ties,
To them the bonds of honour; who resign'd   355
Their country to preserve them, and now seek
In England an asylum—well deserve
To find that (every prejudice forgot,
Which pride and ignorance teaches), we for them
Feel as our brethren; and that English hearts,   360
Of just compassion ever own the sway,
As truly as our element, the deep,
Obeys the mild dominion of the Moon[.]—
This they *have* found; and may they find it still!
Thus may'st thou, Britain, triumph!—May thy foes,   365
By Reason's gen'rous potency subdued,
Learn, that the God thou worshippest, delights
In acts of pure humanity!—May thine
Be still such bloodless laurels! nobler far
Than those acquir'd at Cressy or Poictiers,   370
Or of more recent growth, those well bestow'd
On him who stood on Calpe's blazing height
Amid the thunder of a warring world,
Illustrious rather from the crowds he sav'd
From flood and fire, than from the ranks who fell   375
Beneath his valour!—Actions such as these,
Like incense rising to the Throne of Heaven,
Far better justify the pride, that swells
In British bosoms, than the deafening roar
Of Victory from a thousand brazen throats,   380
That tell with what success wide-wasting War
Has by our brave Compatriots thinned the world.

 END OF BOOK I.

Line 370. **Cressy or Poictiers**: two crucial battles (1346, 1356) in the efforts of Edward III
to establish his claim to the French throne.

Line 372. **him ... height**: George Augustus Eliott (1717–90), who commanded Gibraltar
through its siege by the Spanish (1779–83), was knighted for his courage and perseverance.

THE EMIGRANTS

BOOK THE SECOND

Quippe ubi fas versum atque nefas: tot bella per orbem
Tam multæ scelerum facies; non ullus aratro
Dignus honos: squalent abductis arva colonis,
Et curva[e] rigidum falces conflantur in ensem[.]
Hinc movet Euphrates, illinc Germania bellum[;]
Vicinæ ruptis inter se legibus urbes
Arma ferunt: sævit toto Mars impius orbe.

Vergil, *Georgics*. lib. i.505–11

Book II

SCENE, *on an Eminence on one of those Downs, which afford to the South
a View of the Sea; to the North of the Weald of Sussex.*

TIME, *an Afternoon in April, 1793.*

Long wintry months are past; the Moon that now
Lights her pale crescent even at noon, has made
Four times her revolution; since with step,
Mournful and slow, along the wave-worn cliff,
Pensive I took my solitary way,   5
Lost in despondence, while contemplating
Not my own wayward destiny alone,
(Hard as it is, and difficult to bear!)
But in beholding the unhappy lot

Epigraph. "Here right has become wrong and wrong right, so much war spread across the
world, so many aspects of evil. The plow is no longer honored; fields have been emptied of
their tillers; and the curved sickle is beaten into the unbending sword. War erupts on the
Euphrates, in Germany: neighboring states break their treaties and bear forth arms. Uncar-
ing Mars savages the whole world."

April, 1793: Louis XVI was guillotined on 21 January 1793, and in February war was
declared between England and France. These events form the ironic backdrop to the arrival
of spring that Smith celebrates.

Of the lorn Exiles; who, amid the storms   10
Of wild disastrous Anarchy, are thrown,
Like shipwreck'd sufferers, on England's coast,
To see, perhaps, no more their native land,
Where Desolation riots: They, like me,
From fairer hopes and happier prospects driven,   15
Shrink from the future, and regret the past.
But on this Upland scene, while April comes,
With fragrant airs, to fan my throbbing breast,
Fain would I snatch an interval from Care,
That weighs my wearied spirit down to earth;   20
Courting, once more, the influence of Hope
(For "Hope" still waits upon the flowery prime)*
As here I mark Spring's humid hand unfold
The early leaves that fear capricious winds,
While, even on shelter'd banks, the timid flowers   25
Give, half reluctantly, their warmer hues
To mingle with the primroses' pale stars.
No shade the leafless copses yet afford,
Nor hide the mossy labours of the Thrush,
That, startled, darts across the narrow path;   30
But quickly re-assur'd, resumes his task,
Or adds his louder notes to those that rise
From yonder tufted brake; where the white buds
Of the first thorn are mingled with the leaves
Of that which blossoms on the brow of May.   35

Ah! 'twill not be:—So many years have pass'd,
Since, on my native hills, I learn'd to gaze

---

* Shakspeare. ["Hope waits upon the flowery prime" is actually line 13 of Edmund Waller's "To my young Lady Lucy Sidney" (first printed in his *Poems* of 1645), later retitled "To a Very Young Lady."]

Line 14. **Desolation riots:** In March 1793 the Vendée region was engulfed in counterrevolutionary action; the revolt was put down with barbaric severity.

On these delightful landscapes; and those years
Have taught me so much sorrow, that my soul
Feels not the joy reviving Nature brings;   40
But, in dark retrospect, dejected dwells
On human follies, and on human woes.—
What is the promise of the infant year,
The lively verdure, or the bursting blooms,
To those, who shrink from horrors such as War   45
Spreads o'er the affrighted world? With swimming eye,
Back on the past they throw their mournful looks,
And see the Temple, which they fondly hop'd
Reason would raise to Liberty, destroy'd
By ruffian hands; while, on the ruin'd mass,   50
Flush'd with hot blood, the Fiend of Discord sits
In savage triumph; mocking every plea
Of policy and justice, as she shews
The headless corse of one, whose only crime
Was being born a Monarch—Mercy turns,   55
From spectacle so dire, her swol'n eyes;
And Liberty, with calm, unruffled brow
Magnanimous, as conscious of her strength
In Reason's panoply, scorns to distain
Her righteous cause with carnage, and resigns   60
To Fraud and Anarchy the infuriate crowd.—
    What is the promise of the infant year
To those, who (while the poor but peaceful hind
Pens, unmolested, the encreasing flock
Of his rich master in this sea-fenc'd isle)   65
Survey, in neighbouring countries, scenes that make
The sick heart shudder; and the Man, who thinks,
Blush for his species? *There* the trumpet's voice
Drowns the soft warbling of the woodland choir;
And violets, lurking in their turfy beds   70

Line 55. **Monarch**: Louis XVI, executed two months earlier.   Line 59. **distain**: sully.
Line 68. **trumpet's voice**: call to arms.

Beneath the flow'ring thorn, are stain'd with blood.
There fall, at once, the spoiler and the spoil'd;
While War, wide-ravaging, annihilates
The hope of cultivation; gives to Fiends,
The meagre, ghastly Fiends of Want and Woe,   75
The blasted land—There, taunting in the van
Of vengeance-breathing armies, Insult stalks;
And, in the ranks, "Famine, and Sword, and Fire,
Crouch for employment."*—Lo! the suffering world,
Torn by the fearful conflict, shrinks, amaz'd,   80
From Freedom's name, usurp'd and misapplied,
And, cow'ring to the purple Tyrant's rod,
Deems *that* the lesser ill—Deluded Men!
Ere ye prophane her ever-glorious name,
Or catalogue the thousands that have bled   85
Resisting her; or those, who greatly died
Martyrs to *Liberty*—revert awhile
To the black scroll, that tells of regal crimes
Committed to destroy her; rather count
The hecatombs of victims, who have fallen   90
Beneath a single despot; or who gave
Their wasted lives for some disputed claim
Between anointed robbers: Monsters both!†
"Oh! Polish'd perturbation—golden care!"°
So strangely coveted by feeble Man   95
To lift him o'er his fellows;—Toy, for which
Such showers of blood have drench'd th'affrighted earth—
Unfortunate *his* lot, whose luckless head

---

* Shakspeare [*Henry V*, Prologue, lines 7–8].

† Such was the cause of quarrel between the Houses of York and Lancaster [in England's Wars of the Roses]; and of too many others, with which the page of History reproaches the reason of man.

° Shakspeare [*II Henry IV*, IV.v. 23].

Line 82. **purple Tyrant's rod**: absolute monarchy.   Line 90. **hecatombs**: ritual sacrifices.
Line 98. **his lot**: Louis XVI.

Thy jewel'd circlet, lin'd with thorns, has bound;
And who, by custom's laws, obtains from thee   100
Hereditary right to rule, uncheck'd,
Submissive myriads: for untemper'd power,
Like steel ill form'd, injures the hand
It promis'd to protect—Unhappy France!
If e'er thy lilies, trampled now in dust,   105
And blood-bespotted, shall again revive
In silver splendour, may the wreath be wov'n
By voluntary hands; and Freemen, such
As England's self might boast, unite to place
The guarded diadem on *his* fair brow,   110
Where Loyalty may join with Liberty
To fix it firmly.—In the rugged school
Of stern Adversity so early train'd,
His future life, perchance, may emulate
That of the brave Bernois,* so justly call'd   115
The darling of his people; who rever'd
The Warrior less, than they ador'd the Man!
But ne'er may Party Rage, perverse and blind,
And base Venality, prevail to raise
To public trust, a wretch, whose private vice   120
Makes even the wildest profligate recoil;
And who, with hireling ruffians leagu'd, has burst

---

* Henry the Fourth of France. It may be said of this monarch, that had all the French sovereigns resembled him, despotism would have lost its horrors; yet he had considerable failings, and his greatest virtues may be chiefly imputed to his education in the School of Adversity. [Henry IV, who reigned from 1589 to 1610, founded the Bourbon royal line after the extinction of the Valois dynasty and struggled throughout his reign to enforce amity between rival Catholic and Protestant factions. He was assassinated by the Catholic fanatic Francois Ravaillac. In Smith's political conception, though suffering a similar fate, the first Bourbon king thus stands as a natural foil to what she presumed was the last Bourbon monarch, Louis XVI.]

Lines 105–108. **If e'er thy lilies … voluntary hands**: If France once again accepts a monarch, let it be voluntarily and within a constitutional structure like England's.

Line 120. **wretch**: This attack appears directed at Jean-Paul Marat, the most violent of the Jacobin propagandists, who was assassinated by Charlotte Corday later in 1793.

The laws of Nature and Humanity!
Wading, beneath the Patriot's specious mask,
And in Equality's illusive name,   125
To empire thro' a stream of kindred blood—
Innocent prisoner!—most unhappy heir
Of fatal greatness, who art suffering now
For all the crimes and follies of thy race;
Better for thee, if o'er thy baby brow   130
The regal mischief never had been held:
Then, in an humble sphere, perhaps content,
Thou hadst been free and joyous on the heights
Of Pyrennean mountains, shagg'd with woods
Of chestnut, pine, and oak: as on these hills   135
Is yonder little thoughtless shepherd lad,
Who, on the slope abrupt of downy turf
Reclin'd in playful indolence, sends off
The chalky ball, quick bounding far below;
While, half forgetful of his simple task,   140
Hardly his length'ning shadow, or the bells'
Slow tinkling of his flock, that supping tend
To the brown fallows in the vale beneath,
Where nightly it is folded, from his sport
Recall the happy idler.—While I gaze   145
On his gay vacant countenance, my thoughts
Compare with his obscure, laborious lot,
Thine, most unfortunate, imperial Boy!
Who round thy sullen prison daily hear'st
The savage howl of Murder, as it seeks   150
Thy unoffending life: while sad within

Line 127. **prisoner**: Louis, heir presumptive to the throne of France, was seven years old when his father was executed. He died in 1795. At the point of Smith's writing he was imprisoned with other members of the royal family.

Line 143. **brown fallows**: plowed but uncultivated land.

Line 148. **imperial Boy**: the child Louis, heir presumptive.

Thy wretched Mother, petrified with grief,
Views thee with stony eyes, and cannot weep!—
Ah! much I mourn thy sorrows, hapless Queen!
And deem thy expiation made to Heaven   155
For every fault, to which Prosperity
Betray'd thee, when it plac'd thee on a throne
Where boundless power was thine, and thou wert rais'd
High (as it seem'd) above the envious reach
Of destiny! Whate'er thy errors were,   160
Be they no more remember'd; tho' the rage
Of Party swell'd them to such crimes, as bade
Compassion stifle every sigh that rose
For thy disastrous lot—More than enough
Thou hast endur'd; and every English heart,   165
Ev'n those, that highest beat in Freedom's cause,
Disclaim as base, and of that cause unworthy,
The Vengeance, or the Fear, that makes thee still
A miserable prisoner!—Ah! who knows,
From sad experience, more than I, to feel   170
For thy desponding spirit, as it sinks
Beneath procrastinated fears for those
More dear to thee than life! But eminence
Of misery is thine, as once of joy;
And, as we view the strange vicissitude,   175
We ask anew, where happiness is found?—
Alas! in rural life, where youthful dreams
See the Arcadia that Romance describes,
Not even Content resides!—In yon low hut
Of clay and thatch, where rises the grey smoke   180
Of smold'ring turf, cut from the adjoining moor,
The labourer, its inhabitant, who toils
From the first dawn of twilight, till the Sun
Sinks in the rosy waters of the West,

Line 152. **Mother**: Marie Antoinette, queen of France.   Line 181. **smold'ring turf**: peat.

Finds that with poverty it cannot dwell;   185
For bread, and scanty bread, is all he earns
For him and for his household[.]—Should Disease,
Born of chill wintry rains, arrest his arm,
Then, thro' his patch'd and straw-stuff'd casement, peeps
The squalid figure of extremest Want;   190
And from the Parish the reluctant dole,
Dealt by th'unfeeling farmer, hardly saves
The ling'ring spark of life from cold extinction:
Then the bright Sun of Spring, that smiling bids
All other animals rejoice, beholds,   195
Crept from his pallet, the emaciate wretch
Attempt, with feeble effort, to resume
Some heavy task, above his wasted strength,
Turning his wistful looks (how much in vain!)
To the deserted mansion, where no more   200
The owner (gone to gayer scenes) resides,
Who made even luxury, Virtue; while he gave
The scatter'd crumbs to honest Poverty.—
But, tho' the landscape be too oft deform'd
By figures such as these, yet Peace is here,   205
And o'er our vallies, cloath'd with springing corn,
No hostile hoof shall trample, nor fierce flames
Wither the wood's young verdure, ere it form
Gradual the laughing May's luxuriant shade;
For, by the rude sea guarded, we are safe,   210
And feel not evils such as with deep sighs
The Emigrants deplore, as they recal
The Summer past, when Nature seem'd to lose
Her course in wild distemperature, and aid,
With seasons all revers'd, destructive War.   215
    Shuddering, I view the pictures they have drawn
Of desolated countries, where the ground,
Stripp'd of its unripe produce, was thick strewn
With various Death—the war-horse falling there
By famine, and his rider by the sword.   220

The moping clouds sail'd heavy charg'd with rain,
And bursting o'er the mountains['] misty brow,
Deluged, as with an inland sea, the vales;*
Where, thro' the sullen evening's lurid gloom,
Rising, like columns of volcanic fire,   225
The flames of burning villages illum'd
The waste of water; and the wind, that howl'd
Along its troubled surface, brought the groans
Of plunder'd peasants, and the frantic shrieks
Of mothers for their children; while the brave,   230
To pity still alive, listen'd aghast
To these dire echoes, hopeless to prevent
The evils they beheld, or check the rage,
Which ever, as the people of one land
Meet in contention, fires the human heart   235
With savage thirst of kindred blood, and makes
Man lose his nature; rendering him more fierce
Than the gaunt monsters of the howling waste.
      Oft have I heard the melancholy tale,
Which, all their native gaiety forgot,   240
These Exiles tell—How Hope impell'd them on,
Reckless of tempest, hunger, or the sword,
Till order'd to retreat, they know not why,
From all their flattering prospects, they became
The prey of dark suspicion and regret:†   245
Then, in despondence, sunk the unnerv'd arm

---

* From the heavy and incessant rains during the last campaign, the armies were often compelled to march for many miles through marshes overflowed; suffering the extremities of cold and fatigue. The peasants frequently misled them; and, after having passed these inundations at the hazard of their lives, they were sometimes under the necessity of crossing them a second and a third time; their evening quarters after such a day of exertion were often in a wood without shelter; and their repast, instead of bread, unripe corn, without any other preparation than being mashed into a sort of paste.

† It is remarkable, that notwithstanding the excessive hardships to which the army of the Emigrants was exposed, very few in it suffered from disease till they began to retreat; then it was that despondence consigned to the most miserable death many brave men who deserved a better fate; and then despair impelled some to suicide, while others fell by mutual wounds, unable to survive disappointment and humiliation.

Of gallant Loyalty[.]—At every turn
Shame and disgrace appear'd, and seem'd to mock
Their scatter'd squadrons; which the warlike youth,
Unable to endure, often implor'd,   250
As the last act of friendship, from the hand
Of some brave comrade, to receive the blow
That freed the indignant spirit from its pain.
To a wild mountain, whose bare summit hides
Its broken eminence in clouds; whose steeps   255
Are dark with woods; where the receding rocks
Are worn by torrents of dissolving snow,
A wretched Woman, pale and breathless, flies!
And, gazing round her, listens to the sound
Of hostile footsteps[.]—No! it dies away: 260
Nor noise remains, but of the cataract,
Or surly breeze of night, that mutters low
Among the thickets, where she trembling seeks
A temporary shelter—clasping close
To her hard-heaving heart her sleeping child,   265
All she could rescue of the innocent groupe
That yesterday surrounded her[.]—Escap'd
Almost by miracle! Fear, frantic Fear,
Wing'd her weak feet: yet, half repentant now
Her headlong haste, she wishes she had staid   270
To die with those affrighted Fancy paints
The lawless soldier's victims[.]—Hark! again
The driving tempest bears the cry of Death,
And, with deep sullen thunder, the dread sound
Of cannon vibrates on the tremulous earth;   275
While, bursting in the air, the murderous bomb
Glares o'er her mansion. Where the splinters fall,
Like scatter'd comets, its destructive path
Is mark'd by wreaths of flame!—Then, overwhelm'd
Beneath accumulated horror, sinks   280
The desolate mourner; yet, in Death itself,
True to maternal tenderness, she tries

To save the unconscious infant from the storm
In which she perishes; and to protect
This last dear object of her ruin'd hopes   285
From prowling monsters, that from other hills,
More inaccessible, and wilder wastes,
Lur'd by the scent of slaughter, follow fierce
Contending hosts, and to polluted fields
Add dire increase of horrors[.]—But alas!   290
The Mother and the Infant perish both!—
     The feudal Chief, whose Gothic battlements
Frown on the plain beneath, returning home
From distant lands, alone and in disguise,
Gains at the fall of night his Castle walls,   295
But, at the vacant gate, no Porter sits
To wait his Lord's admittance!—In the courts
All is drear silence!—Guessing but too well
The fatal truth, he shudders as he goes
Thro' the mute hall; where, by the blunted light   300
That the dim moon thro' painted casements lends,
He sees that devastation has been there:
Then, while each hideous image to his mind
Rises terrific, o'er a bleeding corse
Stumbling he falls; another interrupts   305
His staggering feet—all, all who us'd to rush
With joy to meet him—all his family
Lie murder'd in his way!—And the day dawns
On a wild raving Maniac, whom a fate
So sudden and calamitous has robb'd   310
Of reason; and who round his vacant walls
Screams unregarded, and reproaches Heaven! —
Such are thy dreadful trophies, savage War!
And evils such as these, or yet more dire,
Which the pain'd mind recoils from, all are thine—   315
The purple Pestilence, that to the grave
Sends whom the sword has spar'd, is thine; and thine
The Widow's anguish and the Orphan's tears!—

Woes such as these does Man inflict on Man;
And by the closet murderers, whom we style   320
Wise Politicians, are the schemes prepar'd,
Which, to keep Europe's wavering balance even,
Depopulate her kingdoms, and consign
To tears and anguish half a bleeding world!—
    Oh! could the time return, when thoughts like these   325
Spoil'd not that gay delight, which vernal Suns,
Illuminating hills, and woods, and fields,
Gave to my infant spirits—Memory come!
And from distracting cares, that now deprive
Such scenes of all their beauty, kindly bear   330
My fancy to those hours of simple joy,
When, on the banks of Arun, which I see
Make its irriguous course thro' yonder meads,
I play'd; unconscious then of future ill!
There (where, from hollows fring'd with yellow broom,   335
The birch with silver rind, and fairy leaf,
Aslant the low stream trembles) I have stood,
And meditated how to venture best
Into the shallow current, to procure
The willow herb of glowing purple spikes,   340
Or flags, whose sword-like leaves conceal'd the tide,
Startling the timid reed-bird from her nest,
As with aquatic flowers I wove the wreath,
Such as, collected by the shepherd girls,
Deck in the villages the turfy shrine,   345
And mark the arrival of propitious May.—
How little dream'd I then the time would come,
When the bright Sun of that delicious month
Should, from disturb'd and artificial sleep,
Awaken me to never-ending toil,   350
To terror and to tears!—Attempting still,
With feeble hands and cold desponding heart,

Line 333. **irriguous**: irrigating.   Line 341. **flags**: wild iris.

To save my children from the o'erwhelming wrongs,
That have for ten long years been heap'd on me !—
The fearful spectres of chicane and fraud   355
Have, Proteus like, still chang'd their hideous forms
(As the Law lent its plausible disguise),
Pursuing my faint steps; and I have seen
Friendship's sweet bonds (which were so early form'd,)
And once I fondly thought of amaranth   360
Inwove with silver seven times tried) give way,
And fail; as these green fan-like leaves of fern
Will wither at the touch of Autumn's frost.
Yet there *are those*, whose patient pity still
Hears my long murmurs; who, unwearied, try   365
With lenient hands to bind up every wound
My wearied spirit feels, and bid me go
"Right onward"*— a calm votary of the Nymph,
Who, from her adamantine rock, points out
To conscious rectitude the rugged path,   370
That leads at length to Peace!—Ah! yes, my friends
Peace will at last be mine; for in the Grave
Is Peace—and pass a few short years, perchance
A few short months, and all the various pain
I now endure shall be forgotten there,   375
And no memorial shall remain of me,
Save in your bosoms; while even *your* regret
Shall lose its poignancy, as ye reflect
What complicated woes that grave conceals!
But, if the little praise, that may await   380

---

* Milton, Sonnet 22d ["Cyriac, this three years' day," line 9].

Line 354. **on me**: another reference to litigation over the trust fund for Smith's children established by her father-in-law, still many years from being settled.

Line 360. **amaranth**: the flower of paradise; thus, immortal.

Line 369. **adamantine**: of extreme hardness, unbreakable.

Line 373. **pass ... years**: after a few years pass.

The Mother's efforts, should provoke the spleen
Of Priest or Levite; and they then arraign
The dust that cannot hear them; be it yours
To vindicate my humble fame; to say,
That, not in selfish sufferings absorb'd,   385
"I gave to misery all I had, my tears."*
And if, where regulated sanctity
Pours her long orisons to Heaven, my voice
Was seldom heard, that yet *my prayer* was made
To him who hears even silence; not in domes   390
Of human architecture, fill'd with crowds,
But on these hills, where boundless, yet distinct,
Even as a map, beneath are spread the fields
His bounty cloaths; divided here by woods,
And there by commons rude, or winding brooks,   395
While I might breathe the air perfum'd with flowers,
Or the fresh odours of the mountain turf;
And gaze on clouds above me, as they sail'd
Majestic: or remark the reddening north,
When bickering arrows of electric fire   400
Flash on the evening sky—I made my prayer
In unison with murmuring waves that now
Swell with dark tempests, now are mild and blue,
As the bright arch above; for all to me
Declare omniscient goodness; nor need I   405
Declamatory essays to incite
My wonder or my praise, when every leaf
That Spring unfolds, and every simple bud,

* Gray [Thomas Gray, "He gave to Mis'ry all he had, a tear." From the poet's own epitaph, in "Elegy Written in a Country Church-Yard," line 123].

Line 382. **Priest or Levite**: those who judge by a strict code.
Line 387. **regulated sanctity**: formal religion.
Line 388. **long orisons**: lengthy prayers, perhaps too protracted to be counted sincere.
Line 395. **commons rude**: uncultivated common grazing land.
Line 400. **arrows of electric fire**: the aurora borealis, or northern lights.

More forcibly impresses on my heart
His power and wisdom—Ah! while I adore   410
That goodness, which design'd to all that lives
Some taste of happiness, my soul is pain'd
By the variety of woes that Man
For Man creates—his blessings often turn'd
To plagues and curses: Saint-like Piety,   415
Misled by Superstition, has destroy'd
More than Ambition; and the sacred flame
Of Liberty becomes a raging fire,
When Licence and Confusion bid it blaze.
From thy high throne, above yon radiant stars,   420
O Power Omnipotent! with mercy view
This suffering globe, and cause thy creatures cease,
With savage fangs, to tear her bleeding breast:
Restrain that rage for power, that bids a Man,
Himself a worm, desire unbounded rule   425
O'er beings like himself: Teach the hard hearts
Of rulers, that the poorest hind, who dies
For their unrighteous quarrels, in thy sight
Is equal to the imperious Lord, that leads
His disciplin'd destroyers to the field.—   430
May lovely Freedom, in her genuine charms,
Aided by stern but equal Justice, drive
From the ensanguin'd earth the hell-born fiends
Of Pride, Oppression, Avarice, and Revenge,
That ruin what thy mercy made so fair!   435
Then shall these ill-starr'd wanderers, whose sad fate
These desultory lines lament, regain
Their native country; private vengeance then
To public virtue yield; and the fierce feuds,
That long have torn their desolated land,   440
May (even as storms, that agitate the air,
Drive noxious vapours from the blighted earth)
Serve, all tremendous as they are, to fix
The reign of Reason, Liberty, and Peace!

Uncollected Poems

In 1811, five years after Smith's death, Elizabeth Inchbald in her multi-volume collection of *Modern Drama* identified the comedy, *What is She?*, produced in 1799, as having been authored by Smith. Since Inchbald was herself a major writer of comedy during this decade and an acquaintance of Smith's, she is not likely to have advanced this attribution without cause. The comedy is well-written, though it is perhaps overly complicated in its plot: it opened at Covent Garden on 27 April 1799 and ran for just five nights, which would constitute a failure that an author might understandably suppress. Smith herself never alludes to the play, but she lived in London from the beginning of 1798 until early in 1800, and we have few letters or other records of her doings during this period. She did mix freely with an intellectual and literary set; both the company she kept and her association with the contemporary theater are underscored by her having written the prologue to Godwin's tragedy *Antonio* late in 1800. She had been asked as early as the 1780s to write for the stage (see Sonnet 29, page 32), and her intimate knowledge of its conditions can be gleaned from her verses "Written for the benefit of a distressed player" (see page 99). The Prologue and three drafts for an Epilogue bound with the manuscript of the play submitted for clearance by the censor, John Larpent, do reveal characteristic interests of Smith's. The reference in the Prologue to Monimia, heroine of Otway's *The Orphan*, recalls the numerous allusions to Otway in her early sonnets as well as the main female character by the same name in Smith's novel *The Old Manor House* (1793). The knowing class satire in Epilogues [A] and [B] suggests this novelist's concern with a broad social panorama. Epilogue [C] in its move from sardonic remarks about lawyers to its allegory of a garden seems particularly redolent of Smith's concerns at this point in her career.

Hymn to love and life

Twin stars of light! whose blended rays
Illuminate the darkest road
Where fortune's roving exile strays,
When doubt and care the wanderer load,
And drive him far from joy's abode.   5

Propitious Love and smiling Hope!
Be you my guides, and guardian powers,
If, doom'd with adverse fate to cope,
I quit in Honour's rigid hours
These dear, these bliss-devoted towers.   10

Yet here, O still, most radiant! here
(Attend this prayer of fond concern)
To beauty's bosom life endear,
Presaging as ye brightly burn
The rapture of my blest return.   15

Sonnet to the Forest Ytene*

Along thy wood-lanes wild, or shrubby lawns,
Or hollow dells, or glens befring'd with thorn;
Where from its ferny lair, at early morn,

---

* the New Forest.

Hymn to love and life. From Smith's *The Old Manor House.* Written by Orlando Somerive
as he contemplates the fruition of his expectations in love and inheritance. It is probable
that the poem was never reprinted, or reworked to improve its improvisatory character,
because it is so closely tied to the particular situation of its putative author, who has just
accepted a commission in the army and faces being shipped to America to fight the rebel-
lious colonists.

Sonnet to the Forest Ytene. From Smith's *Minor Morals* (1800), an educational book for
children, this sonnet is composed by the young and exemplary Charlotte Amiel to celebrate
the New Forest near Southampton, the largest preserve of woodland in England.

The forester alarms the timid fawn,
I would 'twere mine to wander;—or when fade   5
The gleams of evening into shadowy night:
What time on many a stem or grassy blade
The glow-worm hangs her fairy emerald light,
I would behold the moon-beams fall among
The far retiring trees, and lengthening glades,   10
And listen the low wind, that thro' the shades
Conveys the night-bird's soft love-labour'd song:
For here the soul unruffled feels its powers,
And seeks the Hermit Peace within his forest bowers.

Prologue to *What is She?*
A comedy, in five acts

'Twas said, long since, by various moral sages
That man's short life comprises diff'rent ages;
From childhood first, to manhood we attain,
And then, alas! to childhood sink again.
The same progressions mark Dramatic taste,   5
When manhood 'twixt two infancy's is plac'd.
When first the scene, the moral world display'd,
The Muses limp'd without Mechanic Aid:
Then Bards and Monsters labour'd side by side,
And equal fame, and equal gains divide.   10
Together Actors, Carpenters rehearse,
And the wing'd Griffin helps the hobbling verse.
The saddest tale demands (the heart to seize)
Confed'rate lightning, and the show'r of peas;
Nor wit, nor pathos Audiences require,   15

Sonnet to the Forest Ytene. Line 11. **listen**: listen to.

Line 12. **night-bird's ... song**: the song of the nightingale.

Prologue to *What is She?* Line 9. **Bards**: Conditions in the Elizabethan theater required playwrights like Shakespeare to work intimately with the actors.

Line 14. **show'r of peas**: to mimic the sound of a storm.

But quaint conceits, and dragons, storms & fire.
 At length Taste's manhood came, the Stage improv'd,
Without a Storm Monimia's sorrows mov'd;
Then Love and Valentine could charm the Fair,
Tho' not one Cupid dangled in the Air: 20
"To Scenic Monsters Bevil was preferr'd
Nor found a rival—in some fierce Blue-Beard."
Th'empassion'd verse, Wit's pointed moral aim,
The Audience charm'd, and fix'd the Author's fame.
 But all must change—behold the Muses mourn,   25
And, drooping, see Taste's infancy return;
Again the Bard calls forth red-stocking'd legions,
And show'rs of fire from the infernal regions;
Again, storms darken the Theatric sky,
And strung on ropes the fearful Cupids fly: 30
Again pale ghosts stalk tunefully along,
And end their visit, just as ends the song.
The siege, th'explosion, nightly concourse draws,
And Castles burn and fall—with vast applause!
 To-night a female Scribe, less bold, appears,   35
She dreads to pull the house about your ears;
Her inexperienc'd Muse no plan durst form,
To raise the Spectre, or direct the Storm;
And if her pen no genuine plaudits steal,
From ears—to eyes she offers no appeal;   40
Her Muse, tho' humble, scorns extrinsic art,
And asks her meed—from judgment and the heart.

Line 18. **Monimia**: heroine of Thomas Otway's *The Orphan* (1680).

Line 19. **Valentine**: Valentine Legend is the lover of Angelica in William Congreve's *Love for Love* (1695).

Line 21. **Bevil**: the gentlemanly ideal of Richard Steele's *Conscious Lovers* (1722).

Line 22. **Blue-Beard**: This wife-murderer entered literary renown (and the stock melodrama) through Charles Perrault's fairy tales.

Lines 25–34: **change … applause**: In the 1790s a taste for elaborate spectacle began to have a pronounced effect on all the productions mounted in the London theaters. To Smith's mind the stage is returning to the conditions of two centuries earlier.

Epilogue [A] to *What is She?*

"What is she[?"]—Aye, there's the important question,
Which ask'd too late, oft proves of hard digestion:
And he who stays till past the Honey Moon
May find he asks too late—and knows too soon[.]
But precept often fails without example,   5
So, with your leave, I'll give a little sample[.]
    Squire Fiscky, a Rake of old renown,
By years admonish'd, and quite prudent grown,
Resolves, for virtue's sake, to take a wife:
But ah! far from the Scenes of modern life,   10
He seeks some Miss, whom man with terror seizes,
Who hangs her head, and "does as Papa pleases."
Charm'd with simplicity beyond his hopes,
He weds, and what she is, he finds—when she elopes.
    Sir Tinsel Dash loves elegance and spirit,   15
And shew and beauty thinks the only merit;
So weds a toast, whom half mankind adore.
But gain'd a husband—the gay Farce is o'er,
And she, of taste & beauty late the pattern,
Becomes a misshap'd dowdy, and a slattern.   20
    Not so Lord Dove—he's for a quiet life,
And long he fears to risk domestic strife,
Till lur'd by gentle Julia's placid tone,
Who, ne'er to wield the female weapon's known,
In whom the silent graces seem to centre—   25
His dear[-]lov'd ease the Peer resolves to venture.
The vow pronounc'd—Ma'am's ministry begins[.]
Behold the Ins all Outs, the Outs all Ins!
All's put to rout—Dogs, Servants, horses new—

Line 11. **whom ... seizes**: i.e., is seized with terror by the thought of a man.
Line 17. **toast**: an object of many admirers.

My Lord, I can't endure your formal crew!   30
In fine, ere yet the wedding feast is cold
The gentle Julia proves a very scold.
　　　　But while I thus teach caution from our Play,
What, prays our Authoress, the Ladys say[.]
Ah! here like Hotspur's Kate I prudent grow,   35
And will not tell you what I do not know[.]
Thus much she bids me say—that, Beauty's friend,
She only paints its follies—to amend:
That, while to Warn—her fancy Zephyrine drew
She copy'd her Eugenia from you: 40
And if the justice of the sketch you own,
By your support the likeness will be shewn:
Exert your influence in her heroine's cause,
And what she is, is fix'd by your applause[.]

Epilogue [B] to *What is She?*

No more the quizzish Bewley's destin'd wife,
And yet the Votary of modish life;
In Fashion's rounds again my fame to seek,
In Air an Amazon, in dress a Greek,
I come, a Heroine, with destructive aim,   5
To beat yon Covert for the Critic Game;
The Season's late; but *Birds of prey* none fear
To shoot without a licence—all the Year:
Behold me then—piece levell'd with my eye,
Prepar'd at flocks of Critics to let fly—   10
Yet stay—for in a random shot, who knows

Epilogue [A]. Line 35. **Kate:** the wife of Hotspur in *I Henry IV.*

Lines 39–40: **Zephyrine ... Eugenia:** characters in the play.

Epilogue [B]. This epilogue was spoken by Miss Betterton, the actress who played the main female character, Lady Zephyrine Mutable.

But the same blow may wound both friends and foes.
Suppose, then, ere I take a hostile station,
I try the system—of conciliation;
And still, tho' folly may the truth disguise,   15
Woman's best weapons are her tongue and eyes.
First, that gaunt Critic clad in Iron Grey,
Who seems to frown perdition on our Play,
Would he but smile!—do, Ma'am, make him look up,
Oh, ho! he's harmless—but in haste to sup.   20
The Spark above, just come with eager stride,
Bespurr'd—bebooted—express from Cheapside;
His alter'd eye bodes us no hostile fit,
A Maiden Aunt has spy'd him from the Pit;
In vain you shirk your damsel, and look shy,   25
Friend Tom, you'll have a lecture by and by.
    What says that Beau? a Crop—but don't deride it,
His three-cock't hat is big enough to hide it;
Tho' nightly here—'tis not the Play's his hobby,
He only criticizes in the Lobby.   30
Ye martial youths, who decorate our rows,
Who menace nothing but your Country's foes;
No Female vainly can your suffrage crave,
You must be merciful, because you're brave—
And last, and loudest, you, my friends above,   35
Some by our Play led here, and some by love;
Your honest fronts—seek not behind to hide,
I see you all—your Sweethearts by your side,
No low'ring Critic[-]brows 'mongst you I find,
But John at Betty smirks, and looks so kind: 40

Lines 21–22. **Spark**: a young dandy; his "damsel" (line 25) may not be of the best reputation.

Line 27. **Crop**: an ambiguous reference, which could allude either to modishly short hair or to the riding crop of a man on the hunt for prey.

Line 30. **Lobby**: The lobbies and antechambers of the major theaters were notorious sites for prostitutes to congregate.

Don't, Betty, cheer him with one smile to-night,
'Till he applaud our Play with all his might.
That jolly Tar, by Kate from Rotherhithe brought—
With Bard or Critic ne'er disturbs *his* thought,
He only comes to make the Gallery ring   45
With "Rule, Brittania," and "God save the King";
Oh! may those patriot strains long echo here,
The sweetest music to a British ear.
Yet, while on well known kindness I presume,
Our Authoress, trembling, waits from you her doom.   50

Epilogue [C] to *What is She?*

And so to set two brothers by the ears,
And spin a law-suit out for 15 years,
No other reason by the Bard is found,
Than one poor simple plot of Garden ground[.]
Had a parterre so glowing, and so gay,   5
As that I saw before me, caus'd our play,
The contest had been noble—here we find
As in a Garden, Nature's hand entwin'd
With art and elegance, the blushing Rose
With lillies mixt, see Beauty's cheeks disclose[;]   10
Carnations, Pinks, gay Tulips meet our eyes,
And Belles surrounded oft by butterflys.
Some fruit we boast—by Plums we mean rich Cits[;]
Critics are Crabs, and pine-Apples are Wits.

Epilogue [B] to *What is She?* Line 43. **Rotherhithe:** the area of the docks on the south side of the the Thames east of London.

Epilogue [C] to *What is She?* Line 5. **parterre:** The author joins two meanings of the word: a raised section of a theater and a patterned flowerbed.

Line 12. **butterflys:** young bachelors who circulate among the women.

Line 13. **Cits:** wealthy merchants and bankers who work in the City.

Line 14. **Crabs:** crabapples: hence, sour.

Here too the laurel blooms, and many a Bard   15
Receives from your kind hand its sweet reward[.]
There is a plant, which, when the lark upsprings
To meet the russet mantled morn, & wings
Its flight towards the East, from lovely bed
Of Parent Earth just rears its dewy head,   20
And if approach'd by rude, ungentle hand,
Shrinks in itself, and ceases to expand:
But shou'd the Sun its influence warm diffuse
It opens lovely in a thousand hues,
And thus the Muse in chill suspense retires   25
Till your applause awaken all her fires[.]

Prologue to William Godwin, *Antonio: or, The Soldier's Return*

The haughty Spaniard, who, with hopeless eye,
O'er Calpe's Straits sees British banners fly,
Was, (ere in slothful bigotry was lost
His ardent courage) glory's proudest boast;
The sacred cross to Asia's realms he bore,   5
And, in his own deep woods, the invading Moor
Met in fierce contest: Each undaunted Son
Of both Castiles, or nobler Arragon,
And they, who on the rude Biscayan shore

Prologue to William Godwin, *Antonio: or The Soldier's Return*. Line 2. **Calpe's Straits**: the Straits of Gibralter.

Line 6. **the invading Moor**: Moslems invaded Spain from North Africa in 711 and by 719 had conquered the entire Iberian peninsula.

Line 8. **both Castiles**: Old Castile, a province of north-central Spain, was reconquered from the Moslems in the early eleventh century; by 1085 the capital of New Castile, Toledo, had also been liberated. **Arragon**: In the thirteenth century Aragon was an independent kingdom combining eastern Spain and southwestern France.

Line 9. **Biscayan shore**: Asturia or Navarre, present Basque territory, a mountainous region never conquered by the Moslems.

Heard the vast billows of the Atlantic roar, 10
All, by the fire of martial glory led,
Beneath her crimson banner fought and bled:
High beat each heart in *her* imperious cause,
And, owning hers, disdain'd all other laws.
The Torch of love, no more a lambent flame, 15
Serv'd but to light them to their idol—Fame.
While all that sooths *our* age, or charms *our* youth,
In female tenderness and female truth,
Bliss, that, to all but man, high heaven denies,
Homeborn delights, domestic charities, 20
They tasted not: nor knew they to rejoice
That reason, sweetest in a woman's voice,
Still bids the lover, husband, friend adore,
When transcient beauty fascinates no more:
From Prototypes like these, who lived, we know, 25
And fought and died, three hundred years ago,
Our Poet to-night his hero draws,
The fierce, vindictive slave of honour's laws:—
By softer passions mov'd, to nature true,
His lovely *heroine* he describes from *you,* 30
Women of England!—Lo a bard unknown
Covets your favour—yet in abject tone
He scorns to plead—more general this appeal
Shall be, to all who *think,* to all who *feel.*
Of party guiltless, shunning all offense, 35
Trusting alone to nature, truth and sense,
To this whole audience he his cause confides,
Where British Candour hears, & British taste decides.

Lines 27–30. **hero … heroine:** In Godwin's play Don Antonio de Almanza so divides the affections of his sister Helena from her husband, Don Gusman, Duke of Zuniga, that he incites the Duke to kill him.

Line 35. **Of party guiltless:** Godwin, a major figure in the radical agitation of the 1790s, was so worried about his play being shouted down from the pit, that he submitted it to several friends, among them Coleridge and Lamb, to make sure that no possible cause for such a political reaction existed in the text.

Conversations Introducing Poetry

{ 1804 }

These poems (along with "Studies by the sea" and "Flora," republished with *Beachy Head*) were printed as exemplary texts in Smith's innovative *Conversations Introducing Poetry, Chiefly on Subjects of Natural History for the Use of Children and Young Persons* (1804), in which Mrs. Talbot instructs her children George and Emily simultaneously in natural lore and poetic forms and usage. Occasionally, other texts are intruded, most notably by the children's "aunt," who is actually Charlotte Smith's sister Catherine Anne Dorset: she first established her independent credentials as a children's author in 1806 and reprinted her contributions to Smith's volume in the first collection of her popular favorites, *The Peacock at Home, and Other Poems,* in 1809. Until the verses that come late in the two-volume *Conversations,* Smith's efforts are very much directed to a child's needs and level of comprehension, with the poems serving as mnemonic devices for retaining information and as instruments of moral and ecological education. As is her usual practice, Smith identifies her natural subjects with their scientific names at the end of each volume. Where such an identification coincides with the subject and contents of the verse (in contrast to other subjects of conversation in prose), the note is reprinted here.

To a green-chafer, on a white rose

You dwell within a lovely bower,
Little chafer, gold and green,
Nestling in the fairest flower,
The rose of snow, the garden's queen.

There you drink the chrystal dew,   5
And your shards* as emeralds bright
And corselet, of the ruby's hue,
Hide among the petals white.

Your fringed feet may rest them there,
And there your filmy wings may close,   10
But do not wound the flower so fair
That shelters you in sweet repose.

Insect! be not like him who dares
On pity's bosom to intrude,
And then that gentle bosom tears   15
With baseness and ingratitude.

---

* shards. *Elytra.*

Title. green-chafer: *Scarabeus nobilis.*

Line 6. shards: Mrs. Talbot glosses: "the outward wings of beetles, and such insects, which under them have another pair of light filmy wings, that, when they fly, are spread out; but at other times are folded up under their hard case-like wings, so as not to be perceived" (*Conversations,* I, 7).

Line 7. corselet: again, Mrs. Talbot: "taken from the French word for armour, which was worn to cover the body in battle" (*Conversations,* I, 7).

A walk by the water

Let us walk where reeds are growing,
  By the alders in the mead;
Where the crystal streams are flowing,
  In whose waves the fishes feed.

There the golden carp* is laving,   5
  With the trout, the perch, and bream;†
Mark! their flexile fins are waving,
  As they glance along the stream.

Now they sink in deeper billows,
  Now upon the surface rise;   10
Or from under roots of willows,
  Dart to catch the water-flies.

'Midst the reeds and pebbles hiding,
  See the minnow and the roach;°
Or by water-lillies gliding,   15
  Shun with fear our near approach.

Do not dread us, timid fishes,
  We have neither net nor hook;
Wanderers we, whose only wishes
  Are to read in nature's book.   20

---

* carp. *Cyprinus carpio.*
† trout. *Salmo fario.*   perch. *Perca fluviatilis.*   bream. *Cyprinus brama.*
° minnow. *Cyprinus phoscinus.*   roach. *Cyprinus rutilus.*

Invitation to the bee

Child of patient industry,
Little active busy bee,
Thou art out at early morn,
Just as the opening flowers are born,
Among the green and grassy meads   5
Where the cowslips hang their heads;
Or by hedge-rows, while the dew
Glitters on the harebell* blue.—

Then on eager wing art flown,
To thymy hillocks on the down;   10
Or to revel on the broom;†
Or suck the clover's° crimson bloom;
Murmuring still thou busy bee
Thy little ode to industry!

Go while summer suns are bright,   15
Take at large thy wandering flight;
Go and load thy tiny feet
With every rich and various sweet,
Cling around the flowring thorn,‡
Dive in the woodbine's• honied horn,   20
Seek the wild rose⁋ that shades the dell,
Explore the foxglove's§ freckled bell,

---

* harebell. *Hyacinthus non scriptus.*   † broom. *Spartium scoparium.*
° clover. *Trifolium pratense.*   ‡ thorn. Hawthorn, *Cratega oxyacantha.*
• woodbine. *Lonciera periclymenum.*   ⁋ wild rose. *Rosa canina.*
§ foxglove. *Digitalis purpurea.*

Line 10. **thymy ... down**: small bushes of fragrant thyme are abundant on the South Downs in Sussex, the high chalky grassland overlooking the ocean, where Smith customarily sets her poetry.

Or in the heath flower's fairy cup
Drink the fragrant spirit up.

But when the meadows shall be mown,   25
And summer's garlands overblown;
Then come, thou little busy bee,
And let thy homestead be with me,
There, shelter'd by thy straw-built hive,
In my garden thou shalt live,   30
And that garden shall supply
Thy delicious alchemy;
There for thee, in autumn, blows
The Indian pink* and latest rose,
The mignonette perfumes the air,   35
And stocks, unfading flowers, are there.

Yet fear not when the tempests come,
And drive thee to thy waxen home,
That I shall then most treacherously
For thy honey murder thee.   40

Ah, no!—throughout the winter drear
I'll feed thee, that another year
Thou may'st renew thy industry
Among the flowers, thou little busy bee.

---

* Indian pink. *Dianthus chinensis.*

Line 32. **alchemy**: the transformation of nectar into honey.

The hedge-hog* seen in a frequented path

Wherefore should man or thoughtless boy
Thy quiet harmless life destroy,
Innoxious urchin?—for thy food
Is but the beetle and the fly,
And all thy harmless luxury   5
The swarming insects of the wood.

Should man to whom his God has given
Reason, the brightest ray of heaven,
Delight to hurt, in senseless mirth,
Inferior animals?—and dare   10
To use his power in waging war
Against his brethren of the earth?

Poor creature! to the woods resort,
Lest lingering here, inhuman sport
Should render vain thy thorny case;   15
And whelming water, deep and cold,
Make thee thy spiny ball unfold,
And shew thy simple negro face!

Fly from the cruel; know than they
Less fierce are ravenous beasts of prey,   20
And should perchance these last come near thee[,]

---

* hedgehog. *Erinaceus Europæus.*

Line 3. **Innoxious urchin**: innocuous, harmless; urchin, on the analogy of sea urchin, is a syn-
onym for the spiny hedgehog.

Line 15. **thorny case**: spiny hide.

Line 17. **spiny ball**: hedgehogs protect themselves by rolling into a ball and distending their
spines.

Line 18. **negro**: black. The hedgehog's fur, by contrast, is brown.

And fox or martin cat assail,
Thou, safe within thy coat of mail,
May cry—Ah! noli me tangere.

The early butterfly

Trusting the first warm day of spring,
When transient sunshine warms the sky,
Light on his yellow spotted wing
Comes forth the early butterfly.

With wavering flight, he settles now   5
Where pilewort* spreads its blossoms fair,
Or on the grass where daisies† blow,
Pausing, he rests his pinions there.

But insect! in a luckless hour
Thou from thy winter home hast come,   10
For yet is seen no luscious flower
With odour rich, and honied bloom.

And these that to the early day
Yet timidly their bells unfold,
Close with the sun's retreating ray,   15
And shut their humid eyes of gold.

---

* pilewort. *Ranunculus ficaria.*   † daisy. *Bellis perennis.*

The hedge-hog seen in a frequented path. Line 22. **martin cat**: marten.

Line 24. **noli me tangere**: a common Latin tag, meaning "do not touch me." The accent of *tangere* falls on the first syllable: precocious George Talbot questions whether his mother can rightly claim a poetic license allowing her to force a mispronunciation of the Latin so as to rhyme with "near thee" of line 22 (*Conversations,* I, 47).

The early butterfly. The children's critical sophistication increases: "It is difficult, George," cautions Mrs. Talbot, "to say anything that is not mere commonplace on so obvious and hackneyed a subject"; but she nonetheless has produced these "few stanzas to the butterfly, called Rhamni, which makes its appearance early in March" (*Conversations,* I, 52).

For night's dark shades then gather round,
And night-winds whistle cold and keen,
And hoary frost will crisp the ground,
And blight the leaves of budding green!   20

And thou, poor fly! so soft and frail,
May'st perish ere returning morn,
Nor ever, on the summer gale,
To taste of summer sweets be borne!

Thus unexperienc'd rashness will presume   25
On the fair promise of life's opening day,
Nor dreams how soon the adverse storms may come,
"That hush'd in grim repose, expect their evening prey."

The moth

When dews fall fast, and rosy day
Fades slowly in the west away,
While evening breezes bend the future sheaves;
Votary of vesper's humid light,
The moth, pale wanderer of the night,   5
From his green cradle comes, amid the whispering leaves.

The birds on insect life that feast
Now in their woody coverts rest,
The swallow* slumbers in his dome of clay,

---

* swallow. *Hirundo rustica.*

The early butterfly. Line 28. **That ... prey:** Thomas Gray, "The Bard," line 76.

The moth. "Like verses on the butterfly, any attempt on the subject of the moth may perhaps be trite," acknowledges Mrs. Talbot (*Conversations,* I, 56).

Line 4. **Votary ... light:** lover of dewy moonlight; attracted to candlelight.

And of the numerous tribes who war   10
On the small denizens of air,
The shrieking bat* alone is on the wing for prey.

Eluding him, on lacey plume
The silver moth enjoys the gloom,
Glancing on tremulous wing thro' twilight bowers,   15
Now flits where warm nasturtiums† glow,
Now quivers on the jasmine bough,
And sucks with spiral tongue the balm of sleeping flowers.

Yet if from open casement stream
The taper's bright aspiring beam,   20
And strikes with comet ray his dazzled sight;
Nor perfum'd leaf, nor honied flower,
To check his wild career have power,
But to the attracting flame he takes his rapid flight.

Round it he darts in dizzy rings,   25
And soon his soft and powder'd wings
Are singed; and dimmer grow his pearly eyes,
And now his struggling feet are foil'd,
And scorch'd, entangled, burnt, and soil'd,
His fragile form is lost—the wretched insect dies!   30

---

* bat. *Vespertilis murinus.*

† nasturtium. *Tropæolum majus.* This is one of the flowers which is said to have a sort of glory, or light halo of fire apparently surrounding it, of an evening in dry weather—a phenomenon first observed by one of the daughters of Linnæus. I once thought I saw it in the Summer of 1802.

Lines 19–23. **Yet if ... power**: The second edition of *Conversations* (1819) tries to correct the grammatical awkwardness by making "stream" (line 19) a plural; but the original can be defended as a subjunctive governed by the conditional clause; the real grammatical solecism occurs with "have" of line 23, which governs two singular nouns linked by "nor."

Emblem too just of one, whose way
Thro the calm vale of life might lay,
Yet lured by vanity's illusive fires
Far from that tranquil vale aside,
Like this poor insect suicide   35
Follows the fatal light, and in its flame expires.

To the snow-drop*

Like pendant flakes of vegetating snow,
　　The early herald of the infant year,
Ere yet the adventurous Crocus† dares to blow
　　Beneath the orchard boughs, thy buds appear.

While still the cold north-east ungenial lowers,   5
　　And scarce the hazel° in the leafless copse
Or sallows‡ shew their downy powder'd flowers,
　　The grass is spangled with thy silver drops.

Yet, when those pallid blossoms shall give place
　　To countless tribes of richer hue and scent,   10
Summer's gay blooms, and Autumn's yellow race,
　　I shall thy pale inodorous bells lament.

---

* Snow-drop. *Galanthus nivalis.*　　† Crocus. *Crocus vernus.*
° hazel. *Corylus avellana.*　　‡ sallows. *Salix caprea.*

The moth. Line 32. **lay**: the common solecism for *lie.*

To the snowdrop. Title. The earliest of spring flowers, famous for sometimes blooming amid a blanket of snow, the snowdrop is a favorite subject of women poets of this period (e.g., Barbauld, Robinson). By way of introducing her poem, Mrs. Talbot quotes Anna Barbauld's couplet: "As Flora's breath, by some transforming power, / Had chang'd an icicle into a flower" (*Conversations,* I, 95).

Line 5. **north-east**: the wind off the North Sea.　　Line 7. **sallows**: willows.

So journeying onward in life's varying track,
    Even while warm youth its bright illusion lends,
Fond Memory often with regret looks back   15
    To childhood's pleasures, and to infant friends.

Violets*

Sweet Violets! from your humble beds
Among the moss, beneath the thorn,
You rear your unprotected heads,
And brave the cold and cheerless morn
Of early March; not yet are past   5
The wintry cloud, the sullen blast,
Which, when your fragrant buds shall blow,
May lay those purple beauties low.
Ah, stay awhile, till warmer showers
And brighter suns shall cheer the day;   10
Sweet Violets stay, till hardier flowers
Prepare to meet the lovely May.
Then from your mossy shelter come,
And rival every richer bloom;
For though their colours gayer shine,   15
Their odours do not equal thine.
And thus real merit still may dare to vie,
With all that wealth bestows, or pageant heraldry.

---

* Violets. *Viola odorata.*

Violets. Title. Mrs. Talbot notes that "some of the lines are entirely taken from a little poem, I believe written by Mr. Gifford" (*Conversations,* I, 96). William Gifford was a prominent satirist who became editor of the *Quarterly Review* when it was founded in 1810. It was common for authors of the time to publish minor verse in newspapers or magazines; and this appears the kind of piece to which Mrs. Talbot refers.

Line 18. **pageant heraldry**: an ancestry paraded before others.

To a butterfly* in a window

Escaped thy place of wintry rest,
And in the brightest colours drest,
Thy new-born wings prepared for flight,
Ah! do not, Butterfly, in vain
Thus flutter on the crystal pane,   5
But go! and soar to life and light.

High on the buoyant Summer gale
Thro' cloudless ether thou may'st sail,
Or rest among the fairest flowers;
To meet thy winnowing friends may'st speed,   10
Or at thy choice luxurious feed
In woodlands wild, or garden bowers.

Beneath some leaf of ample shade
Thy pearly eggs shall then be laid,
Small rudiments of many a fly;   15
While thou, thy frail existence past,
Shall shudder in the chilly blast,
And fold thy painted wings and die!

Soon fleets thy transient life away;
Yet short as is thy vital day,   20
Like flowers that form thy fragrant food;
Thou, poor Ephemeron, shalt have fill'd
The little space thy Maker willed,
And all thou know'st of life be good.

---

* Admirable Butterfly. *Papilis atalanta.* [Mrs. Talbot notes that this butterfly is also called the Colonel and is black with scarlet and white spots.]

Line10. **winnowing**: with wings fanning.   Line 15. **small rudiments**: embryonic forms.
Line 22. **Ephemeron**: lasting a day.

Wild flowers

Fair rising from her icy couch,
Wan herald of the floral year,
The Snow-drop* marks the Spring's approach,
Ere yet the Primrose† groups appear,
Or peers the Arum° from its spotted veil,   5
Or odorous Violets‡ scent the cold capricious gale.

Then thickly strewn in woodland bowers
Anemonies• their stars unfold;
There spring the Sorrel's¶ veined flowers,
And rich in vegetable gold   10
From calyx pale, the freckled Cowslip§ born,
Receives in amber cups the fragrant dews of morn.

Lo! the green Thorn◻ her silver buds
Expands, to May's enlivening beam;
Hottonia◊ blushes on the floods;   15
And where the slowly trickling stream

---

* Snow-drop. *Galanthus.*   † Primrose. *Primula vulgaris.*

° *Arum maculatum.* Cuckoo Pint, or Lords and Ladies.   ‡ Violets. *Viola odorata.*

• Anemonies. Wood Anemone, *Anemone nemorosa.*

¶ Sorrel. Wood sorrel, *Oxalis acetosella.*   § Cowslip. *Primula veris major.*

◻Thorn. White Thorn or May, *Cratægus.*   ◊ Hottonia. Water Violet, *Palustris.*

Title. This poem first appeared in Smith's *Minor Morals* (1800), an educational book for children, under the title "The Kalendar of Flora." There, the maternal figure, Mrs. Belmour, acknowledging that she "studied less to make the poetry fine than comprehensible" (page 72), contrives this poem to be memorized by her children and their friends so they will learn the names of common plants in their vicinity. The idea of dating the year through the successive seasons of flowers is traditional, though in *Conversations Introducing Poetry* no mention is made of this aspect of the poem. One might compare it with "The horologe of the fields" (published with *Beachy Head*) in which Smith measures the hours of the day by the opening and closing of flowers.

Line 11. **calyx:** husk; an obscure line whose sense is that the cowslip is born out of its calyx or husk.

Mid grass and spiry rushes stealing glides,
Her lovely fringed flowers fair Menyanthes* hides.

In the lone copse or shadowy dale,
Wild cluster'd knots of Harebells† blow,   20
And droops the Lily of the vale°
O'er Vinca's‡ matted leaves below,
The Orchis• race with varied beauty charm,
And mock the exploring bee, or fly's aerial form.

Wound in the hedgerow's oaken boughs,   25
The Woodbine's¶ tassels float in air,
And blushing, the uncultured Rose§
Hangs high her beauteous blossoms there;
Her fillets there the purple Nightshade¤ weaves,
And the Brionia◊ winds her pale and scolloped leaves.   30

To later Summer's fragrant breath
Clemati's** feathery garlands dance;
The hollow Foxglove†† nods beneath,
While the tall Mullein's°° yellow lance,
Dear to the meally tribe of evening, towers,   35
And the weak Galium‡‡ weaves its myriad fairy flowers.

---

* *Menyanthis trifolia.* Buck Bean or Bob Bean.   †Harebell. *Hyacinth non scriptus.*

° Lily. Lilly of the Valley, *Convallaria majalis.*   ‡ *Vinca major* and *minor.* Periwinkle.

• Orchis. Fly and Bee Orchis. Orchis *apifera* and *muscifera* or *Ophrys infectifera,* and *Orchis Adrachnites.*

¶ Woodbine. *Lonicera.*

§ Rose. Wild rose, *Rosa canina,* Dog Rose, *Rosa Eglanteria,* Sweet Briar.

¤ Nightshade. *Solanum dulcamara.*   ◊ Brionia. *Byronia dioica,* Byrony.

** *Clematis vitalba.* Virgin's Bower, or Traveller's Joy.   †† Foxglove. *Digitalis.*

°° Mullein. Moth Mullein, *Verbascum thapsus.*

‡‡ Galium. *Galium verum,* Yellow Lady's Bed-straw.

Line 35. **meally tribe:** moths.

Sheltering the coot's or wild duck's nest,
And where the timid halcyon hides,
The Willow-herb,* in crimson drest,
Waves with Arundo† o'er the tides;   40
And there the bright Nymphea° loves to lave,
Or spreads her golden orbs‡ upon the dimpling wave.

And thou! by pain and sorrow blest,
Papaver!• that an opiate dew
Conceal'st beneath thy scarlet vest,   45
Contrasting with the Corn flower⁵ blue,
Autumnal months behold thy gauzy leaves
Bend in the rustling gale, amid the tawny sheaves.

From the first bud whose venturous head
The Winter's lingering tempest braves,   50
To those which mid the foliage dead
Sink latest to their annual grave,
All are for food, for health, or pleasure given,
And speak in various ways the bounteous hand of Heaven.

The close of summer

Farewell ye banks, where late the primrose growing,
Among fresh leaves its pallid stars display'd,
And the ground-ivy's§ balmy flowers blowing,
Trail'd their festoons along the grassy shade.

---

* Willow-herb. *Epilobium hirsutum.*   † *Arundo.* Reed.
° Nymphea. *Nymphea alba,* White Water-Lily.
‡ golden orbs. *Nymphea lutea,* Yellow Water- Lily.   • *Papaver.* Common Poppy.
⁵ Corn flower. *Centaurea cyanus.*   § ground-ivy. *Glecoma hederacea.*

The close of summer. Line 3. **blowing:** in blossom.

Farewell! to richer scenes and Summer pleasures,   5
Hedge-rows, engarlanded with many a wreath,
Where the wild roses hang their blushing treasures,
And to the evening gale the woodbines breathe.

Farewell! the meadows, where such various showers
Of beauty lurked, among the fragrant hay;   10
Where orchis* bloomed with freak'd and spotted flowers,
And lychnis† blushing like the new born day.

The burning dog-star, and the insatiate mower,
Have swept or wither'd all this floral pride;
And mullein's° now, or bugloss'‡ lingering flower,   15
Scarce cheer the green lane's parched and dusty side.

His busy sickle now the months-man wielding,
Close are the light and fragile poppies shorn,
And while the golden ears their stores are yielding,
The azure corn-flowers fall among the corn.   20

The woods are silent too, where loudly flinging
Wild notes of rapture to the western gale,
A thousand birds their hymns of joy were singing,
And bade the enchanting hours of Spring time hail!

The stock-dove• now is heard, in plaintive measure,   25
The cricket shrill, and wether's drowsy bell,

---

* orchis. *Orchis maculata,* and others.   † lychnis. *Lychnis dioica.*
° mullein. *Verbascum thapsus.*   ‡ bugloss. *Lycopsis arvensis.*
• stock-dove. *Columbo oenas.*

Line 17. **months-man:** George provides the gloss: "One who is hired by the farmer, to work for him for a month, during harvest; for which time the men have in proportion more wages, than at any other time of the year" (*Conversations,* I, 191).

Line 26. **wether:** castrated sheep.

But to the sounds and scents of vernal pleasure,
Music and dewy airs, a long farewell!

Yet tho' no beauteous wreaths adorn the season,
Nor birds sing blythe, nor sweets the winds diffuse,   30
This riper period, like the age of reason,
Tho' stript of loveliness, is rich in use.

The wheat-ear*

From that deep shelter'd solitude,
Where in some quarry wild and rude,
Your feather'd mother reared her brood,
            Why, pilgrim, did you brave
The upland winds so bleak and keen,   5
To seek these hills?—whose slopes between
Wide stretch'd in grey expanse is seen,
            The Ocean's toiling wave?

Did instinct bid you linger here,
That broad and restless Ocean near,   10
And wait, till with the waning year
            Those northern gales arise,
Which, from the tall cliff's rugged side

---

* *Motacilla Oenanthe.* These birds frequent open stony places, warrens, downs, &c. They
build in stone quarries, old rabbit holes, &c. making their nest of dry grass, feathers and
horsehair. They lay six or eight eggs. They feed on earthworms and flies, and in Autumn,
when fat, are esteemed a great delicacy, and caught in great numbers on the hills between
Eastbourne and those above Brighthelmstone. They are sometime caught more to the west-
ward, but are not found so fat as those taken on the more eastern downs. The females arrive
there in March; the male birds not till a fortnight afterwards; in September they all disap-
pear. About the stone quarries in Somersetshire, they are, it is said, observed at all times of
the year, but I do not remember to have heard that they are taken for the table in any other
part of England. Mr. White in his *Natural History* [Gilbert White (1720–93), *Natural His-
tory of Selborne*, 1789] calls the Wheat-ear "the Sussex bird." It does not seem to be ascer-
tained, whether or not they migrate to France, or other parts of the continent.—Some birds
seem to be only partially migrants, and do not all leave the countries where they are bred.

Shall give your soft light plumes to glide,
Across the channel's refluent tide,   15
      To seek more favoring skies?

Alas! and has not instinct said
That luxury's toils for you are laid,
And that by groundless fears betray'd
      You ne'er perhaps may know   20
Those regions, where the embowering vine
Loves round the luscious fig to twine,
And mild the Suns of Winter shine,
      And flowers perennial blow.

To take you, shepherd boys prepare   25
The hollow turf, the wiry snare,
Of those weak terrors well aware,
      That bid you vainly dread
The shadows floating o'er the downs,
Or murmuring gale, that round the stones   30
Of some old beacon,* as it moans,
      Scarce moves the thistle's head.

And if a cloud obscure the Sun
With faint and fluttering heart you run,
And to the pitfall you should shun   35
      Resort in trembling haste;

---

* I have often wished to know, whether the very large stones of many hundred weight, which are to be seen on the very highest of the South downs, within a few miles of the sea, surrounded generally by a trench, and very different from any stones to be found within many miles, were not artificial, and made by cementing a great number of smaller stones together. I think I have read, that some of the immense circles of stones supposed to have been the temples of the Druids, were by some enquirers believed to have been thus composed. But these are questions which I have generally been stared at for making.

Line 22. **fig**: Smith's note to "Written for the benefit of a distressed player," lines 4–5, suggests the oblique relevance of this imagery.

Line 25. **shepherd boys**: The subject is treated again in *Beachy Head,* lines 461-65.

While, on that dewy cloud so high,
The lark, sweet minstrel of the sky,
Sings in the morning's beamy eye,
    And bathes his spotted breast.   40

Ah! simple bird, resembling you
Are those, that with distorted view
Thro' life some selfish end pursue,
    With low inglorious aim;
They sink in blank oblivious night,   45
While minds superior dare the light,
And high on honor's glorious height
    Aspire to endless fame!

An evening walk by the sea-side

'Tis pleasant to wander along on the sand,
Beneath the high cliff that is hallowed in caves;
When the fisher has put off his boat from the land,
And the prawn-catcher* wades thro' the short rippling waves.

While fast run before us the sandling† and plover,   5
Intent on the crabs and the sand-eels to feed,
And here on a rock which the tide will soon cover,
We'll find us a seat that is tapestried with weed.

---

* It is usual to see, in certain states of the tide, women and strong boys wading through the shallow waves; pushing before them a net, fastened to a pole, to catch Prawns, *Cancer serratus,* and Shrimp, *Cancer Cragon.* On some part[s] of the coast, the former are caught in ozier pots placed among the rocks, in the same manner as for lobsters.

† Sandlings, or Sanderlings, Sea Plovers, Sandpipers, all of the genus *Tringa;* these birds, of which there are many varieties, live on sea insects among the rocks, and on the sands; many of them appear in March, and retire in September or October; some remain throughout the year.

Bright gleam the white sails in the slant rays of even,
And stud as with silver the broad level main,   10
While glowing clouds float on the fair face of Heaven,
And the mirror-like water reflects them again.

How various the shades of marine vegetation,
Thrown here the rough flints and the pebbles among,
The feather'd conferva* of deepest carnation,   15
The dark purple slake and the olive sea thong.†

While Flora herself unreluctantly mingles
Her garlands with those that the Nereids have worn,
For the yellow horned poppy° springs up on the shingles,
And convolvulas‡ rival the rays the morn.   20

But now to retire from the rock we have warning,
Already the water encircles our seat,
And slowly the tide of the evening returning,
The moon beam reflects in the waves at our feet.

Ah! whether as now the mild Summer sea flowing,   25
Scarce wrinkles the sands as it murmurs on shore,
Or fierce wintry whirlwinds impetuously blowing
Bid high maddening surges resistlessly roar;

---

* *conferva.* Of this sea weed there is great variety. Some of a deep crimson, others pale red, green, white, or purple; they resemble tufts, or are branched, and appear like small leafless trees.

† slake or sloke. *Ulva umbilicalis.*   sea thong. *Fucus elongatus.*

° yellow horned poppy. *Glaucium chelidonium.*

‡ convolvulas. *Convolvulus Soldinella.* This plant is not frequent on the Southern coast, but in the West, and about Weymouth, it is common.

Line 18. **Nereids**: sea-nymphs.

That Power, which can put the wide waters in motion,
Then bid the vast billows repose at His word;   30
Fills the mind with deep reverence, while Earth, Air, and Ocean,
Alike of the universe speak him the Lord.

The heath

Even the wide Heath, where the unequal ground
Has never on its rugged surface felt
The hand of Industry, though wild and rough,
Is not without its beauty; here the furze,*
Enrich'd among its spines, with golden flowers   5
Scents the keen air; while all its thorny groups
Wide scatter'd o'er the waste are full of life;
For 'midst its yellow bloom, the assembled chats†
Wave high the tremulous wing, and with shrill notes,
But clear and pleasant, cheer the extensive heath.   10
Linnets in numerous flocks frequent it too,
And bashful, hiding in these scenes remote
From his congeners, (they who make the woods
And the thick copses echo to their song)
The heath-thrush makes his domicile; and while   15
His patient mate with downy bosom warms
Their future nestlings, he his love lay sings
Loud to the shaggy wild[.]—the Erica° here,
That o'er the Caledonian hills sublime

---

* furze. *Ulex.* It is in some countries [regions] called Gorse, in others Whin. It is sometimes sown for fences, and to make coverts for the protection of game; but is naturally produced on heaths and waste grounds. There is a dwarf sort of it[:]—It is sometimes chopped small and given to horses to eat, and is cut and stacked up, to burn lime with.

† chats. Whin Chats, *Motacilla rubetra.* Stone Chats. *Motacilla rubicola.*

° Erica. Common Heath, *Erica vulgaris.* Cross-leaved Heath, *Erica tetralix.* Fine leaved Heath, *Erica cenerea*[.]–Of these last there are varieties, pink, blush colour, and white[.]–Cornish Heath, *Erica,* is found only, I believe in that county.

Line 13. **congeners**: of the same genus.   Line 19. **Caledonian hills**: Scottish highlands.

Spreads its dark mantle (where the bees delight   20
To seek their purest honey), flourishes,
Sometimes with bells like Amethysts, and then
Paler, and shaded like the maiden's cheek
With gradual blushes—Other while, as white
As rime that hangs upon the frozen spray.   25
Of this, old Scotia's hardy mountaineers
Their rustic couches form; and there enjoy
Sleep, which beneath his velvet canopy
Luxurious idleness implores in vain!
Between the matted heath and ragged gorse   30
Wind natural walks of turf, as short and fine
As clothe the chalky downs; and there the sheep
Under some thorny bush, or where the fern
Lends a light shadow from the Sun, resort,
And ruminate or feed; and frequent there   35
Nourish'd by evening mists, the mushroom* spreads
From a small ivory bulb, his circular roof[,]
The fairies['] fabled board[.]—Poor is the soil,
And of the plants that clothe it few possess
Succulent moisture; yet a parasite   40
Clings even to them; for its entangling stalk
The wire[-]like dodder† winds; and nourishes,
Rootless itself, its small white flowers on them.
So to the most unhappy of our race
Those, on whom never prosperous hour has smiled,   45
Towards whom Nature as a step-dame stern
Has cruelly dealt; and whom the world rejects[,]

---

* mushroom. *Fungus Agaric.* Of these there is an infinite variety, but one only is usually
eaten in England. Though the Italians, French, and more particularly the Russians consider
as very excellent food many Fungus's which we think unwholesome, and turn from with dis-
gust. It is certain, however, that several of them are of a poisonous quality.

† dodder. *Cuscuta.* There are of this plant two sorts, the greater and lesser Dodder. It sup-
ports itself on the sap of the plant to which it adheres.

Line 38. **board**: dining table.

To these forlorn ones, ever there adheres
Some self-consoling passion; round their hearts
Some vanity entwines itself; and hides,   50
And is perhaps in mercy given to hide,
The mortifying sad realities
Of their hard lot.

Ode to the missel thrush*

The Winter Solstice scarce is past,
Loud is the wind, and hoarsely sound
The mill-streams in the swelling blast,
And cold and humid is the ground[;]
When, to the ivy, that embowers   5
Some pollard tree, or sheltering rock,
The troop of timid warblers flock,
And shuddering wait for milder hours.

---

* Missel Thrush. *Turdus visivorous.* Mr. White, in his account of singing birds [in the *Natural History of Selborne*], puts this among those whose song ceases before Midsummer. It is certainly an error. This remarkable bird, which cannot be mistaken for any other, began to sing so early as the second week of January; and now I hear him uttering a more clamorous song, the 8th of July, between the flying showers. Whenever the weather is windy or changeable, he announces it by a variety of loud notes. There is only one bird of this kind within hearing, who sang last year to the beginning of August. His food consists of berries and insects, but principally, the former. The fruit of the Hawthorn, *Mesphilus,* Elder, *Sambucus,* Spindletree, *Euonymus,* Sloe, *Prunus,* and Holly, *Ilex,* occasionally supply him; but the Misseltoe, *Viscum,* from whence he takes his name of *viscivorous,* is his favourite food. As bird-lime is often made of its glutinous berries, and this thrush is supposed to encrease the Misseltoe by depositing the seeds he has swallowed on other trees, he is said in a Latin proverb to propagate the means of his own destruction.

Title. Mrs. Talbot introduces the subject so: "It would ... be difficult to find any thing new to say of that most charming of our feathered musicians [the nightingale, on which Smith had written three sonnets]—but there is a bird, which[,] if it does not sing so exquisitely, is yet usually heard with great pleasure, since it announces the approach of Spring, even before the earliest plants appear, and often in the first days of January. It is also a thrush, the largest of English singing birds, and feeds much on the berries of missletoe; and because of its loud notes from the top of some high tree, in blowing, or showery weather, the country people in Hampshire, and Sussex, call it the storm-cock" (*Conversations,* II, 60).

While thou! the leader of their band,
Fearless salut'st the opening year;   10
Nor stay'st, till blow the breezes bland
That bid the tender leaves appear:
But, on some towering elm or pine,
Waving elate thy dauntless wing,
Thou joy'st thy love notes wild to sing,   15
Impatient of St. Valentine!

Oh, herald of the Spring! while yet
No harebell scents the woodland lane,
Nor starwort fair, nor violet,
Braves the bleak gust and driving rain,   20
'Tis thine, as thro' the copses rude
Some pensive wanderer sighs along,
To soothe him with thy cheerful song,
And tell of Hope and Fortitude!

For thee then, may the hawthorn bush,   25
The elder, and the spindle tree,
With all their various berries blush,
And the blue sloe abound for thee!
For thee, the coral holly glow
Its arm'd and glossy leaves among,   30
And many a branched oak be hung
With thy pellucid missletoe.

Still may thy nest, with lichen lin'd,
Be hidden from the invading jay,
Nor truant boy its covert find,   35
To bear thy callow young away;
So thou, precursor still of good,
O, herald of approaching Spring,

Line 32. **pellucid**: shining with light.

Shalt to the pensive wanderer sing
Thy song of Hope and Fortitude.   40

Ode to the olive tree*

Altho' thy flowers minute, disclose
No colours rivalling the rose,
   And lend no odours to the gale;
While dimly thro' the pallid green
Of thy long slender leaves, are seen   5
   Thy berries pale;

Yet for thy virtues art thou known,
And not the Anana's burnish'd cone,
   Or golden fruits that bless the earth
Of Indian climes, however fair,   10
Can with thy modest boughs compare,
   For genuine worth.

Man, from his early Eden driven,
Receiv'd thee from relenting Heaven,
   And thou the whelming surge above,   15
Symbol of pardon, deign'd to rear
Alone thy willowy head, to cheer
   The wandering dove.

---

* Olive Tree. *Olea Europa.* Oil, however useful, either at our tables or in the Materia Medica [contemporary medical encyclopedia], is yet more so on the continent: a Spanish table presents almost every kind of food prepared with oil. It is also much used in Italy and the South of France; and I have known English people, after a long residence in those countries, declare, that being accustomed to eat fine and pure oil, they had no longer any wish for the indispensable article of English luxury, butter. The inflammation arising from the stings of venomous reptiles or insects is removed by an application of olive oil. If poured on the water, it makes the rough waves subside. Olives are planted in little groves, round the farms, or as they are called Bastides, in the South of France.

Line 8. **Anana's burnish'd cone**: the pineapple.

Tho' no green whispering shade is thine,
Where peasant girls at noon recline,   20
    Or, while the village tabor plays,
Gay vine-dressers, and goatherds, meet
To dance with light unwearied feet
        On holidays;

Yet doth the fruit thy sprays produce,   25
Supply what ardent Suns refuse,
    Nor want of grassy lawn or mead,
To pasture milky herds, is found
While fertile Olive groves surround
        The lone Bastide.   30

Thou stillest the wild and troubled waves,
And as the human tempest raves
    When Wisdom bids the tumult cease;
Thee, round her calm majestic brows
She binds; and waves thy sacred boughs,   35
        Emblems of Peace!

Ah! then, tho' thy wan blossoms bear
No odours for the vagrant air,
    Yet genuine worth belongs to thee;
And Peace and Wisdom, powers divine,   40
Shall plant thee round the holy shrine
        Of Liberty!

Line 21. **tabor**: a small drum.

To the fire-fly of Jamaica,
seen in a collection

How art thou alter'd! since afar,
Thou seem'dst a bright earth wandering star;
When thy living lustre ran,
Tall majestic trees between,
And Guazume, or Swietan,*   5
Or the Pimento's† glossy green,
As caught their varnish'd leaves, thy glancing light
Reflected flying fires, amid the moonless night.

From shady heights, where currents spring,
Where the ground dove° dips her wing,   10
Winds of night reviving blow,
Thro' rustling fields of maize and cane,‡
And wave the Coffee's• fragrant bough;
But winds of night, for thee in vain
May breathe, of the Plumeria's¶ luscious bloom,   15
Or Granate's scarlet buds, or Plinia's mild perfume.§

The recent captive, who in vain,
Attempts to break his heavy chain,

---

* Guazume. *Theobroma guazuma*, Great Cedar of Jamaica.   *Swietan*. Mahogani.

† Pimento. *Myrtus Pimento*, Jamaica All-spice.

° ground dove. A small dove which creeps on the ground, is very frequent in the woods of Jamaica. I have not been able to find its Linnæan name.

‡ cane. *Saccharum officinarum*.   • Coffee. *Coffea arabica*.

¶ Plumeria, commonly called Tree Jasmin, a most beautiful and odorous plant.

§ Granate. *Punica granata*, Pomegranate. Plinia. *Plinia pedunculata*, a fragrant native of tropical countries.

Title. Identified by Mrs. Talbot as the *Fulgora lanternaria*. Abolition of the slave trade from British dominions was at this point an issue of great public debate: the Abolition bill was finally passed by the British parliament in 1807, three years after this poem with its strong antislavery undertones was published.

And find his liberty in flight;
Shall no more in terror hide,   20
From thy strange and doubtful light,
In the mountain's cavern'd side,*
Or gully deep, where gibbering monkies cling,
And broods the giant bat,† on dark funereal wing.

Nor thee his darkling steps to aid,   25
Thro' the forest's pathless shade,
Shall the sighing Slave invoke;
Who, his daily task perform'd,
Would forget his heavy yoke;
And by fond affections warm'd,   30
Glide to some dear sequester'd spot, to prove,
Friendship's consoling voice, or sympathising love.°

Now, when sinks the Sun away,
And fades at once the sultry day,
Thee, as falls the sudden night,   35
Never Naturalist shall view,
Dart with corruscation bright,
Down the cocoa‡ avenue;
Or see thee give, with transient gleams to glow,
The green Banana's head, or Shaddock's loaded bough.•   40

---

* The wretched Negro, fearing punishment, or driven to despair by continual labour, often secretes himself in these obscure recesses, and preys in his turn on his oppressor at the hazard of his life.

† Bats bigger than crows are found in the gullies and caverns among the woods of Jamaica. And monkeys hide there, sallying forth in numbers to prey on the canes and fruit.

° After the toils of the day, the poor African often walks many miles, and for a few hours loses the sense of his misery among his friends and companions.

‡ cocoa. Coco-nut tree, *Cocos*.

• Banana. *Musa Paradisiacus*, Plantain or Banana. The Shaddock, which is I believe sometimes vulgarly called the forbidden fruit, is shaped like a lemon with the colour of an orange; it is sometimes as big as the largest melon; but not very good to eat. At least those I have formerly seen brought from Barbadoes were worth nothing.

Line 25. **darkling**: in the dark.

Ah! never more shalt thou behold,
The midnight Beauty,* slow unfold
Her golden zone, and thro' the gloom
To thee her radiant leaves display,
More lovely than the roseate bloom   45
Of flowers, that drink the tropic day;
And while thy dancing flames around her blaze,
Shed odours more refin'd, and beam with brighter rays.

The glass thy faded form contains,
But of thy lamp no spark remains;   50
That lamp, which through the palmy grove,
Floated once with sapphire beam,
As lucid as the star of Love,
Reflected in the bickering stream;
Transient and bright! so human meteors rise,   55
And glare and sink, in pensive REASON's eyes.

Ye dazzling comets that appear
In Fashion's rainbow atmosphere,
Lightning and flashing for a day;
Think ye, how fugitive your fame?   60
How soon from her light scroll away,
Is wafted your ephemeron name?
Even tho' on canvas still your forms are shewn,
Or the slow chisel shapes the pale resembling stone.

Let vaunting OSTENTATION trust   65
The pencil's art, or marble bust,
While long neglected modest worth

---

* Whoever has seen the *Cactus grandiflora,* and been gratified with its scent, must acknowledge it to be one of the most magnificent and delicious productions of vegetable nature. [Mrs. Talbot notes, it "is said, though incorrectly, to open exactly at midnight" (*Conversations*, II, 91).]

Line 62. **ephemeron**: ephemeral, lasting a day.

Unmark'd, unhonor'd, and unknown,
Obtains at length a little earth,
Where kindred merit weeps alone;   70
Yet there, tho' VANITY no trophies rear,
Is FRIENDSHIP's long regret, and true AFFECTION's tear!

Lines composed in passing through
a forest in Germany*

If, when tomorrow's Sun with upward ray,
Gilds the wide spreading oak, and burnish'd pine,
Destin'd to mingle here with foreign clay,
Pale, cold, and still, should sleep this form of mine;
The Day-star, with as lustrous warmth would glow,   5
And thro' the ferny lairs and forest shades,
With sweetest woodscents fraught, the air would blow,
And timid wild deer, bound along the glades;
While in a few short months, to clothe the mould,
Would velvet moss and purple melic rise,   10
By Heaven's pure dewdrops water'd, clear and cold,
And birds innumerous sing my obsequies;
But, in my native land, no faithful maid
To mourn for me, would pleasure's orgies shun;
No sister's love my long delay upbraid;   15
No mother's anxious love demand her son.
Thou, only thou, my friend, would feel regret,
My blighted hopes and early fate deplore;
And, while my faults thou'dst palliate or forget,
Would half rejoice, I felt that fate no more.   20

---

* These two short poems [the first is "Verses supposed to have been written in the New Forest, in early spring," page 107] have before been printed. [Both ostensibly productions of "a despondent young man" who is Mrs. Talbot's acquaintance, the first had been earlier published in *Marchmont* and in the second volume of *Elegiac Sonnets;* these "Lines" were included in the fourth volume of Smith's last publication of fiction, *Letters of a Solitary Wanderer,* published in 1802. There they are presented as written by the narrator while crossing a tract known for harboring robbers.]

To a geranium* which flowered
during the winter
Written in autumn

Native of Afric's arid lands,
Thou, and thy many-tinctur'd bands,
Unheeded and unvalued grew,
While Caffres crush'd beneath the sands
Thy pencill'd flowers of roseate hue.   5

But our cold northern sky beneath,
For thee attemper'd zephyrs breathe,
And art supplies the tepid dew,
That feeds, in many a glowing wreath,
Thy lovely flowers of roseate hue.   10

Thy race, that spring uncultur'd here,
Decline with the declining year,
While in successive beauty new,
Thine own light bouquets fresh appear,
And marbled leaves of cheerful hue.   15

---

* Of Geraniums and Pelagorniums, there are almost innumerable varieties. The plants of
that species that grow here are some of the prettiest ornaments of our hedgerows, meadows,
and downs; but the exotic sorts, which have long been among the most desirable furniture
of the Conservatory, are principally natives of Africa. A friend of mine, who has visited the
Cape of Good Hope, described to me the splendid appearance of these beautiful flowers
covering the rocks and sand hills; many of the most elegant growing as luxuriantly as docks
or mallows do here; while others rise to the size of large shrubs.

Line 4. **Caffres**: "The race of men inhabiting the country about the Cape of Good Hope are
so called," explains Mrs. Talbot (*Conversations*, II, 119).

Now buds and bells of every shade,
By Summer's ardent eye survey'd,
No more their gorgeous colours shew;
And even the lingering asters* fade,
With drooping heads of purple hue.   20

But naturalized in foreign earth,
'Tis thine, with many a beauteous birth,
As if in gratitude they blew,
To hang, like blushing trophies forth,
Thy pencill'd flowers of roseate hue.   25

Oh then, amidst the wintry gloom,
Those flowers shall dress my cottage room,
Like friends in adverse fortune true;
And soothe me with their roseate bloom,
And downy leaves of vernal hue.   30

---

* asters. The Asters are almost the last ornament of our gardens; they blow late, and give the
appearance of gaiety when the more beautiful flowers are gone.

Line 17. **ardent eye**: the fiery sun.

To the mulberry-tree*
On reading the oriental aphorism, "by patience and labour the mulberry-leaf becomes satin"

Hither, in half blown garlands drest,
Advances the reluctant Spring,
And shrinking, feels her tender breast
Chill'd by Winter's snowy wing;
Nor wilt thou, alien as thou art, display   5
Or leaf, or swelling bud, to meet the varying day.

Yet, when the mother of the rose,
Bright June, leads on the glowing hours,
And from her hands luxuriant throws
Her lovely groups of Summer flowers;   10
Forth from thy brown and unclad branches shoot
Serrated leaves and rudiments of fruit.

And soon those boughs umbrageous spread
A shelter from Autumnal rays,
While gay beneath thy shadowy head,   15
His gambols happy childhood plays;

---

* *Morus nigra*, the common Mulberry. The mulberry tree, a native of Italy, is cultivated not only for its grateful fruit, but for the more lucrative purpose of supplying food to silk-worms. The leaves of the white mulberry are preferred for this purpose in Europe; but in China, where the best silk is made, the silk-worms are fed with the leaves of the *Morus Tartaricus*. From the bark of another species, *Morus papyrifera,* the Japanese make paper, and the inhabitants of the South Sea Islands, the cloth which serves them for apparel. Woodville's Med. Bot. [William Woodville, *Medical Botany, containing systematic and general descriptions, with plates, of all the medicinal plants, indigenous and exotic, comprehended in the catalogues of the Materia Medica...*, 3 volumes. London: James Philips, 1790–93.]

Line 1. **half blown garlands**: buds only partially open.

Lines 5–6. **Nor ... day**: Mrs. Talbot glosses this: "Pliny, the Roman naturalist, calls [it] the wisest of trees because, even in Italy, it does not put forth its leaves till the cold weather is certainly gone" (*Conversations*, II, 134).

Eager, with crimson fingers to amass
Thy ruby fruit, that strews the turfy grass.

But where, festoon'd with purple vines,*
More freely grows thy graceful form,   20
And skreen'd by towering Appenines,
Thy foliage feeds the spinning worm;
PATIENCE and INDUSTRY protect thy shade,
And see, by future looms, their care repaid.

They mark the threads, half viewless wind
That form the shining light cocoon,   25
Now tinted as the orange rind,
Or paler than the pearly moon;
Then at their summons in the task engage,
Light active youth, and tremulous old age.

The task that bids thy tresses green   30
A thousand varied hues assume,
There colour'd like the sky serene,
And mocking here the rose's bloom;
And now, in lucid volumes lightly roll'd,
Where purple clouds are starr'd with mimic gold.   35

But not because thy veined leaves.
Do to the grey winged moth supply
The nutriment, whence Patience weaves
The monarch's velvet canopy;   40
Thro' his high domes, a splendid radiance throws,
And binds the jewell'd circlet on his brows;

---

* In Italy, the vines are often seen hanging in festoons from tree to tree in the plantations of mulberry trees.

Line 21. **skreen'd**: screened.

And not, that thus transform'd, thy boughs,
Now as a cestus clasp the fair,
Now in her changeful vestment flows,   45
And filets now her plaited hair;
I praise thee; but that I behold in thee
The triumph of unwearied Industry.

'Tis, that laborious millions owe
To thee, the source of simple food   50
In Eastern climes; or where the Po
Reflects thee from his classic flood;
While useless INDOLENCE may blush, to view
What PATIENCE, INDUSTRY, and ART, can do.

Line 44. **cestus**: belt or girdle.   Line 46. **filets**: ties with ribbons.

Beachy Head, Fables, and Other Poems

{ 1807 }

ADVERTISEMENT

As the following Poems were delivered to the Publisher as early as the month of May last, it may not be thought improper to state the circumstances that have hitherto delayed their appearance.

The fulfilling this duty to the public has since devolved to other hands; for alas! the admired author is now unconscious of their praise or censure, having fallen a victim to a long and painful illness, on the 28th of October last.

The delay which since that period has taken place, has been occasioned partly by the hope of finding a preface to the present publication, which there was some reason to suppose herself had written, and partly from an intention of annexing a short account of her life; but it having been since decided to publish biographical memoirs, and a selection of her correspondence, on a more enlarged plan, and under the immediate authority of her own nearest relatives, it was thought unnecessary; and the motives for deferring the publication are altogether removed.

The public, who have received the several editions of Mrs. Smith's former Poems with unbounded approbation, will, without doubt, admit the claims of the present work to an equal share of their favour; and her friends and admirers cannot fail of being highly gratified in observing, that although most of the Poems included in this volume were composed during the few and short intervals of ease which her infirmities permitted her to enjoy; yet they bear the most unquestionable evidence of the same undiminished genius, spirit, and imagination, which so imminently distinguished her former productions.

The Poem entitled BEACHY HEAD is not completed according to the original design. That the increasing debility of its author has been the cause of its being left in an imperfect state, will it is hoped be a sufficient apology.

Line 14. **nearest relatives:** This would seem an allusion to Catherine Anne Dorset, Charlotte Smith's sister, who prepared a memoir to introduce a selection of her works for a series that was discontinued. This biographical sketch was finally published by Walter Scott in his *Lives of the Novelists* (1821).

There are two Poems in this collection, viz. FLORA, and STUDIES BY   30
THE SEA, which have already been published in Mrs. Smith's *Conversa-
tions for the Use of Children and Young Persons;* but as many of her
friends considered them as misplaced in that work, and not likely to fall
under the general observation of those who were qualified to appreciate
their superior elegance and exquisite fancy, and had expressed a desire of
seeing them transplanted into a more congenial soil, the Publisher, with
his usual liberality, has permitted them to reappear in the present
volume.

JANUARY 31, 1807.

BEACHY HEAD

On thy stupendous summit, rock sublime!
That o'er the channel rear'd, half way at sea
The mariner at early morning hails,*
I would recline; while Fancy should go forth,
And represent the strange and awful hour   5
Of vast concussion;† when the Omnipotent
Stretch'd forth his arm, and rent the solid hills,
Bidding the impetuous main flood rush between
The rifted shores, and from the continent
Eternally divided this green isle.   10
Imperial lord of the high southern coast!
From thy projecting head-land I would mark
Far in the east the shades of night disperse,
Melting and thinned, as from the dark blue wave
Emerging, brilliant rays of arrowy light   15
Dart from the horizon; when the glorious sun
Just lifts above it his resplendent orb.
Advances now, with feathery silver touched,
The rippling tide of flood; glisten the sands,
While, inmates of the chalky clefts that scar   20
Thy sides precipitous, with shrill harsh cry,
Their white wings glancing in the level beam,
The terns, and gulls, and tarrocks, seek their food,°
And thy rough hollows echo to the voice

---

* In crossing the Channel from the coast of France, Beachy-Head is the first land made.

† Alluding to an idea that this Island was once joined to the continent of Europe, and torn from it by some convulsion of Nature. I confess I never could trace the resemblance between the two countries. Yet the cliffs about Dieppe, resemble the chalk cliffs on the Southern coast. But Normandy has no likeness whatever to the part of England opposite to it.

° Terns. *Sterna hirundo*, or Sea Swallow. Gulls. *Larus canus*. Tarrocks. *Larus tridactylus*.

Line 15. **arrowy light**: dawn; the first 100 lines circumscribe a summer day.

Of the gray choughs,* and ever restless daws,   25
With clamour, not unlike the chiding hounds,
While the lone shepherd, and his baying dog,
Drive to thy turfy crest his bleating flock.

The high meridian of the day is past,
And Ocean now, reflecting the calm Heaven,   30
Is of cerulean hue; and murmurs low
The tide of ebb, upon the level sands.
The sloop, her angular canvas shifting still,
Catches the light and variable airs
That but a little crisp the summer sea,   35
Dimpling its tranquil surface.

                                        Afar off,
And just emerging from the arch immense
Where seem to part the elements, a fleet
Of fishing vessels stretch their lesser sails;
While more remote, and like a dubious spot   40
Just hanging in the horizon, laden deep,
The ship of commerce richly freighted, makes
Her slower progress, on her distant voyage,
Bound to the orient climates, where the sun
Matures the spice within its odorous shell,   45
And, rivalling the gray worm's filmy toil,

---

* gray choughs. *Corvus Graculus*, Cornish Choughs, or, as these birds are called by the
Sussex people, Saddle-backed Crows, build in great numbers on this coast.

Line 29. **high meridian**: noon.

Line 39. **lesser sails**: the ships, not employing their main sails, proceed at half-speed
dragging their nets.

Line 40. **dubious spot**: the perspective is to the southwest, where this commercial vessel, an
Indiaman, embarks from England's major southern harbor of Portsmouth.

Line 46. **filmy toil**: the creation of silk.

Bursts from its pod the vegetable down;*
Which in long turban'd wreaths, from torrid heat
Defends the brows of Asia's countless casts.
There the Earth hides within her glowing breast   50
The beamy adamant,† and the round pearl
Enchased in rugged covering; which the slave,
With perilous and breathless toil, tears off
From the rough sea-rock, deep beneath the waves.
These are the toys of Nature; and her sport   55
Of little estimate in Reason's eye:
And they who reason, with abhorrence see
Man, for such gaudes and baubles, violate
The sacred freedom of his fellow man—
Erroneous estimate! As Heaven's pure air,   60
Fresh as it blows on this aërial height,
Or sound of seas upon the stony strand,
Or inland, the gay harmony of birds,
And winds that wander in the leafy woods;
Are to the unadulterate taste more worth   65
Than the elaborate harmony, brought out
From fretted stop, or modulated airs
Of vocal science.—So the brightest gems,
Glancing resplendent on the regal crown,
Or trembling in the high born beauty's ear,   70
Are poor and paltry, to the lovely light
Of the fair star, that as the day declines

---

* Cotton. *Gossypium herbaceum.*   [Throughout the nineteenth century the trade in cotton was essential to Britain's commercial preeminence in clothmaking.]

† Diamonds, the hardest and most valuable of precious stones. For the extraordinary exertions of the Indians in diving for the pearl oysters, see the account of the Pearl fisheries in [Robert] Percival's *View of Ceylon* [*An Account of the Island of Ceylon* (1803; 2nd ed.1805)].

Line 49. **casts**: India's castes.   Line 52. **Enchased**: encased.

Line 67. **fretted stop**: finger position on a stringed instrument.

Line 72. **fair star**: Venus, the evening star.

Attendent on her queen, the crescent moon,
Bathes her bright tresses in the eastern wave.
For now the sun is verging to the sea,   75
And as he westward sinks, the floating clouds
Suspended, move upon the evening gale,
And gathering round his orb, as if to shade
The insufferable brightness, they resign
Their gauzy whiteness; and more warm'd, assume   80
All hues of purple. There, transparent gold
Mingles with ruby tints, and sapphire gleams,
And colours, such as Nature through her works
Shews only in the ethereal canopy.
Thither aspiring Fancy fondly soars,   85
Wandering sublime thro' visionary vales,
Where bright pavilions rise, and trophies, fann'd
By airs celestial; and adorn'd with wreaths
Of flowers that bloom amid elysian bowers.
Now bright, and brighter still the colours glow,   90
Till half the lustrous orb within the flood
Seems to retire: the flood reflecting still
Its splendor, and in mimic glory drest;
Till the last ray shot upward, fires the clouds
With blazing crimson; then in paler light,   95
Long lines of tenderer radiance, lingering yield
To partial darkness; and on the opposing side
The early moon distinctly rising, throws
Her pearly brilliance on the trembling tide.

The fishermen, who at set seasons pass   100
Many a league off at sea their toiling night,
Now hail their comrades, from their daily task
Returning; and make ready for their own,
With the night tide commencing:—The night tide
Bears a dark vessel on, whose hull and sails   105

Mark her a coaster from the north. Her keel
Now ploughs the sand; and sidelong now she leans,
While with loud clamours her athletic crew
Unload her; and resounds the busy hum
Along the wave-worn rocks. Yet more remote   110
Where the rough cliff hangs beetling o'er its base,
All breathes repose; the water's rippling sound
Scarce heard; but now and then the sea-snipe's* cry
Just tells that something living is abroad;
And sometimes crossing on the moonbright line,   115
Glimmers the skiff, faintly discern'd awhile,
Then lost in shadow.

             Contemplation here,
High on her throne of rock, aloof may sit,
And bid recording Memory unfold
Her scroll voluminous—bid her retrace   120
The period, when from Neustria's hostile shore
The Norman launch'd his galleys, and the bay
O'er which that mass of ruin† frowns even now
In vain and sullen menace, then received
The new invaders; a proud martial race,   125

---

* In crossing the channel this bird is heard at night, uttering a short cry, and flitting along near the surface of the waves. The sailors call it the Sea Snipe; but I can find no species of sea bird of which this is the vulgar name. A bird so called inhabits the Lake of Geneva.

† Pevensey Castle.

Line 119. **recording Memory**: history.   Line 121. **Neustria's hostile shore**: Normandy.

Of Scandinavia* the undaunted sons,
Whom Dogon, Fier-a-bras, and Humfroi led
To conquest: while Trinacria to their power
Yielded her wheaten garland; and when thou,

---

* The Scandinavians (modern Norway, Sweden, Denmark, Lapland, &c.) and other inhabitants of the north, began towards the end of the 8th century, to leave their inhospitable climate in search of the produce of more fortunate countries.

The North-men made inroads on the coasts of France; and carrying back immense booty, excited their compatriots to engage in the same piratical voyages: and they were afterwards joined by numbers of necessitous and daring adventurers from the coasts of Provence and Sicily.

In 844, these wandering innovators had a great number of vessels at sea; and again visiting the coasts of France, Spain, and England, the following year they penetrated even to Paris: and the unfortunate Charles the Bald, king of France, purchased at a high price, the retreat of the banditti he had no other means of repelling.

These successful expeditions continued for some time; till Rollo, otherwise Raoul, assembled a number of followers, and after a descent on England, crossed the channel, and made himself master of Rouen, which he fortified. Charles the Simple, unable to contend with Rollo, offered to resign to him some of the northern provinces, and to give him his daughter in marriage. Neustria, since called Normandy, was granted to him, and afterwards Brittany. He added the more solid virtues of the legislator to the fierce valour of the conqueror—converted to Christianity, he established justice, and repressed the excesses of his Danish subjects, till then accustomed to live only by plunder. His name became the signal for pursuing those who violated the laws; as well as the cry of Haro, still so usual in Normandy. The Danes and Francs produced a race of men celebrated for their valour; and it was a small party of these that in 983, having been on a pilgrimage to Jerusalem, arrived on their return at Salerno, and found the town surrounded by Mahometans, whom the Salernians were bribing to leave their coast. The Normans represented to them the baseness and cowardice of such submission; and notwithstanding the inequality of their numbers, they boldly attacked the Saracen camp, and drove the infidels to their ships. The prince of Salerno, astonished at their successful audacity, would have loaded them with the marks of his gratitude; but refusing every reward, they returned to their own country, from whence, however, other bodies of Normans passed into Sicily (anciently called Trinacria); and many of them entered into the service of the emperor of the East, others of the Pope, and the duke of Naples was happy to engage a small party of them in defence of his newly founded duchy. Soon afterwards three brothers of Coutance, the sons of Tancred de Hauteville, Guillaume Fier-a-bras, Drogon, and Humfroi, joining the Normans established at Aversa, became masters of the fertile island of Sicily; and Robert Guiscard joining them, the Normans became sovereigns both of Sicily and Naples (Parthenope). How William, the natural son of Robert, duke of Normandy, possessed himself of England, is too well known to be repeated here. William sailing from St. Valori, landed in the bay of Pevensey; and at the place now called Battle, met the English forces under Harold: an esquire (ecuyer) called Taillefer, mounted on an armed horse, led on the Normans, singing in a thundering tone the war song of Rollo. He threw himself among the English, and was killed on the first onset. In a marsh not far from Hastings, the skeletons of an armed man and horse were found a few years since, which are believed to have belonged to the Normans, as a party of their horse, deceived in the nature of the ground, perished in the morass.

Parthenope! within thy fertile bay   130
Receiv'd the victors—

           In the mailed ranks
Of Normans landing on the British coast
Rode Taillefer; and with astounding voice
Thunder'd the war song daring Roland sang
First in the fierce contention: vainly brave,   135
One not inglorious struggle England made—
But failing, saw the Saxon heptarchy
Finish for ever.——Then the holy pile,*
Yet seen upon the field of conquest, rose,
Where to appease heaven's wrath for so much blood,   140
The conqueror bade unceasing prayers ascend,
And requiems for the slayers and the slain.
But let not modern Gallia form from hence
Presumptuous hopes, that ever thou again,
Queen of the isles! shalt crouch to foreign arms.   145
The enervate sons of Italy may yield;
And the Iberian, all his trophies torn
And wrapp'd in Superstition's monkish weed,
May shelter his abasement, and put on
Degrading fetters. Never, never thou!   150
Imperial mistress of the obedient sea;
But thou, in thy integrity secure,
Shalt now undaunted meet a world in arms.

England! 'twas where this promontory rears
Its rugged brow above the channel wave,   155

---

* Battle Abbey was raised by the Conqueror, and endowed with an ample revenue, that masses might be said night and day for the souls of those who perished in battle.

Line 137. **Saxon heptarchy**: the seven contiguous kingdoms of Saxon England.
Lines 146–47. **Italy ... Iberian**: Napoleon had conquered both Italy and the Iberian peninsula.

Parting the hostile nations, that thy fame,
Thy naval fame was tarnish'd, at what time
Thou, leagued with the Batavian, gavest to France*
One day of triumph—triumph the more loud,
Because even then so rare. Oh! well redeem'd,   160
Since, by a series of illustrious men,
Such as no other country ever rear'd,
To vindicate her cause. It is a list
Which, as Fame echoes it, blanches the cheek
Of bold Ambition; while the despot feels   165
The extorted sceptre tremble in his grasp.

From even the proudest roll by glory fill'd,
How gladly the reflecting mind returns
To simple scenes of peace and industry,
Where, bosom'd in some valley of the hills   170
Stands the lone farm; its gate with tawny ricks
Surrounded, and with granaries and sheds,
Roof'd with green mosses, and by elms and ash
Partially shaded; and not far remov'd
The hut of sea-flints built; the humble home   175

---

* In 1690, King William being then in Ireland, Tourville, the French admiral, arrived on the coast of England. His fleet consisted of seventy-eight large ships, and twenty-two fire-ships. Lord Torrington, the English admiral, lay at St. Helens, with only forty English and a few Dutch ships; and conscious of the disadvantage under which he should give battle, he ran up between the enemy's fleet and the coast, to protect it. The queen's council, dictated to by Russel, persuaded her to order Torrington to venture a battle. The orders Torrington appears to have obeyed reluctantly: his fleet now consisted of twenty-two Dutch and thirty-four English ships. Evertson, the Dutch admiral, was eager to obtain glory; Torrington, more cautious, reflected on the importance of the stake. The consequence was, that the Dutch rashly sailing on were surrounded, and Torrington, solicitous to recover this false step, placed himself with difficulty between the Dutch and French;—but three Dutch ships were burnt, two of their admirals killed, and almost all their ships disabled. The English and Dutch declining a second engagement, retired towards the mouth of the Thames. The French, from ignorance of the coast, and misunderstanding among each other, failed to take all the advantage they might have done of this victory.

Line 167. **roll**: historical chronicle or list.

Of one, who sometimes watches on the heights,*
When hid in the cold mist of passing clouds,
The flock, with dripping fleeces, are dispers'd
O'er the wide down; then from some ridged point
That overlooks the sea, his eager eye   180
Watches the bark that for his signal waits
To land its merchandize:—Quitting for this
Clandestine traffic his more honest toil,
The crook abandoning, he braves himself
The heaviest snow-storm of December's night,   185
When with conflicting winds the ocean raves,
And on the tossing boat, unfearing mounts
To meet the partners of the perilous trade,
And share their hazard. Well it were for him,
If no such commerce of destruction known,   190
He were content with what the earth affords
To human labour; even where she seems
Reluctant most. More happy is the hind,
Who, with his own hands rears on some black moor,
Or turbary, his independent hut   195
Cover'd with heather, whence the slow white smoke
Of smouldering peat arises——A few sheep,
His best possession, with his children share
The rugged shed when wintry tempests blow;
But, when with Spring's return the green blades rise   200
Amid the russet heath, the household live
Joint tenants of the waste throughout the day,
And often, from her nest, among the swamps,

---

* The shepherds and labourers of this tract of country, a hardy and athletic race of men, are almost universally engaged in the contraband trade, carried on for the coarsest and most destructive spirits, with the opposite coast. When no other vessel will venture to sea, these men hazard their lives to elude the watchfulness of the Revenue officers, and to secure their cargoes.

Line 195. **turbary**: peat bog.   Line 202. **waste**: uncultivated wild.

Where the gemm'd sun-dew* grows, or fring'd buck-bean,
They scare the plover,† that with plaintive cries   205
Flutters, as sorely wounded, down the wind.
Rude, and but just remov'd from savage life
Is the rough dweller among scenes like these,
(Scenes all unlike the poet's fabling dreams
Describing Arcady)—But he is free;   210
The dread that follows on illegal acts
He never feels; and his industrious mate
Shares in his labour. Where the brook is traced
By crouding osiers, and the black coot° hides
Among the plashy reeds, her diving brood,   215
The matron wades; gathering the long green rush
That well prepar'd hereafter lends its light
To her poor cottage, dark and cheerless else
Thro' the drear hours of Winter. Otherwhile
She leads her infant group where charlock grows   220
"Unprofitably gay,"‡ or to the fields,
Where congregate the linnet and the finch,
That on the thistles, so profusely spread,
Feast in the desert; the poor family
Early resort, extirpating with care   225
These, and the gaudier mischief of the ground;
Then flames the high rais'd heap; seen afar off

---

* sun-dew. *Drosera rotundifolia.*   buck-bean. *Menyanthes trifoliatum.*
† plover. *Tringa vanellus.*   ° coot. *Fulica aterrima.*
‡ "With blossom'd furze, unprofitably gay." Goldsmith [*The Deserted Village*, line 194].

Line 206. **as sorely wounded:** feigning injury to distract attention from her nest.
Line 210. **Arcady:** a pastoral ideal.   Line 214. **osiers:** willows.
Line 216. **rush:** dried reeds burned for light by the English peasantry in place of expensive candles.
Line 220. **charlock:** wild mustard, poisonous to sheep.

Like hostile war-fires flashing to the sky.*
Another task is theirs: On fields that shew
As angry Heaven had rain'd sterility, 230
Stony and cold, and hostile to the plough,
Where clamouring loud, the evening curlew† runs
And drops her spotted eggs among the flints;
The mother and the children pile the stones
In rugged pyramids;—and all this toil 235
They patiently encounter; well content
On their flock bed to slumber undisturb'd
Beneath the smoky roof they call their own.
Oh! little knows the sturdy hind, who stands
Gazing, with looks where envy and contempt 240
Are often strangely mingled, on the car
Where prosperous Fortune sits; what secret care
Or sick satiety is often hid,
Beneath the splendid outside: *He* knows not
How frequently the child of Luxury 245
Enjoying nothing, flies from place to place
In chase of pleasure that eludes his grasp;
And that content is e'en less found by him,
Than by the labourer, whose pick-axe smooths
The road before his chariot; and who doffs 250
What *was* an hat; and as the train pass on,
Thinks how one day's expenditure, like this,
Would cheer him for long months, when to his toil
The frozen earth closes her marble breast.

---

* The Beacons formerly lighted up on the hills to give notice of the approach of an enemy. These signals would still be used in case of alarm, if the Telegraph [semaphore signals] now substituted could not be distinguished on account of fog or darkness.

† curlew. *Charadrius oedienemus.*

Line 230. **As:** as if.   Line 237. **flock bed:** mattress stuffed with waste wool from shearing.

Ah! who *is* happy? Happiness! a word   255
That like false fire, from marsh effluvia born,
Misleads the wanderer, destin'd to contend
In the world's wilderness, with want or woe—
Yet *they* are happy, who have never ask'd
What good or evil means. The boy   260
That on the river's margin gaily plays,
Has heard that Death is there[.]—He knows not Death,
And therefore fears it not; and venturing in
He gains a bullrush, or a minnow—then,
At certain peril, for a worthless prize,   265
A crow's, or raven's nest, he climbs the boll
Of some tall pine; and of his prowess proud,
Is for a moment happy. Are *your* cares,
Ye who despise him, never worse applied?
The village girl is happy, who sets forth   270
To distant fair, gay in her Sunday suit,
With cherry colour'd knots, and flourish'd shawl,
And bonnet newly purchas'd. So is he
Her little brother, who his mimic drum
Beats, till he drowns her rural lovers' oaths   275
Of constant faith, and still increasing love;
Ah! yet a while, and half those oaths believ'd,
Her happiness is vanish'd; and the boy
While yet a stripling, finds the sound he lov'd
Has led him on, till he has given up   280
His freedom, and his happiness together.
I once was happy, when while yet a child,
I learn'd to love these upland solitudes,
And, when elastic as the mountain air,

Line 256. **false fire**: ignis fatuus, will-o'-the-wisp.   Line 266. **boll**: bole, trunk.

Line 278. **vanish'd**: She may suffer the disgrace of an illegitimate birth; or, properly married, find herself (like Smith) victimized by her husband, as the ensuing lines depict.

Line 281. **together**: i.e. has become a soldier in a real war.

Line 284. **elastic**: buoyant, resilient.

To my light spirit, care was yet unknown   285
And evil unforseen:—Early it came,
And childhood scarcely passed, I was condemned,
A guiltless exile, silently to sigh,
While Memory, with faithful pencil, drew
The contrast; and regretting, I compar'd   290
With the polluted smoky atmosphere
And dark and stifling streets, the southern hills
That to the setting Sun, their graceful heads
Rearing, o'erlook the frith, where Vecta* breaks
With her white rocks, the strong impetuous tide,   295
When western winds the vast Atlantic urge
To thunder on the coast[.]—Haunts of my youth!
Scenes of fond day dreams, I behold ye yet!
Where 'twas so pleasant by thy northern slopes
To climb the winding sheep-path, aided oft   300
By scatter'd thorns: whose spiny branches bore
 Small woolly tufts, spoils of the vagrant lamb
There seeking shelter from the noon-day sun;
And pleasant, seated on the short soft turf,
To look beneath upon the hollow way   305
While heavily upward mov'd the labouring wain,
 And stalking slowly by, the sturdy hind
To ease his panting team, stopp'd with a stone
The grating wheel.

                    Advancing higher still
The prospect widens, and the village church   310
But little, o'er the lowly roofs around

---

* Vecta. The Isle of Wight, which breaks the force of the waves when they are driven by
south-west winds against this long and open coast. It is somewhere described as "Vecta
shouldering the Western Waves."

Line 294. **frith**: firth, a long, narrow inlet from the sea.
Line 305. **hollow way**: road through a depression.   Line 306. **wain**: cart.

Rears its gray belfry, and its simple vane;
Those lowly roofs of thatch are half conceal'd
By the rude arms of trees, lovely in spring,*
When on each bough, the rosy-tinctur'd bloom   315
Sits thick, and promises autumnal plenty.
For even those orchards round the Norman Farms,
Which, as their owners mark the promis'd fruit,
Console them for the vineyards of the south,
Surpass not these.

     Where woods of ash, and beech,   320
And partial copses, fringe the green hill foot,
 The upland shepherd rears his modest home,
There wanders by, a little nameless stream
That from the hill wells forth, bright now and clear,
Or after rain with chalky mixture gray,   325
But still refreshing in its shallow course,
The cottage garden; most for use design'd,
Yet not of beauty destitute. The vine
Mantles the little casement; yet the briar
Drops fragrant dew among the July flowers;   330
And pansies rayed, and freak'd and mottled pinks
Grow among balm, and rosemary and rue
There honeysuckles flaunt, and roses blow
Almost uncultured: Some with dark green leaves
Contrast their flowers of pure unsullied white;   335
Others, like velvet robes of regal state
Of richest crimson, while in thorny moss

---

* Every cottage in this country has its orchard; and I imagine that not even those of
Herefordshire, or Worcestershire, exhibit a more beautiful prospect, when the trees are in
bloom, and the "Primavera candida e vermiglia" ["pure and rosy Spring," Petrarch, Sonnet
310, line 4], is every where so enchanting.

Line 316. **autumnal plenty**: harvest of apples.
Line 332. **balm ... rue**: herbs used for medicine and seasoning.

Enshrined and cradled, the most lovely, wear
The hues of youthful beauty's glowing cheek.—
With fond regret I recollect e'en now   340
In Spring and Summer, what delight I felt
Among these cottage gardens, and how much
Such artless nosegays, knotted with a rush
By village housewife or her ruddy maid,
Were welcome to me; soon and simply pleas'd.   345

An early worshipper at Nature's shrine,
I loved her rudest scenes—warrens, and heaths,
And yellow commons, and birch-shaded hollows,
And hedge rows, bordering unfrequented lanes
Bowered with wild roses, and the clasping woodbine   350
Where purple tassels of the tangling vetch*
With bittersweet, and bryony inweave,†
And the dew fills the silver bindweed's° cups—
I loved to trace the brooks whose humid banks
Nourish the harebell, and the freckled pagil;‡   355
And stroll among o'ershadowing woods of beech,
Lending in Summer, from the heats of noon
A whispering shade; while haply there reclines
Some pensive lover of uncultur'd flowers,
Who, from the tumps with bright green mosses clad,   360
Plucks the wood sorrel,˙ with its light thin leaves,
Heart-shaped, and triply folded; and its root
Creeping like beaded coral; or who there

---

* vetch. *Vicia sylvatica.*   † bittersweet. *Solanum dulcamara.* bryony. *Bryonia alba.*
° bindweed. *Convolvulus sepium.*
‡ harebell. *Hyacinthus non scriptus.* pagil. *Primula veris.*   • sorrel. *Oxalis acetosella.*

Line 347. **warrens:** uncultivated land set aside for animal life, particularly rabbits.
Line 359. **uncultur'd flowers:** wildflowers.
Line 360. **tumps:** small hillocks raised above the boggish turf.

Gathers, the copse's pride, anémones,*
With rays like golden studs on ivory laid   365
Most delicate: but touch'd with purple clouds,
Fit crown for April's fair but changeful brow.

Ah! hills so early loved! in fancy still
I breathe your pure keen air; and still behold
Those widely spreading views, mocking alike   370
The Poet and the Painter's utmost art.
And still, observing objects more minute,
Wondering remark the strange and foreign forms
Of sea-shells; with the pale calcareous soil
Mingled, and seeming of resembling substance.†   375
Tho' surely the blue Ocean (from the heights
Where the downs westward trend, but dimly seen)
Here never roll'd its surge. Does Nature then
Mimic, in wanton mood, fantastic shapes
Of bivalves, and inwreathed volutes, that cling   380
To the dark sea-rock of the wat'ry world?
Or did this range of chalky mountains, once°

---

* anémones. *Anemóne nemorosa.* It appears to be settled on late and excellent authorities, that this word should not be accented on the second syllable, but on the penultima. I have however ventured the more known accentuation, as more generally used, and suiting better the nature of my verse.

† Among the crumbling chalk I have often found shells, some quite in a fossil state and hardly distinguishable from chalk. Others appeared more recent; cockles, muscles, and periwinkles, I well remember, were among the number; and some whose names I do not know. A great number were like those of small land snails. It is now many years since I made these observations. The appearance of sea-shells so far from the sea excited my surprise, though I then knew nothing of natural history. I have never read any of the late theories of the earth, nor was I ever satisfied with the attempts to explain many of the phenomena which call forth conjecture in those books I happened to have had access to on this subject.

° The theory here slightly hinted at, is taken from an idea started by Mr. White [Gilbert White (1720–93), *The History of Selbourne* (1789)].

Line 367. **April's ... brow:** anemones bloom in early spring.

Line 374. **calcareous:** chalky.

Line 380. **bivalves:** double-shelled mollusks: e.g., clams and oysters.   **volutes:** spiral-shelled mollusks: e.g., periwinkles, conchs.

Form a vast bason, where the Ocean waves
Swell'd fathomless? What time these fossil shells,
Buoy'd on their native element, were thrown   385
Among the imbedding calx: when the huge hill
Its giant bulk heaved, and in strange ferment
Grew up a guardian barrier, 'twixt the sea
And the green level of the sylvan weald.

Ah! very vain is Science' proudest boast,   390
And but a little light its flame yet lends
To its most ardent votaries; since from whence
These fossil forms are seen, is but conjecture,
Food for vague theories, or vain dispute,
While to his daily task the peasant goes,   395
Unheeding such inquiry; with no care
But that the kindly change of sun and shower,
Fit for his toil the earth he cultivates.
As little recks the herdsman of the hill,
Who on some turfy knoll, idly reclined,   400
Watches his wether flock, that deep beneath
Rest the remains of men, of whom is left*
No traces in the records of mankind,
Save what these half obliterated mounds
And half fill'd trenches doubtfully impart   405
To some lone antiquary; who on times remote,
Since which two thousand years have roll'd away,
Loves to contemplate. He perhaps may trace,
Or fancy he can trace, the oblong square

---

* These Downs are not only marked with traces of encampments, which from their forms are called Roman or Danish; but there are numerous tumuli [burial mounds] among them. Some of which having been opened a few years ago, were supposed by a learned antiquary to contain the remains of the original natives of the country.

Line 389. **weald**: the Sussex weald, the woodland valley inland from the downs.
Line 399. **recks**: reckons; considers.   Line 401. **wether**: castrated male sheep.

Where the mail'd legions, under Claudius,* rear'd   410
The rampire, or excavated fossé delved;
What time the huge unwieldy Elephant†
Auxiliary reluctant, hither led,
From Afric's forest glooms and tawny sands,
First felt the Northern blast, and his vast frame   415
Sunk useless; whence in after ages found,
The wondering hinds, on those enormous bones

Gaz'd; and in giants° dwelling on the hills
Believed and marvell'd—

---

* That the legions of Claudius [10 B.C.–54 A.D.] were in this part of Britain appears certain. Since this emperor received the submission of Cantii, Atrebates, Irenobates, and Regni, in which latter denomination were included the people of Sussex.

† In the year 1740, some workmen digging in the park at Burton in Sussex, discovered, nine feet below the surface, the teeth and bones of an elephant; two of the former were seven feet eight inches in length. There were besides these, tusks, one of which broke in removing it, a grinder not at all decayed, and a part of the jaw-bone, with bones of the knee and thigh, and several others. Some of them remained very lately at Burton House, the seat of John Biddulph, Esq. Others were in possession of the Rev. Dr. Langrish, minister of Petworth at that period, who was present when some of these bones were taken up, and gave it as his opinion, that they had remained there since the universal deluge [that is, from the time of Noah's Ark]. The Romans under the Emperor Claudius probably brought elephants into Britain. Milton, in the Second Book of his History [of Britain], in speaking of the expedition, says that "He [who waiteth ready with a huge preparation, as if not safe anough amidst the flowr of all his Romans,] like a great eastern king, with armed elephants, marched [marches] through Gallia." This is given on the authority of Dion Cassius, in his Life of the Emperor Claudius. It has therefore been conjectured, that the bones found at Burton might have been those of one of these elephants, who perished there soon after its landing; or dying on the high downs, one of which, called Duncton Hill, rises immediately above Burton Park, the bones might have been washed down by the torrents of rain, and buried deep in the soil. They were not found together, but scattered at some distance from each other. The two tusks were twenty feet apart. I had often heard of the elephant's bones at Burton, but never saw them; and I have no books to refer to. I think I saw, in what is now called the National Museum at Paris, the very large bones of an elephant, which were found in North America: though it is certain that this enormous animal is never seen in its natural state, but in the countries under the torrid zone of the old world. I have, since making this note, been told that the bones of the rhinoceros and hippopotamus have been found in America.

° The peasants believe that the large bones sometimes found belonged to giants, who formerly lived on the hills. The devil also has a great deal to do with the remarkable forms of hill and vale: the Devil's Punch Bowl, the Devil's Leaps, and the Devil's Dyke, are names given to deep hollows, or high and abrupt ridges, in this and the neighbouring county.

Line 411. **rampire**: rampart, barrier.   **fossé**: ditch, trench.

Hither, Ambition come!
Come and behold the nothingness of all   420
For which you carry thro' the oppressed Earth,
War, and its train of horrors—see where tread
The innumerous hoofs of flocks above the works
By which the warrior sought to register
His glory, and immortalize his name[.]—   425
The pirate Dane,* who from his circular camp
Bore in destructive robbery, fire and sword
Down thro' the vale, sleeps unremember'd here;
And here, beneath the green sward, rests alike
The savage native,† who his acorn meal   430
Shar'd with the herds, that ranged the pathless woods;
And the centurion, who on these wide hills
Encamping, planted the Imperial Eagle.
All, with the lapse of Time, have passed away,
Even as the clouds, with dark and dragon shapes,   435
Or like vast promontories crown'd with towers,
Cast their broad shadows on the downs: then sail
Far to the northward, and their transient gloom
Is soon forgotten.

But from thoughts like these,
By human crimes suggested, let us turn   440
To where a more attractive study courts
The wanderer of the hills; while shepherd girls
Will from among the fescue° bring him flowers,
Of wonderous mockery; some resembling bees

---

* The incursions of the Danes were for many ages the scourge of this island.

† The Aborigines of this country lived in woods, unsheltered but by trees and caves; and were probably as truly savage as any of those who are now termed so.

° The grass called Sheep's Fescue, (*Festuca ovina*) clothes these Downs with the softest turf.

Line 433. **Imperial Eagle**: the standard of the Roman Empire.

In velvet vest, intent on their sweet toil,*   445
While others mimic flies,† that lightly sport
In the green shade, or float along the pool,
But here seen perch'd upon the slender stalk,
And gathering honey dew. While in the breeze
That wafts the thistle's plumed seed along,   450
Blue bells wave tremulous. The mountain thyme°
Purples the hassock of the heaving mole,
And the short turf is gay with tormentil,‡
And bird's foot trefoil, and the lesser tribes
Of hawkweed;• spangling it with fringed stars.—   455
Near where a richer tract of cultur'd land
Slopes to the south; and burnished by the sun,
Bend in the gale of August, floods of corn;
The guardian of the flock, with watchful care,¶
Repels by voice and dog the encroaching sheep—   460

---

* *Ophrys apifera*, Bee Ophrys, or Orchis found plentifully on the hills, as well as the next.

† *Ophrys muscifera*. Fly Orchis. Linnæus, misled by the variations to which some of this tribe are really subject, has perhaps too rashly esteemed all those which resemble insects, as forming only one species, which he terms Ophrys insectifera. See *English Botany.*

° Blue bells. *Campanula rotundifolia.* Mountain thyme. *Thymus serpyllum.* "It is a common notion, that the flesh of sheep which feed upon aromatic plants, particularly wild thyme, is superior in flavour to other mutton. The truth is, that sheep do not crop these aromatic plants, unless now and then by accident, or when they are first turned on hungry to downs, heaths, or commons; but the soil and situations favourable to aromatic plants, produce a short sweet pasturage, best adapted to feeding sheep, whom nature designed for mountains, and not for turnip grounds and rich meadows. The attachment of bees to this, and other aromatic plants, is well known." Martyn's Miller [Thomas Martyn, *The Gardener's and Botanist's Dictionary ... by the late Philip Miller ... To Which Are Now Added a Complete Enumeration and Description of All Plants* (1797–1807)].

‡ tormentil. *Tormentilla reptans.*

• bird's foot trefoil. *Trifolium ornithopoides.*   hawkweed. *Hieracium,* many sorts.

¶ The downs, especially to the south, where they are less abrupt, are in many places under the plough; and the attention of the shepherds is there particularly required to keep the flocks from trespassing.

Line 452. **hassock ... mole**: a tuft of grass being forced up by a ridge forming in watery ground.

While his boy visits every wired trap*
That scars the turf; and from the pit-falls takes
The timid migrants,† who from distant wilds,
Warrens, and stone quarries, are destined thus
To lose their short existence. But unsought   465
By Luxury yet, the Shepherd still protects
The social bird,° who from his native haunts
Of willowy current, or the rushy pool,
Follows the fleecy croud, and flirts and skims,
In fellowship among them.

             Where the knoll   470
More elevated takes the changeful winds,
The windmill rears its vanes; and thitherward
With his white load, the master travelling,
Scares the rooks rising slow on whispering wings,
While o'er his head, before the summer sun   475
Lights up the blue expanse, heard more than seen,
The lark sings matins; and above the clouds
Floating, embathes his spotted breast in dew.
Beneath the shadow of a gnarled thorn,
Bent by the sea blast‡ from a seat of turf   480

---

* Square holes cut in the turf, into which a wire noose is fixed, to catch Wheatears. Mr. White [*History of Selbourne*] says, that these birds (*Motacilla oenanthe*) are never taken beyond the river Adur, and Beding Hill; but this is certainly a mistake.

† These birds are extremely fearful, and on the slightest appearance of a cloud, run for shelter to the first rut, or heap of stone, that they see.

° The Yellow Wagtail. *Motacilla flava*. It frequents the banks of rivulets in winter, making its nest in meadows and corn-fields. But after the breeding season is over, it haunts downs and sheepwalks, and is seen constantly among the flocks, probably for the sake of the insects it picks up. In France the shepherds call it *La Bergeronette*, and say it often gives them, by its cry, notice of approaching danger.

‡ The strong winds from the south-west occasion almost all the trees, which on these hills are exposed to it, to grow the other way.

Line 473. **With … master**: the farmer, bringing grain to the mill.

With fairy nosegays strewn, how wide the view!*
Till in the distant north it melts away,
And mingles indiscriminate with clouds:
But if the eye could reach so far, the mart
Of England's capital, its domes and spires   485
Might be perceived—Yet hence the distant range
Of Kentish hills,† appear in purple haze;
And nearer, undulate the wooded heights,
And airy summits,° that above the mole
Rise in green beauty; and the beacon'd ridge   490
Of Black-down‡ shagg'd with heath, and swelling rude
Like a dark island from the vale; its brow
Catching the last rays of the evening sun
That gleam between the nearer park's old oaks,
Then lighten up the river, and make prominent   495
The portal, and the ruin'd battlements•
Of that dismantled fortress; rais'd what time
The Conqueror's successors fiercely fought,
Tearing with civil feuds the desolate land.
But now a tiller of the soil dwells there,   500
And of the turret's loop'd and rafter'd halls
Has made an humbler homestead—Where he sees,
Instead of armed foemen, herds that graze

---

* So extensive are some of the views from these hills, that only the want of power in the human eye to travel so far, prevents London itself being discerned. Description falls so infinitely short of the reality, that only here and there, distinct features can be given.

† A scar of chalk in a hill beyond Sevenoaks in Kent, is very distinctly seen of a clear day.

° The hills about Dorking in Surry; over almost the whole extent of which county the prospect extends.

‡ This is an high ridge, extending between Sussex and Surry. It is covered with heath, and has almost always a dark appearance. On it is a telegraph.

• In this country there are several of the fortresses or castles built by Stephen of Blois [King of England, 1135–54], in his contention for the kingdom, with the daughter of Henry the First, the empress Matilda. Some of these are now converted into farm houses.

Line 489. **mole**: the cliffs that descend to the sea.

Along his yellow meadows; or his flocks
At evening from the upland driv'n to fold—   505

In such a castellated mansion once
A stranger chose his home; and where hard by
In rude disorder fallen, and hid with brushwood
Lay fragments gray of towers and buttresses,
Among the ruins, often he would muse—   510
His rustic meal soon ended, he was wont
To wander forth, listening the evening sounds
Of rushing milldam, or the distant team,
Or night-jar, chasing fern-flies:* the tir'd hind
Pass'd him at nightfall, wondering he should sit   515
On the hill top so late: they from the coast
Who sought bye paths with their clandestine load,
Saw with suspicious doubt, the lonely man
Cross on their way: but village maidens thought

---

* Dr. Aikin remarks, I believe, in his essay "On the Application of Natural History to the Purposes of Poetry," how many of our best poets have noticed the same circumstance, the hum of the Dor Beetle *(Scaraboeus stercorarius)* among the sounds heard by the evening wanderer. [In *An Essay on the Application of Natural History to Poetry* (London: J. Johnson, 1777), 7–8, John Aikin, the brother of Anna Barbauld, compares the usage of Shakespeare's *Macbeth*, Milton's "Lycidas," Gray's "Elegy Written in a Country Church-Yard," and Collins' "Ode to Evening."] I remember only one instance in which the more remarkable, though by no means uncommon noise, of the Fern Owl, or Goatsucker, is mentioned. It is called the Night Hawk, the Jar Bird, the Churn Owl, and the Fern Owl, from its feeding on the *Scaraboeus solstitialis,* or Fern Chafer, which it catches while on the wing with its claws, the middle toe of which is long and curiously serrated, on purpose to hold them. It was this bird that was intended to be described in the Forty-second Sonnet [Smith's *Sonnets;* see page 40]. I was mistaken in supposing it as visible in November; it is a migrant, and leaves this country in August. I had often seen and heard it, but I did not then know its name or history. It is called Goatsucker *(Caprimulgus),* from a strange prejudice taken against it by the Italians, who assert that it sucks their goats; and the peasants of England still believe that a disease in the backs of their cattle, occasioned by a fly, which deposits its egg under the skin, and raises a boil, sometimes fatal to calves, is the work of this bird, which they call a Puckeridge. Nothing can convince them that their beasts are not injured by this bird, which they therefore hold in abhorrence.

Line 513. **rushing milldam:** a dam in a stream creating sufficient force of water to drive a mill.

Line 517. **Who ... load:** smugglers.

His senses injur'd; and with pity say   520
That he, poor youth! must have been cross'd in love—
For often, stretch'd upon the mountain turf
With folded arms, and eyes intently fix'd
Where ancient elms and firs obscured a grange,
Some little space within the vale below,   525
They heard him, as complaining of his fate,
And to the murmuring wind, of cold neglect
And baffled hope he told.—The peasant girls
These plaintive sounds remember, and even now
Among them may be heard the stranger's songs.   530

        Were I a Shepherd on the hill
            And ever as the mists withdrew
        Could see the willows of the rill
        Shading the footway to the mill
            Where once I walk'd with you—   535

        And as away Night's shadows sail,
            And sounds of birds and brooks arise,
        Believe, that from the woody vale
        I hear your voice upon the gale
            In soothing melodies;   540

        And viewing from the Alpine height,
            The prospect dress'd in hues of air,
        Could say, while transient colours bright
        Touch'd the fair scene with dewy light,
            'Tis, that *her* eyes are there!   545

        I think, I could endure my lot
            And linger on a few short years,
        And then, by all but you forgot,

Line 524. **grange**: farm.

Sleep, where the turf that clothes the spot
   May claim some pitying tears.   550

For 'tis not easy to forget
   One, who thro' life has lov'd you still,
And you, however late, might yet
With sighs to Memory giv'n, regret
   The Shepherd of the Hill.   555

Yet otherwhile it seem'd as if young Hope
Her flattering pencil gave to Fancy's hand,
And in his wanderings, rear'd to sooth his soul
Ideal bowers of pleasure—Then, of Solitude
And of his hermit life, still more enamour'd,   560
His home was in the forest; and wild fruits
And bread sustain'd him. There in early spring
The Barkmen* found him, e'er the sun arose;
There at their daily toil, the Wedgecutters†
Beheld him thro' the distant thicket move.   565
The shaggy dog following the truffle hunter,°
Bark'd at the loiterer; and perchance at night
Belated villagers from fair or wake,
While the fresh night-wind let the moonbeams in
Between the swaying boughs, just saw him pass,   570
And then in silence, gliding like a ghost
He vanish'd! Lost among the deepening gloom.—
But near one ancient tree, whose wreathed roots

---

* As soon as the sap begins to rise, the trees intended for felling are cut and barked. At which time the men who are employed in that business pass whole days in the woods.

† The wedges used in ship-building are made of beech wood, and great numbers are cut every year in the woods near the Downs.

° Truffles are found under the beech woods, by means of small dogs trained to hunt them by the scent.

Line 554. **regret**: remember with regret.

Form'd a rude couch, love-songs and scatter'd rhymes,
Unfinish'd sentences, or half erased,   575
And rhapsodies like this, were sometimes found—

Let us to woodland wilds repair
    While yet the glittering night-dews seem
To wait the freshly-breathing air,
    Precursive of the morning beam,   580
That rising with advancing day,
Scatters the silver drops away.

An elm, uprooted by the storm,
    The trunk with mosses gray and green,
Shall make for us a rustic form,   585
    Where lighter grows the forest scene;
And far among the bowery shades,
Are ferny lawns and grassy glades.

Retiring May to lovely June
    Her latest garland now resigns;   590
The banks with cuckoo-flowers* are strewn,
    The woodwalks blue with columbines,†
And with its reeds, the wandering stream
Reflects the flag-flower's° golden gleam.

There, feathering down the turf to meet,   595
    Their shadowy arms the beeches spread,
While high above our sylvan seat,
    Lifts the light ash its airy head;
And later leaved, the oaks between
Extend their boughs of vernal green.   600

---

* cuckoo-flowers. *Lychnis dioica.* Shakespeare describes the Cuckoo buds as being yellow [in *Love's Labour's Lost* V.ii.894]. He probably meant the numerous Ranunculi, or March marigolds *(Caltha palustris)* which so gild the meadows in Spring; but poets have never been botanists. The Cuckoo flower is the *Lychnis floscuculi.*

† columbines. *Aquilegia vulgaris.* ° flag-flower. *Iris pseudacorus.*

The slender birch its paper rind
    Seems offering to divided love,
And shuddering even without a wind
    Aspins, their paler foliage move,
As if some spirit of the air   605
Breath'd a low sigh in passing there.

The Squirrel in his frolic mood,
    Will fearless bound among the boughs;
Yaffils* laugh loudly thro' the wood,
    And murmuring ring-doves tell their vows;   610
While we, as sweetest woodscents rise,
Listen to woodland melodies.

And I'll contrive a sylvan room
    Against the time of summer heat,
Where leaves, inwoven in Nature's loom,   615
    Shall canopy our green retreat;
And gales that "close the eye of day"†
Shall linger, e'er they die away.

And when a sear and sallow hue
    From early frost the bower receives,   620
I'll dress the sand rock cave for you,
    And strew the floor with heath and leaves,
That you, against the autumnal air
May find securer shelter there.

The Nightingale will then have ceas'd   625
    To sing her moonlight serenade;

---

* Yaffils. Woodpeckers (*Picus*); three or four species in Britain.

† "And [Thy] liquid notes that close the eye of day." Milton [Sonnet 1, "O nightingale," line 5]. The idea here meant to be conveyed is of the evening wind, so welcome after a hot day of Summer, and which appears to sooth and lull all nature into tranquillity.

But the gay bird with blushing breast,*
   And Woodlarks† still will haunt the shade,
And by the borders of the spring
Reed-wrens° will yet be carolling.   630

The forest hermit's lonely cave
   None but such soothing sounds shall reach,
Or hardly heard, the distant wave
   Slow breaking on the stony beach;
Or winds, that now sigh soft and low,   635
Now make wild music as they blow.

And then, before the chilling North
   The tawny foliage falling light,
Seems, as it flits along the earth,
   The footfall of the busy Sprite,   640
Who wrapt in pale autumnal gloom,
Calls up the mist-born Mushroom.

Oh! could I hear your soft voice there,
   And see you in the forest green
All beauteous as you are, more fair   645
   You'ld look, amid the sylvan scene,
And in a wood-girl's simple guise,
Be still more lovely in mine eyes.

Ye phantoms of unreal delight,
   Visions of fond delirium born!   650
Rise not on my deluded sight,
   Then leave me drooping and forlorn

---

* The Robin, (*Motacilla rubecula*) which is always heard after other songsters have ceased to sing.

† The Woodlark, (*Alauda nemorosa*) sings very late.

° Reed-wrens, (*Motacilla arundinacea*) sing all the summer and autumn, and are often heard during the night.

To know, such bliss can never be,
Unless Amanda loved like me.

The visionary, nursing dreams like these,   655
Is not indeed unhappy. Summer woods
Wave over him, and whisper as they wave,
Some future blessings he may yet enjoy.
And as above him sail the silver clouds,
He follows them in thought to distant climes,   660
Where, far from the cold policy of this,
Dividing him from her he fondly loves,
He, in some island of the southern sea,*
May haply build his cane-constructed bower
Beneath the bread-fruit, or aspiring palm,   665
With long green foliage rippling in the gale.
Oh! let him cherish his ideal bliss—
For what is life, when Hope has ceas'd to strew
Her fragile flowers along its thorny way?
And sad and gloomy are his days, who lives   670
Of Hope abandon'd!

             Just beneath the rock
Where Beachy overpeers the channel wave,
Within a cavern mined by wintry tides
Dwelt one,† who long disgusted with the world

---

* An allusion to the visionary delights of the newly discovered islands [Polynesia,
particularly Tahiti], where it was at first believed men lived in a state of simplicity and
happiness; but where, as later enquiries have ascertained, that exemption from toil, which
the fertility of their country gives them, produces the grossest vices; and a degree of
corruption that late navigators think will end in the extirpation of the whole people in a few
years.

† In a cavern almost immediately under the cliff called Beachy Head, there lived, as the
people of the country believed, a man of the name of Darby, who for many years had no
other abode than this cave, and subsisted almost entirely on shell-fish. He had often
administered assistance to ship-wrecked mariners; but venturing into the sea on this
charitable mission during a violent equinoctial storm, he himself perished. As it is above
thirty years since I heard this tradition of Parson Darby (for so I think he was called): it may
now perhaps be forgotten.

And all its ways, appear'd to suffer life   675
Rather than live; the soul-reviving gale,
Fanning the bean-field, or the thymy heath,
Had not for many summers breathed on him;
And nothing mark'd to him the season's change,
Save that more gently rose the placid sea,   680
And that the birds which winter on the coast
Gave place to other migrants; save that the fog,
Hovering no more above the beetling cliffs
Betray'd not then the little careless sheep*
On the brink grazing, while their headlong fall   685
Near the lone Hermit's flint-surrounded home,
Claim'd unavailing pity; for his heart
Was feelingly alive to all that breath'd;
And outraged as he was, in sanguine youth,
By human crimes, he still acutely felt   690
For human misery.

           Wandering on the beach,
He learn'd to augur from the clouds of heaven,
And from the changing colours of the sea,
And sullen murmurs of the hollow cliffs,
Or the dark porpoises,† that near the shore   695
Gambol'd and sported on the level brine
When tempests were approaching: then at night
He listen'd to the wind; and as it drove
The billows with o'erwhelming vehemence
He, starting from his rugged couch, went forth   700
And hazarding a life, too valueless,
He waded thro' the waves, with plank or pole
Towards where the mariner in conflict dread
Was buffeting for life the roaring surge;

---

* Sometimes in thick weather the sheep feeding on the summit of the cliff, miss their
footing, and are killed by the fall.

† Dark porpoises. *Delphinus phocœna.*

And now just seen, now lost in foaming gulphs,   705
The dismal gleaming of the clouded moon
Shew'd the dire peril. Often he had snatch'd
From the wild billows, some unhappy man
Who liv'd to bless the hermit of the rocks.
But if his generous cares were all in vain,   710
And with slow swell the tide of morning bore
Some blue swol'n cor'se to land; the pale recluse
Dug in the chalk a sepulchre—above
Where the dank sea-wrack mark'd the utmost tide,
And with his prayers perform'd the obsequies   715
For the poor helpless stranger.

                             One dark night
The equinoctial wind blew south by west,
Fierce on the shore;—the bellowing cliffs were shook
Even to their stony base, and fragments fell
Flashing and thundering on the angry flood.   720
At day-break, anxious for the lonely man,
His cave the mountain shepherds visited,
Tho' sand and banks of weeds had choak'd their way—
He was not in it; but his drowned cor'se
By the waves wafted, near his former home   725
Receiv'd the rites of burial. Those who read
Chisel'd within the rock, these mournful lines,
Memorials of his sufferings, did not grieve,
That dying in the cause of charity
His spirit, from its earthly bondage freed,   730
Had to some better region fled for ever.

Line 714. **sea-wrack:** the line of refuse, particularly seaweed, on the shore.

FABLES

NOTES TO THE FABLES

These are old stories, which I have endeavoured to tell with such a degree of novelty as natural history can lend them. They have been so often repeated, that probably the original inventors have been long since forgotten. La Fontaine, whose graceful simplicity in such light narrative has been universally allowed, is the most usually referred to.

La Fontaine, in his manner of telling the story of Les deux Pigeons [Book IX, Fable 2], calls them *Friends*. But the proverbial conjugal fidelity of this race of birds, makes it seem more natural to describe them as the pigeon and his mate. If it be objected, that the Truant Dove is represented as repeating the apology of Henry the Fourth of France—"Toujours perdrix, toujours Chapon bouilli ne vaut rien" [If you always have boiled partridge or capon, it is nothing special]; and that his partner talks from Shakspeare; I must take refuge under the authority of Chaucer; or rather his polisher Dryden; who makes his Dame Partlet quote Galen and Cato, while Chanticleer explains Latin sentences:

> "For in the days of yore the birds of parts,
> Were bred to speak and sing; and learn the liberal arts."
> ["The Cock and the Fox; or, the Tale of the Nun's Priest," lines 91–92]

In fact, if the mind momentarily acquiesces in the absurdity of animals having the passions and the faculties of man, every thing else may be granted. It might be necessary to apologize for inserting these fables; but that which Prior and Cowper, and so many other of the most eminent writers have not disdained, can never need any defence.

La Fontaine begins the second Fable here inserted—"L'Alouette met ses Petits, avec le Maître d'un Champ" [Book IV, Fable 22]—thus:

> Ne t'attends qu'à toi seul, c'est un commun proverbe;
> Voici comme Esope le mit
> En credit."

There is nothing I am more desirous of avoiding, even in a trifle like this, than the charge of plagiarism. I must in the present instance defend myself by stating, that so long since as April 1805, Mr. [Joseph] Johnson [publisher of *Beachy Head*] was in possession of the MS copy of this

251

Fable. In July 1806, a friend brought with her from London, a volume called *The Birds of Scotland, with other Poems* [by James Grahame (Edinburgh: Blackwood's, 1806); passages quoted, with some liberty, from pages 2–3, 42], in which I read, what, if my fable had been first published, I might perhaps have thought very like an imitation. My lines of the Lark are:

> "————But like a dart
> From his low homestead with the morning springs,   40
> And far above the floating vapour sings,
> At such an height,
> That even the shepherd lad upon the hill,
> Hearing his matin note so shrill,
> With shaded eyes against the lustre bright,
> Scarce sees him twinkling in a *flood of light*—"

Mr. Graham, in a more lengthened description, says of the Lark:

> "————————————He towers
> In loftier poise, with sweeter fuller pipe,
> Cheering the ploughman at his furrow end,   50
> The while he clears the share; or listening, leans
> Upon his paddle staff; and with rais'd hand
> Shadows his half-shut eyes, striving to scan
> The songster melting in the *flood of light*—"

The extreme resemblance of these passages may be accounted for, however, by the observation very justly made, that natural objects being equally visible to all, it is very probable that descriptions of such objects will be often alike.

I cannot help remarking another coincidence. My lines on the female Lark sitting, are: 60

> "She leaves her nest reluctant and in haste,
> And scarce allows herself to taste
> A dew drop and a few small seeds—"

Mr. Graham says of the Wren:

> "————never flitting off,
> Save when the morning Sun is high, to drink
> A dew drop from the nearest flower cup—".

The dictatorial owl

Within a hollow elm, whose scanty shade
    But half acknowledg'd the returning spring,
A female Owl her domicile had made;
    There, through the live-long day with folded wing
And eyes half-clos'd she sat; eyes black and round,   5
    Like berries that on deadly nightshade grow,
And full white face demure, and look profound,
    That ever seem'd some evil to foreknow;
Still with sententious saws she overflow'd,
And birds of omen dark frequented her abode.   10

Thither, to profit by her learned lore,
    Repair'd the daw, the magpie, and the crow[;]
Malicious tongues indeed *did* say, that more
    Of the vain world's affairs they wont to know,
And there discuss, than, 'mid the night's deep noon,   15
    To hear wise axioms from her whisker'd beak,
Or to chaunt solemn airs to hail the moon;
    But only worldlings thus, she said, would speak,
And, that more sapient judges did opine
Their converse was most pure, and held on themes divine.   20

She for the errours of the feather'd nation
    Griev'd very sorely. "They were all infected
With vanities that wanted reformation,
    And to erroneous notions were subjected;
Addicted too to sportiveness and joke,   25
    To song and frolic, and profane delight;"

Line 6. **deadly nightshade**: the poison belladonna.   Line 9. **saws**: proverbial sayings.
Line 12. **daw**: jackdaw, a kind of crow.
Line 14. **wont**: an older, nonreflexive usage: were wont.
Line 15. **night's deep noon**: midnight.
Line 18. **worldlings**: cynics without spiritual interests.

But Strixaline declar'd, the feather'd folk
  Should be to grave demeanour given quite;
Nor, while rejoicing in the new-born spring,
Should cooing dove be heard, or woodlark carolling.   30

She often had to tell, in piteous tone,
  How a poor chough by some sad chance was shent;
Or of some orphan cuckoo left alone
  She would declaim; and then with loud lament,
To do them good, she'd their disasters tell,   35
  And much deplore the faults they had committed;
Yet "hop'd, poor creatures! they might still do well."
  And sighing, she would say, how much she pitied
Birds, who, improvident resolv'd to wed,
Which in such times as these to certain ruin led!   40

To her 'twas music, when grown gray with age,
  Some crow caw'd loud her praise, with yellow bill,
And bade her in the wholesome task engage,
  Mid the plum'd race new maxims to instill;
The raven, ever famous for discerning,   45
  Of nose most exquisite for all good things,
Declar'd she was a fowl of wondrous learning;
  And that no head was ever 'twixt two wings
So wise as hers. Nor female since the pope,
Ycleped Joan, with Strixaline could cope.   50

This, in process of time, so rais'd her pride,
  That ev'ry hour seem'd lost, till she had shown
How science had to her no light denied,
  And what prodigious wisdom was her own!
So, no more shrinking from the blaze of day,   55
  Forth flew she. It was then those pleasant hours,

Line 32. **chough**: a kind of crow.   **shent**: disgraced, put to shame (archaic).
Line 50. **Joan**: the legendary female pope of the ninth century.

When village girls, to hail propitious May,
　　Search the wild copses and the fields for flow'rs,
And gayly sing the yellow meads among,
　　And ev'ry heart is cheer'd, and all look fresh and young.   60

His nest amid the orchard's painted buds
　　The bulfinch wove; and loudly sung the thrush
In the green hawthorn; and the new-leav'd woods,
　　The golden furze, and holly's guarded bush,
With song resounded: tree-moss gray enchas'd   65
　　The chaffinch's soft house; and the dark yew
Receiv'd the hedge sparrow, that careful plac'd
　　Within it's bosom eggs as brightly blue
As the calm sky, or the unruffled deep,
When not a cloud appears, and ev'n the Zephyrs sleep.   70

There is a sundial near a garden fence,
　　Which flow'rs, and herbs, and blossom'd shrubs surround.
And Strixaline determin'd, that from thence
　　She to the winged creatures would expound
Her long collected store. There she alighted,   75
　　And, though much dazzled by the noon's bright rays,
In accents shrill a long discourse recited;
　　While all the birds, in wonder and amaze,
Their songs amid the coverts green suspended,
Much marvelling what Strixaline intended!   80

But when she told them, never joyous note
　　Should by light grateful hearts to Heav'n be sung,
And still insisted, that from ev'ry throat,
　　Dirges, the knell of cheerful Hope, be rung;
While, quitting meadows, wilds, and brakes, and trees,   85

Line 64. **holly's guarded bush**: that is, edged by prickles.　　Line 65. **enchas'd**: encased.

Line 76. **noon's bright rays**: owls sleep during the day: Strixaline, by extension, is out of her element.

She bade them among gloomy ruins hide;
   Nor finch nor white-throat wanton on the breeze,
     Nor reed lark warble by the river side;
They were indignant each, and stood aloof,
Suspecting all this zeal but mask'd a shrewd Tartuffe.   90

Till out of patience they enrag'd surround her,
   Some clamouring cry, that her insidious tongue
Bodes them no good; while others say they've found her
   At ev'ning's close marauding for their young,
When frogs appear'd no more, and mice were scarce.   95
   At length the wryneck, missel thrush, and bunting,
Protested they would end this odious farce,
   And from the dial the baffl'd prater hunting,
With cries and shrieks her hooting they o'erwhelm,
And drive her back for shelter to her elm.   100

There, vanity severely mortified,
   Still on her heart with sharp corrosion prey'd;
No salvo now could cure her wounded pride,
   Yet did she fondly still herself persuade,
That she was born in a reforming hour,   105
   And meant to dictate, govern, and direct;
That wisdom such as hers included pow'r,
   Nor did experience teach her to reflect
How very ill *some folks* apply their labours,
Who think themselves much wiser than their neighbours.   110

Line 90. **Tartuffe**: the title character of Moliere's study of hypocrisy.

Line 95. **frogs … mice**: we are reminded that owls are carnivores.

Line 103. **salvo**: poor excuse.

The jay in masquerade

Within a park's area vast,
  Where grassy slopes and planted glades,
Where the thron'd chesnuts, cones, and mast,
  Strew'd the wide woodland's mingled shades;
From antler'd oaks the acorns shower'd,   5
  As blew the sharp October breeze;
And from the lighter ashes pour'd
  With the first frost their jetty keys.
Attracted there a countless throng
  Of birds resorted to the woods,   10
With various cries, and various song,
  Cheering the cultur'd solitudes.
In the high elms gregarious rooks
  Were heard, loud clam'ring with the daw;
And alders, crowding on the brooks,   15
  The willow wren and halcyon saw;
And where, through reeds and sedges steal
  With slower course th' obstructed tide,
The shieldrake, and the timid teal,
  And water rail, and widgeon hide.   20
The lake's blue wave in plumy pride
  The swan repell'd with ebon foot,
And ducks Muscovian, scarlet-eyed,
  Sail'd social with the dusky coot.
The partridge on the sunny knowl   25
  Securely call'd her running brood,
And here at large the turkeys prowl
  As free as in their native wood;
With quick short note the pheasant crow'd,

Line 1. **park's area:** the grounds of a large estate.   Line 3. **mast:** various nuts.
Line 8. **jetty keys:** black berries.   Line 12. **cultur'd:** cultivated.
Lines 13–14: **rooks ... daw:** varieties of crow.   Line 16. **halcyon:** kingfisher.
Line 25. **knowl:** knoll.

While, scudding through the paddocks spacious,   30
In voice monotonous and loud,
    Was seen the guinea fowl pugnacious.
The mistress who presided here
    Each bird indigenous protected;
While many a feather'd foreigner   35
    Was from remoter climes collected.
A Jay among these scenes was hatch'd,
    Who fancied that indulgent nature
His grace and beauty ne'er had match'd,
    Not ever form'd so fair a creature.   40
His wings, where blues of tend'rest shade
    Declin'd so gradually to jet;
Plumes like gray clouds, that o'er the red
    Float when the summer sun is set;
Like Sachem's diadem, a crest   45
    Rising to mark him for dominion;
In short, that never bird possess'd
    Such charms, was his confirm'd opinion.
Till wand'ring forth one luckless day,
    'Twas his ill fortune to behold   50
A peacock to the sun display,
    Above his lovely shells of gold,
Those shafts, so webb'd, and painted so,
    That they seem'd stol'n from Cupid's wing,
And dipp'd in the ethereal bow   55
    That shines above the show'rs of spring;
And, as the light intensely beam'd,
    Or as they felt the rustling zephyr,
The em'rald crescents brightly gleam'd
    Round lustrous orbs of deep'ning sapphire.   60
Still, on the peacock as he gaz'd,
    The Jay beheld some beauty new,
While high his green panache he rais'd,

Line 30. **paddocks**: grassy lots, pastures.
Line 45. **Sachem's diadem**: Iroquois Indian headdress.   Line 53. **shafts**: tail plumes.

And waved his sinuous neck of blue;
And still with keen and jealous eyes,   65
  The restless, vain, impatient Jay
Or perches near, or round him flies,
  And marks his manners and his way.
For where his shiv'ring train is spread,
  Or near the ant-hills in the copse,   70
Or in the grass along the mead,
  Some radiant feather often drops;
And these, where'er they chanc'd to fall,
  The Jay, with eagerness the prize
Hasten'd to seize, collecting all   75
  These snowy shafts with azure eyes,
Fancying that all this plumage gay
  He could so manage, as to place
Around his form, and thus display
  The peacock's hues, the peacock's grace.   80
He tried, and so adorn'd appear'd,
  Amazing all the folk of feather;
Who, while they gazed at him, were heard
  To join in ridicule together,
Gibing and taunting, as they press   85
  Around, and mock his senseless trouble,
While some pluck off his borrow'd dress,
  Geese hiss, ducks quack, and turkies gobble.
Shrill screams the stare, and long and loud
  The yaffil laughs from aspin gray;   90
Til scarce escaping from the crowd
  With his own plumes, he skulks away.

Be what you are, nor try in vain,
  To reach what nature will deny,
Factitious Art can ne'er attain   95
  The grace of young Simplicity.

Line 63. **panache**: the peacock's crest.   Line 89. **stare**: starling.

And ye, whose transient fame arises
   From that which others write or say,
Learn hence, how common sense despises
   The pilf'ring literary Jay.   100

The truant dove*
from Pilpay

A mountain stream its channel deep
Beneath a rock's rough base had torn;
The cliff, like a vast castle wall, was steep
By fretting rains in many a crevice worn;
But the fern wav'd there, and the mosses crept,   5
And o'er the summit, where the wind
Peel'd from their stems the silver rind,
Depending birches wept—
There, tufts of broom a footing used to find,
And heath and straggling grass to grow,   10
And half-way down from roots enwreathing, broke
The branches of a scathed oak,
And seem to guard the cave below,
Where each revolving year,
Their twins two faithful Doves were wont to rear.   15
Choice never join'd a fonder pair;
To each their simple home was dear,
No discord ever enter'd there;

---

* The varieties of pigeons here named, as Fantail, Carrier, Pouter, Almond Tumbler, and Nun, with many others, are varieties produced by art from the common pigeon. Societies exist in which prizes are given to those who produce birds nearest to the standard of imaginary perfection. A Pouter is a bird of which the crop is capable of being so much distended with wind, that the animal appears to be without a head. On this enlargement of the crop depends the beauty and value of the bird. These Fanciers are to Ornithologists, what Flower Fanciers are to Botanists.

The jay in masquerade. Line 100. **pilf'ring literary Jay**: plagiarist.
The truant dove. Line 8. **Depending**: with branches hanging.

But there the soft affections dwell'd,
And three returning springs beheld   20
Secure within their fortress high
The little happy family.
"Toujours perdrix, messieurs, ne valent rien"—
So did a Gallic monarch once harangue,
And evil was the day whereon our bird   25
This saying heard
From certain new acquaintance he had found;
Who at their perfect ease,
Amid a field of pease,
Boasted to him, that all the country round,   30
The wheat, and oats, and barley, rye and tares,
Quite to the neighb'ring sea, were theirs;
And theirs the oak, and beech-woods, far and near,
For their right noble owner was a peer,
And they themselves luxuriantly were stored   35
In a great dove-cote—to amuse my lord!
"Toujours perdrix ne valent rien." That's strange!
When people once are happy, wherefore change?
So thought our Stock Dove, but communication
With birds in his new friends' exalted station,   40
Whose means of information,
And knowledge of all sorts, must be so ample;
Who saw great folks, and follow'd their example,
Made on the dweller of the cave, impression;
And soon, whatever was his best possession,   45
His sanctuary within the rock's deep breast,
His soft-ey'd partner, and her nest,
He thought of with indiff'rence, then with loathing;

Line 23. **Toujours ... rien**: see Smith's "Note to the Fables." This saying attributed to
Henry IV of France is a favorite maxim of Smith's, which she quotes as well in the preface
to the sixth edition of her *Elegiac Sonnets*.

Line 29. **pease**: older plural form of pea.

Line 37. **Toujours ... rien**: The repetition of the saying reminds us that if the present "right
noble owner" gets bored with partridge, he has an ample supply of doves for dinner.

So much insipid love was good for nothing.—
But sometimes tenderness return'd; his dame   50
So long belov'd, so mild, so free from blame,
How should he tell her, he had learn'd to cavil
At happiness itself, and longed to travel?
His heart still smote him, so much wrong to do her,
He knew not how to break the matter to her.   55
But love, though blind himself, makes some discerning;
His frequent absence, and his late returning,
With ruffled plumage, and with alter'd eyes,
His careless short replies,
And to their couplets coldness or neglect   60
Had made his gentle wife suspect,
All was not right; but she forbore to teaze him,
Which would but give him an excuse to rove:
She therefore tried by every art to please him,
Endur'd his peevish starts with patient love,   65
And when (like other husbands from a tavern)
Of his new notions full he sought his cavern,
She with dissembled cheerfulness "beguiled
The thing she was," and gaily coo'd and smiled.
'Tis not in this most motley sphere uncommon,   70
For man (and so of course more feeble woman)
Most strongly to suspect, what they're pursuing
Will lead them to inevitable ruin,
Yet rush with open eyes to their undoing;
Thus felt the Dove; but in the cant of fashion   75
He talk'd of fate, and of predestination,
And in a grave oration,
He to his much affrighted mate related,

Line 60. **couplets**: twin offspring.   Line 62. **teaze**: interrogate.

Lines 68–69. **beguiled … was**: thus Desdemona in an aside responds to Iago's bantering: "I am not merry; but I do beguile / The thing I am by seeming otherwise" (*Othello*, II.i.123–24).

Line 76. **fate … predestination**: a pedantic trait he shares wtih Chaucer's Chaunticleer.

How he, yet slumb'ring in the egg, was fated,
To gather knowledge, to instruct his kind,   80
By observation elevate his mind,
And give new impulse to Columbian life;
"If it be so," exclaim'd his hapless wife,
"It is *my* fate, to pass my days in pain,
To mourn your love estrang'd, and mourn in vain;   85
Here in our once dear hut to wake and weep,
When your unkindness shall have 'murder'd sleep';
And never that dear hut shall I prepare,
And wait with fondness your arrival there,
While, me and mine forgetting, you will go   90
To some new love." "Why *no,* I tell you *no,*—
What shall I say such foolish fears to cure?
I only mean to make a little tour,
Just—just to see the world around me; then
With new delight, I shall come home again;   95
Such tours are quite the rage—at my return
I shall have much to tell, and you to learn;
Of fashions—some becoming, some grotesque;
Of change of empires, and ideas novel;
Of buildings, Grecian, Gothic, Arabesque,   100
And scenery sublime and picturesque;
And all these things with pleasure we'll discuss—"
"Ah, me! and what are all these things to us?"
"So then, you'd have a bird of genius grovel,
And never see beyond a farmer's hovel?   105

Line 82. **Columbian**: a pun joining *colombe* (French for dove) with the urge to explore after the pattern of Christopher Columbus.

Line 87. **murdered sleep**: *Macbeth,* II.ii.42.

Line 96. **Such tours**: The grand tour of Europe was an essential element in the formation of an eighteenth-century English gentleman.

Line 100. **Grecian ... Arabesque**: current styles of architecture. Smith might be thinking of the Royal Pavilion at Brighton, which had just undergone the first stage of its transformation from a neoclassical original to the oriental fantasy on which the Prince of Wales, later George IV, lavished extravagant sums of money. A local dove, in other words, need not go far for an education.

Ev'n the sand-martin, that inferior creature,
Goes once a year abroad." "It is *his* nature,
But yours, how diff'rent once!" and then she sigh'd,
"There *was* a time, Ah! would that I had died,
Ere you so chang'd! when you'd have perish'd, rather   110
Than this poor breast should heave a single feather
With grief and care; and all this cant of fashion
Would but have rais'd your anger, or compassion.—
O my dear love! You sought not then to range,
But on my changeful neck as fell the light,   115
You sweetly said, you wish'd no other change
Than that soft neck could show; to berries bright
Of mountain ash you fondly could compare
My scarlet feet and bill; my shape and air,
Ah! faithless flatt'rer, did you not declare   120
The soul of grace and beauty centred there?
My eyes, you said, were opals, brightly pink,
Enchas'd in onyx, and you seem'd to think,
Each charm might then the coldest heart enthrall,
Those charms were mine. Alas! I gave you all—   125
Your farthest wand'rings then were but to fetch
The pea, the tare, the beechmast, and the vetch,
For my repast, within my rocky bow'r,
With spleenwort shaded, and the blue-bell's flow'r:
For prospects then you never wish'd to roam,   130
But the best scen'ry was our happy home;
And when, beneath my breast, then fair and young,
Our first dear pair, our earliest nestlings sprung,
And weakly, indistinctly, tried to coo—
Were not those moments picturesque to you?"   135
"Yes, faith, my dear; and all you say is true."
"Oh! hear me then; if thus we have been blest,
If on these wings it was your joy to rest,

Line 123. **Enchas'd:** encased.

Love must from habit still new strength be gaining—"
"From habit? 'tis of that, child, I'm complaining: 140
This everlasting fondness will not be
For birds of flesh and blood. We sha'nt agree,
So why dispute? now prithee don't torment me;
I shall not long be gone; let that content ye:
Pshaw! what a fuss! Come, no more sighs and groans,   145
Keep up your spirits; mind your little ones;
My journey won't be far—my honour's pledg'd—
I shall be back again before they're fledg'd;
Give me a kiss; and now my dear, adieu!"
So light of heart and plumes away he flew;   150
And, as above the shelt'ring rock he springs,
She listen'd to the echo of his wings;
Those well-known sounds, so soothing heretofore,
Which her heart whisper'd she should hear no more.
Then to her cold and widow'd bed she crept,   155
Clasp'd her half-orphan'd young, and wept!
Her recreant mate, by other views attracted,
A very different part enacted;
He sought the dove-cote, and was greeted there
With all that's tonish, elegant, and rare   160
Among the pigeon tribes; and there the rover
Liv'd quite in clover!
His jolly comrades now were blades of spirit;
Their nymphs possess'd most *fascinating* merit;
Nor fail'd our hero of the rock to prove   165
He thought not of inviolable love
To his poor spouse at home. He bow'd and sigh'd,
Now to a Fantail's, now a Cropper's bride;
Then cow'ring low to a majestic Powter,
Declar'd he should not suffer life without her!   170
And then with upturn'd eyes, in phrase still humbler,

Line 148. **fledged**: having grown the feathers necessary for flight. These birds are still nestlings.

Implor'd the pity of an Almond Tumbler;
Next, to a beauteous Carrier's feet he'd run,
And liv'd a week the captive of a Nun:
Thus far in measureless content he revels,   175
And blest the hour when he began his travels.
Yet some things soon occurr'd not quite so pleasant;
He had observ'd, that an unfeeling peasant,
In silence mounting on a ladder high,
Seiz'd certain pigeons just as they could fly,   180
Who never figur'd more, but in a pie:
That was but awkward; then, his lordship's son
Heard from the groom, that 'twould be famous fun
To try on others his unpractis'd gun;
Their fall, the rattling shot, his nerves perplex'd;   185
He thought perhaps it might be his turn next.
It has been seen ere now, that much elated,
To be by some great man caress'd and fêted,
A youth of humble birth, and mind industrious,
Foregoes in evil hour his independence;   190
And, charm'd to wait upon his friend illustrious,
Gives up his time to flatt'ry and attendance.
His patron, smiling at his folly, lets him—
Some newer whim succeeds, and he forgets him.
So far'd our bird; his new friend's vacant stare   195
Told him he scarce remember'd he was there;
And, when he talk'd of living more securely,
This very dear friend, yawning, answer'd, "Surely!
You are quite right to do what's most expedient,
So, au revoir!—Good bye! Your most obedient."   200
Allies in prosp'rous fortune thus he prov'd,
And left them, unregretting, unbelov'd;
Yet much his self-love suffer'd by the shock,
And now, his quiet cabin in the rock,

Line 200. **Your most obedient**: with "servant," the formulaic closing to a letter.

The faithful partner of his ev'ry care,　　　　　　　205
And all the blessings he abandon'd there,
Rush'd on his sick'ning heart; he felt it yearn,
But pride and shame prevented his return;
So wand'ring farther—at the close of day
To the high woods he pensive wing'd his way;　　　210
But new distress at ev'ry turn he found—
Struck by a hawk, and stunn'd upon the ground,
He once by miracle escap'd; then fled
From a wild cat, and hid his trembling head
Beneath a dock; recov'ring, on the wind　　　　　215
He rose once more, and left his fears behind;
And, as above the clouds he soar'd, the light
Fell on an inland rock; the radiance bright
Show'd him his long deserted place of rest,
And thitherward he flew; his throbbing breast　　　220
Dwelt on his mate, so gentle, and so wrong'd,
And on his mem'ry throng'd
The happiness he once at home had known;
Then to forgive him earnest to engage her,
And for his errours eager to atone,　　　　　　　225
Onward he went; but ah! not yet had flown
Fate's sharpest arrow: to decide a wager,
Two sportsmen shot at our deserter; down
The wind swift wheeling, struggling, still he fell,
Close to the margin of the stream, that flow'd　　　230
Beneath the foot of his regretted cell,
And the fresh grass was spotted with his blood;
To his dear home he turn'd his languid view,
Deplor'd his folly, while he look'd his last,
And sigh'd a long adieu!　　　　　　　　　　　235
Thither to sip the brook, his nestlings, led
By their still pensive mother, came;

Line 215. **dock**: a coarse weed.　　Line 233. **languid**: faint, enfeebled.

He saw; and murm'ring forth her dear lov'd name,
Implor'd her pity, and with short'ning breath,
Besought her to forgive him ere his death[.]—   240
And now, how hard in metre to relate
The tears and tender pity of his mate!
Or with what gen'rous zeal his faithful moitie
Taught her now feather'd young, with duteous piety,
To aid her, on their mutual wings to bear,   245
With storklike care,
Their suff'ring parent to the rock above;
There, by the best physician, Love,
His wounds were heal'd[.]—His wand'rings at an end,
And sober'd quite, the husband, and the friend,   250
In proof of reformation and contrition,
Gave to his race this prudent admonition;
Advice, which this, our fabling muse, presumes,
May benefit the *biped without plumes:*
"If of domestic peace you are possess'd,   255
Learn to believe yourself supremely bless'd;
And, gratefully enjoying your condition,
Frisk not about, on whims and fancies strange,
For, ten to one, you for the worse will change;
And 'tis most wise, to check all vain ambition[.]—   260
By such aspiring pride the angels fell;
So love your wife, and know when you are well."

Line 243. **moitie:** moiety; other half.

The lark's nest

A fable from Esop

"Trust only to thyself"; the maxim's sound;
For, though life's choicest blessing be a friend,
Friends do not very much abound;
Or, where they happen to be found,
And greatly thou on *friendship* shouldst depend, 5
Thou'lt find it will not bear
Much wear and tear;
Nay! that even kindred, cousin, uncle, brother,
Has each perhaps to mind his own affair;
Attend to thine then; lean not on another. 10
Esop assures us that the maxim's wise;
And by a tale illustrates his advice:

When April's bright and fickle beams
Saw ev'ry feather'd pair
In the green woodlands, or by willowy streams, 15
Busied in matrimonial schemes,
A Lark, amid the dewy air,
Woo'd, and soon won, a fav'rite fair,
And, in a spot by springing rye protected,
Her labour sometimes shar'd; 20
While she, with bents, and wither'd grass collected,
Their humble domicile prepar'd;
Then, by her duty fix'd, the tender mate
Unwearied press'd
Their future progeny beneath her breast, 25
And little slept and little ate,
While her gay lover, with a careless heart,
As is the custom of his sex,
Full little recks

Line 21. **bents**: a stiff grass; sedge.

The coming family; but like a dart   30
From his low homestead with the morning springs;
And far above the floating vapour sings
At such a height
That even the shepherd-lad upon the hill,
Hearing his matin note so shrill,   35
With shaded eyes against the lustre bright
Scarce sees him twinkling in a flood of light.
But hunger, spite of all her perseverance,
Was one day urgent on his patient bride;
The truant made not his appearance,   40
That her fond care might be a while supplied,—
So, because hunger will not be denied,
She leaves her nest reluctant, and in haste
But just allows herself to taste
A dewdrop, and a few small seeds[.]—   45
Ah! how her flutt'ring bosom bleeds,
When the dear cradle she had fondly rear'd
All desolate appear'd!
And ranging wide about the field she saw
A setter huge, whose unrelenting jaw   50
Had crush'd her half-existing young;
Long o'er her ruin'd hopes the mother hung,
And vainly mourn'd,
Ere from the clouds her wanderer return'd:—
Tears justly shed by beauty, who can stand them?   55
He heard her plaintive tale with unfeign'd sorrow,
But, as his motto was, "Nil desperandum,"
Bade her hope better fortune for tomorrow;
Then from the fatal spot afar, they sought
A safer shelter, having bought   60
Experience, which is always rather dear;
And very near

Line 44. **But ... taste:** only allows herself a taste.

Line 57: **Nil desperandum:** "Despair of nothing" (Horace, *Odes,* I.vii.27).

A grassy headland, in a field of wheat,
They fix'd, with cautious care, their second seat[.]—
But this took time; May was already past,   65
The white thorn had her silver blossoms cast,
And there the Nightingale to lovely June
Her last farewell had sung;
No longer reign'd July's intemp'rate noon,
And high in Heaven the reaper's moon   70
A little crescent hung,
Ere from their shells appear'd the plumeless young.
Oh! then with how much tender care
The busy pair
Watch'd and provided for the panting brood!   75
For then the vagrant of the air,
Soar'd not to meet the morning star,
But, never from the nestlings far,
Explor'd each furrow, ev'ry sod for food;
While his more anxious partner tried   80
From hostile eyes the helpless group to hide;
Attempting now with lab'ring bill to guide
The enwreathing bindweed round the nest;
Now joy'd to see the cornflow'r's azure crest
Above it waving, and the cockle grow,   85
Or poppies throw
Their scarlet curtains round;
While the more humble children of the ground,
Freak'd pansies, fumitory, pimpernel,
Circled with arras light the secret cell.—   90
But who against all evils can provide?
Hid, and o'ershadow'd thus, and fortified,
By teasel, and the scabious' thready disk,
Corn-marygold, and thistles, too much risk
The little household still were doom'd to run,   95

Line 90. **arras**: curtain.

For the same ardent sun,
Whose beams had drawn up many an idle flow'r
To fence the lonely bow'r,
Had by his pow'rful heat
Matur'd the wheat;   100
And chang'd of hue, it hung its heavy head,
While ev'ry rustling gale that blew along,
From neighb'ring uplands, brought the rustic song
Of harvest merriment; then full of dread,
Lest, not yet fully fledg'd, her race   105
The reaper's foot might crush, or reaper's dog might trace,
Or village child, too young to reap or bind,
Loit'ring around, her hidden treasure find;
The mother bird was bent
To move them, ere the sickle came more near;   110
And therefore, when for food abroad she went,
(For now her mate again was on the ramble)
She bade her young report what they should hear:
So the next hour they cried, "They'll all assemble,
The farmer's neighbours, with the dawn of light,   115
Therefore, dear mother, let us move tonight."
"Fear not, my loves," said she, "you need not tremble;
Trust me, if only neighbours are in question,
Eat what I bring, and spoil not your digestion
Or sleep, for this." Next day away she flew,   120
And that no neighbour came was very true;
But her returning wings the Larklings knew,
And quiv'ring round her told, their landlord said,
"Why, John! the reaping must not be delay'd,
By peep of day tomorrow we'll begin,   125
Since now so many of our kin
Have promis'd us their help to set about it."
"Still," quoth the bird, "I doubt it;
The corn will stand tomorrow." So it prov'd;
The morning's dawn arriv'd—but never saw   130

Or uncle, cousin, or brother-in-law;
And not a reaphook mov'd!
Then to his son the angry farmer cried,
"Some folks are little known 'till they are tried;
Who would have thought we had so few well-wishers!   135
What! neither neighbour Dawes, nor cousin Fishers,
Nor uncle Betts, nor e'en my brother Delves,
Will lend a hand, to help us get the corn in?
Well then, let you and me, tomorrow morning,
E'en try what we can do with it ourselves."   140
"Nay," quoth the Lark, "'tis time then to be gone:
What a man undertakes himself is done."
Certes, she was a bird of observation;
For very true it is, that none,
Whatever be his station,   145
Lord of a province, tenant of a mead,
Whether he fill a cottage, or a throne,
Or guard a flock, or guide a nation,
Is very likely to succeed,
Who manages affairs by deputation.   150

The swallow

The gorse* is yellow on the heath,
  The banks with speedwell† flowers are gay,
The oaks are budding; and beneath,
The hawthorn soon will bear the wreath,
  The silver wreath of May.   5

---

* gorse. *Ulex Europæus*, Gorse-Furze, called so in many counties of England.

† speedwell. *Veronica chamædrys*. This elegant flower, though not celebrated like the Primrose, Cowslip, and Daisy, is in all its varieties one of the most beautiful of our indigenous plants.

The lark's nest. Line 131. **Or ... or**: Either ... or.

Line 146. **tenant**: sharecropper.   **mead**: meadow.

The welcome guest of settled Spring,
   The Swallow too is come at last;
Just at sun-set, when thrushes sing,
I saw her dash with rapid wing,
   And hail'd her as she pass'd.   10

Come, summer visitant, attach
   To my reed roof your nest of clay,
And let my ear your music catch
Low twitt'ring underneath the thatch
   At the gray dawn of day.   15

As fables tell, an Indian Sage,*
   The Hindostani woods among,
Could in his desert hermitage,
As if 'twere mark'd in written page,
   Translate the wild bird's song.   20

I wish I did his power possess,
   That I might learn, fleet bird, from thee,
What our vain systems only guess,
And know from what wide wilderness
   You came across the sea.   25

I would a little while restrain
   Your rapid wing, that I might hear
Whether on clouds that bring the rain,
You sail'd above the western main,
   The wind your charioteer.   30

---

* There are two or three fables that relate the knowledge acquired by some Indian recluse, of the language of birds.

Line 12. **reed**: thatched.

In Afric, does the sultry gale
    Thro' spicy bower, and palmy grove,
Bear the repeated Cuckoo's tale?
Dwells *there* a time, the wandering Rail
    Or the itinerant Dove?*   35

Were you in Asia? O relate,
    If there your fabled sister's woes
She seem'd in sorrow to narrate;
Or sings she but to celebrate
    Her nuptials with the rose?†   40

I would enquire how journeying long,
    The vast and pathless ocean o'er,
You ply again those pinions strong,
And come to build anew among°
    The scenes you left before;   45

But if, as colder breezes blow,
    Prophetic of the waning year,
You hide, tho' none know when or how,
In the cliff's excavated brow,‡
    And linger torpid here;   50

---

* The Cuckoo, the Rail, and many species of Doves, are all emigrants.

† Alluding to the Ovidian fable of the Metamorphosis of Procne and Philomela into the Swallow and the Nightingale; and to the oriental story of the Loves of the Nightingale and the Rose; which is told with such elegant extravagance in the Botanic Garden.

° Accurate observers have remarked, that an equal number of these birds return every year to build in the places they frequented before; and that each pair set immediately about repairing a particular nest.

‡ Many persons have supported the idea, that the Hirundines linger concealed among rocks and hollows in a torpid state, and that all do not emigrate.

Line 50. **linger torpid**: hibernate.

Thus lost to life, what favouring dream
    Bids you to happier hours awake;
And tells, that dancing in the beam,
The light gnat hovers o'er the stream,
    The May-fly on the lake?   55

Or if, by instinct taught to know
    Approaching dearth of insect food;
To isles and willowy aits you go,*
And crouding on the pliant bough,
    Sink in the dimpling flood: 60

How learn ye, while the cold waves boom
    Your deep and ouzy couch above,
The time when flowers of promise bloom,
And call you from your transient tomb,
    To light, and life, and love?   65

Alas! how little can be known,
    Her sacred veil where Nature draws;
Let baffled Science humbly own,
Her mysteries understood alone,
    By *Him* who gives her laws.   70

---

* Another opinion is, that the Swallows, at the time they disappear, assemble about rivers and ponds, and a number of them settling on the pliant boughs of willow and osier, sink by their weight into the water; at the bottom of which they remain torpid till the ensuing spring. For the foundation of these various theories see White's *History of Selbourne.*

OTHER POEMS

Flora

Remote from scenes, where the o'erwearied mind
Shrinks from the crimes and follies of mankind,
From hostile menace, and offensive boast,
Peace, and her train of home-born pleasures lost;
To Fancy's reign, who would not gladly turn,   5
And lose awhile the miseries they mourn
In sweet oblivion?—Come then Fancy! deign,
Queen of ideal pleasure, once again
To lend thy magic pencil, and to bring
Such lovely forms, as in life's happier Spring   10
On the green margin of my native Wey,
Before mine infant eyes were wont to play,
And with that pencil, teach me to describe
The enchanting Goddess of the flowery tribe,
Whose first prerogative it is to chase   15
The clouds that hang on languid beauty's face;*
And, while advancing Suns, and tepid showers,
Lead on the laughing Spring's delicious hours,
Bid the wan maid the hues of health assume,
Charm with new grace, and blush with fresher bloom,   20

The vision comes!—While slowly melt away
Night's hovering shades before the eastern ray,
Ere yet declines the morning's humid star,
Fair Fancy brings her; in her leafy car
Flora descends, to dress the expecting earth,   25
Awake the germs, and call the buds to birth,

---

* "The spleen is seldom felt where Flora reigns, / The lowering eye, the petulance, the frown, / And sullen sadness, that do shade, distort, / And mar the face of beauty, when no cause / For such immeasurable grief appears, / These Flora banishes." Cowper [*The Task*, I.455–60].

Line 26. **germs**: seeds.

Bid each hybernacle its cell unfold,
And open silken leaves, and eyes of gold!

   Of forest foliage of the firmest shade
Enwoven by magic hands the Car was made,   30
Oak and the ample Plane, without entwin'd,
And Beech and Ash the verdant concave lined;
The Saxifrage,* that snowy flowers emboss,
Supplied the seat; and of the mural Moss
The velvet footstool rose, where lightly rest   35
Her slender feet in Cypripedium drest.
The tufted Rush† that bears a silken crown,
The floating feathers of the Thistle's° down,
In tender hues of rainbow lustre dyed,
The airy texture of her robe supplied;   40
And wild Convolvulas,‡ yet half unblown,
Form'd with their wreathing buds her simple zone;
Some wandering tresses of her radiant hair
Luxuriant floated on the enamour'd air,
The rest were by the Scandix'• points confin'd,   45
And graced, a shining knot, her hair behind—
While as a sceptre of supreme command,
She waved the Anthoxanthum⁣ⁱ in her hand.

---

* Saxifrage. *Saxifraga hypnoides*, Moss Saxifrage, commonly called Ladies' cushion.

† Rush. *Eriophorum angustifolium.* ° Thistle. *Carduus.*

‡ Convolvulas. *Convolvulus arvensis*, a remarkably pretty plant, but no favourite with the husbandman. [The morning glory is a flowering vine of quick growth and an almost ineradicable root system.]

• Scandix. *Scandix pectum*, Venus's comb, or Shepherd's needle.

⁣ⁱ Anthoxanthum. *Anthoxanthum odoratum*, Vernal Meadow Grass. It is to this grass that hay owes its fine odour.

Line 27. **hybernacle:** hibernacle; winter covering of a bud.

Line 31. **ample Plane:** European cousin to the sycamore.

Line 34. **mural Moss:** moss growing on a wall.   Line 42. **zone:** belt, cincture.

Around the Goddess, as the flies that play
In countless myriads in the western ray,   50
The Sylphs innumerous throng, whose magic powers
Guard the soft buds, and nurse the infant flowers,
Round the sustaining stems weak tendrils bind,
And save the Pollen from dispersing wind,
From Suns too ardent shade their transient hues,   55
And catch in odorous cups translucent dews.
The ruder tasks of others are, to chase
From vegetable life the Insect race,
Breath the polluting thread the Spider weaves,
And brush the Aphis* from the unfolding leaves.   60

For conquest arm'd the pigmy warriors wield
The thorny lance, and spread the hollow shield
Of Lichen† tough; or bear, as silver bright,
Lunaria's° pearly circlet, firm and light.
On the helm'd head the crimson Foxglove‡ glows,   65
Or Scutellaria• guards the martial brows,
While the Leontodon�‍ its plumage rears,
And o'er the casque in waving grace appears;
With stern undaunted eye, one warlike Chief

---

* Aphis. *Aphis,* or *Aphides.* These are the "myriads brushed from Russian wilds;" the blights, cankers, lice, or vermin, to use common phrases, that so often disfigure and destroy the fairest vegetable productions. [Smith refers to Thomson's *Seasons,* "Spring," lines 114–22.]

† Lichen. *Lichen.* Of these many have the forms of shields, when in fructification.

° Lunaria. *Lunaria annua,* Moon wort, usually called Honesty.

‡ Foxglove. *Digitalis purpurea,* common Fox-glove.

• Scutellaria. *Scutellaria galericulata,* small Skull-cap.

�‍ Leontodon. *Leontodon officinalis,* Common Dent-de-lion.

Line 51. **Sylphs:** In *Conversations Introducing Poetry* (II, 166–67) Mrs. Talbot cites the precedent of William Hayley's *Triumphs of Temper* and Erasmus Darwin's *Botanic Garden,* which popularized such fairy-like creatures in late eighteenth-century poetry.

Line 55. **ardent:** fiercely flaming.

Grasps the tall club from Arum's* blood-dropp'd leaf,   70
This with the Burdock's† hooks annoys his foes,
The purple Thorn, *that* borrows from the Rose.
In honeyed nectaries couched, some drive away
The forked insidious Earwig from his prey,
Fearless the scaled Libellula° assail,   75
Dart their keen lances at the encroaching Snail,
Arrest the winged Ant,‡ on pinions light,
And strike the headlong Beetle• in his flight.

Nor less assiduous round their lovely Queen,
The lighter forms of female Fays are seen;   80
Rich was the purple vest Floscella wore,
Spun of the tufts the Tradescantia¶ bore,
The Cistus' § flowers minute her temples graced,
And threads of Yucca¤ bound her slender waist.

From the wild Bee,** whose wondrous labour weaves,   85
In artful folds the Rose's fragrant leaves,

---

* Arum. *Arum maculatum,* vulgarly Cuckoo pint, or Lords and Ladies.

† Burdock's. *Arctium lappa.*

° Libellula. The Dragonfly, or as it is called in the southern countries, the Horse-stinger, though it preys only on other insects. Several sorts of these are seen about water, but its introduction here is a poetical licence, as it does not feed on or injure flowers.

‡ Ant. *Formica.* In one state of their existence the male Ants have wings.

• Beetle. *Scarabeus.*

¶ Tradescantia. The silk-like tuft within the plant called *Tradescantia* appears to the eye composed of very fine filaments; but on examining one of these small silky threads through a microscope, it looks like a string of amethysts.

§ Cistus. *Cistus helianthemum,* Dwarf Cistus.

¤ Yucca. *Yucca,* Thready Yucca, an aloe, I believe.

** the wild Bee. *Apis centuncularis.* This insect weaves or rather cements rose leaves together to form its cell.

Line 81. **Floscella**: in *Conversations Introducing Poetry* Mrs. Talbot explains these fanciful creatures: "The attendant nymphs, Floscella, Petalla, Nectarynia, and Calyxa, you will understand are named after the parts of flowers" (II, 181).

Was borrow'd fair Petalla's light cymarre;
And the Hypericum,* with spangling star,
O'er her fair locks its bloom minute enwreathed;
Then, while voluptuous odours round her breathed,   90
Came Nectarynia; as the arrowy rays
Of lambent fire round pictured Seraphs blaze,
So did the Passiflora's† radii shed
Cerulean glory o'er the Sylphid's head,
While round her form the pliant tendrils twined,   95
And clasp'd the scarf that floated on the wind.

More grave, the para-nymph Calyxa drest;
A brown transparent spatha° formed her vest.
The silver scales that bound her raven hair,
Xeranthemum's‡ unfading calyx bear;   100
And a light sash of spiral Ophrys• press'd
Her filmy tunic, on her tender breast.

But where shall images or words be found
To paint the fair ethereal forms, that round
The Queen of flowers attended? and the while   105
Basked in her eyes, and wanton'd in her smile.

Now towards the earth the gay procession bends,
Lo! from the buoyant air, the Car descends;

---

* Hypericum. An elegant shrub, of which Cowper thus speaks: "Hypericum all bloom, so thick a swarm / Of flowers like flies clothing her slender rods / That scarce a leaf appears" [*The Task*, VI.165–67]. It seems admirably adapted to a fairy garland.

† Passiflora. *Passiflora cerulea*, the Passion flower.

° spatha. The sheath from which many flowers spring such as the Narcissus, &c.

‡ Xeranthemum. The scales of one species of the *Xeranthemum* are particularly elegant.

• Ophrys. *Ophrys spiralis*, Spiral Ophrys, Ladies traces.
The following lines describing well known flowers, notes would be superfluous.

Line 87. **cymarre:** diaphanous chemise.

Line 100. **calyx:** the outermost part of a flower, its cup.

Anticipating then the various year,
Flowers of all hues and every month appear,   110
From every swelling bulb its blossoms rise;
Here blow the Hyacinths of loveliest dyes,
Breathing of heaven; and there her royal brows
Begemmed with pearl, the Crown Imperial shews;
Peeps the blue Gentian from the softning ground,   115
Jonquils and Violets shed their odours round;
High rears the Honeysuck his scallop'd horn;
A snow of blossoms whiten on the Thorn.
Here, like the fatal fruit to Paris given,
That spread fell feuds throughout the fabled Heaven,   120
The yellow Rose her golden globe displays;
There, lovelier still, among their spiny sprays
Her blushing Rivals glow with brighter dyes,
Than paints the Summer Sun, on western skies;
And the scarce ting'd, and paler Rose unveil   125
Their modest beauties to the sighing gale.

      Thro' the deep woodland's wild uncultured scene,
Spreads the soft influence of the floral Queen.
A beauteous pyramid, the Chesnut* rears,
Its crimson tassels on the Larch† appears;   130
The Fir,° dark native of the sullen North,
Owns her soft sway; and slowly springing forth
On the rough Oak‡ are buds minute unfurl'd,
Whose giant produce may command the World!
Each forest thicket feels the balmy air,   135

---

* Chesnut. *Hippocastanum,* Horse chesnut.   † Larch. *Pinus lariæ.*
° Fir. *Pinus sylvestris,* Scotch Fir.   ‡ Oak. *Quercus rober.*

Line 134. **giant ... World**: the timber used to build England's navy.

And plants that love the shade are blowing there,
Rude rocks with Filices and Bryum smile,
And wastes are gay with Thyme and Chamomile.

    Ah! yet prolong the dear delicious dream,
And trace her power along the mountain stream.   140
See! from its rude and rocky source, o'erhung
With female Fern, and glossy Adder's-tongue,*
Slowly it wells, in pure and crystal drops,
And steals soft-gliding thro' the upland copse;
Then murmuring on, along the willowy sides,   145
The Reed-bird whispers, and the Halcyon hides;†
While among Sallows pale, and birchen bowers,
Embarks in Fancy's eye the Queen of flowers[.]—

    O'er her light skiff, of woven bull-rush made,
The water Lily° lends a polish'd shade,   150
While Galium‡ there of pale and silver hue,
And Epilobiums• on the banks that grew,
Form her soft couch; and as the Sylphs divide,
With pliant arms, the still encreasing tide,
A thousand leaves along the stream unfold;   155
Amid its waving swords, in flaming gold
The Iris towers; and here the Arrowhead,¶
And water Crowfoot,§ more profusely spread,

---

* Female fern. *Polypodium, silix femina,* Adder's-tongue. *Asplenium Scolopendrium,* Hart's tongue, more usually called Adder's tongue.

† Reed-bird. *Motacilla salicaria,* the reed Sparrow, or willow Wren. A bird that in a low and sweet note imitates several others, and sings all night. Halcyon. *Alcedo ispida,* The King fisher, or Halcyon, one of the most beautiful of English birds.

° Water lily. *Nymphæa alba.*   ‡ Galium. *Galium palustre,* White Lady's bed straw.

• Epilobiums. Various species of Willow herbs.

¶ Iris. *Iris palustris,* common Flag, or yellow Iris. Arrowhead. *Sagittaria sagittifolia.*

§ Crowfoot. *Ranunculus aquaticus,* white water Crowfoot.

Line 136. **blowing**: in blossom.   Line 147. **Sallows pale**: a kind of willow.

Spangle the quiet current; higher there,
As conscious of her claims, in beauty rare,   160
Her rosy umbels rears the flow'ring Rush,*
While with reflected charms the waters blush.

   The Naiad now the Year's fair Goddess leads,
Thro' richer pastures, and more level meads,
Down to the Sea; where even the briny sands   165
Their product offer to her glowing hands;
For there, by Sea-dews nurs'd, and airs marine,
The Chelidonium† blows; in glaucous green,
Each refluent tide the thorn'd Eryngium° laves
And its pale leaves seem tinctured by the waves;   170
And half way up the clift, whose rugged brow
Hangs o'er the ever[-]toiling Surge below,
Springs the light Tamarisk[.]‡—The summit bare
Is tufted by the Statice;* and there,
Crush'd by the fisher, as he stands to mark   175
Some distant signal, or approaching bark,
The Saltwort's⁋ starry stalks are thickly sown,
Like humble worth, unheeded and unknown!—

---

* Rush. *Butomus umbellatus*, the flow'ring Rush, or water Gladiole, the only native of England of the class *Enneandria hexagynia*.

† Chelidonium. *Chelidonium glaucium*, the horned or sea Poppy.

° Eryngium. *Eryngium maritimum*, Sea Holly.

‡ Tamarisk. *Tamarix gallica*. This elegant plant is not very uncommon on cliffs in the West of England, and was in 1800 to be found on an high rock to the Eastward of the town of Hastings, in Sussex.

• Statice. *Statice armeria*. Sea Pink, Sea Lavender, commonly called Thrift, is frequently used for borders of flower beds. It covers some of the most sterile cliffs.

⁋ Saltwort. *Salsola kali*. This plant when burnt affords a fossile alkali, and is used in the manufacture of glass. The best is brought from the Mediterranean, and forms a considerable article of commerce. It is very frequent on the cliffs on the Sussex coast.

Line 163. **Naiad:** A nymph of the stream escorts Flora to the sea.

Line 168. **blows:** blooms.

From depths where Corals spring from crystal caves,
And break with scarlet branch the eddying waves,   180
Where Algæ* stream, as change the flowing tides,
And where half flower, half fish, the Polyp† hides,
And long tenacious bands of Sea-lace twine
Round palm-shaped leaves empearl'd with Coralline,°
Enamour'd Fancy now the Sea-maids calls,   185
And from their grottos dim, and shell-paved halls,
Charm'd by her voice, the shining train emerge,
And buoyant float above the circling surge[:]
Green Byssus,‡ waving in the sea born gales,
Form'd their thin mantles, and transparent veils[;]   190
Panier'd• in shells, or bound with silver strings
Of silken Pinna,❡ each her trophy brings
Of plants, from rocks and caverns sub-marine,
With leathery branch, and bladder'd buds between;
There its dark folds the pucker'd Laver spread   195
With trees in miniature of various red;
There flag-shaped Olive leaves depending hung,
And fairy fans from glossy pebbles sprung:

---

* Algæ. Sea weeds of many sorts. Sea Lace, line 183, is one of them. *Algae, Fuci* and *Conferva,* include, I believe, all sea plants.

† Polyp. The Polypus, or sea Anemone.

° Corraline. Coralline is, if I do not misunderstand the only book I have to consult, a shelly substance, the work of sea insects, adhering to stones and to sea weeds.

‡ Green Byssus. *Flos aquæ*, Paper Byssus; a semi-transparent substance floating on the waves.

• Panier'd: Panier'd is not perhaps a word correctly English, but it must here be forgiven me. [Indeed, the *Oxford English Dictionary* cites this usage as a verb form the only one in English after the sixteenth century. A pannier was a frame, usually made of whalebone or wire, which extended a lady's gown at the hips, the mode of high fashion in the late eighteenth century.]

❡ Pinna. The Pinna, or Sea-Wing, is contained in a two-valved shell. It consists of fine long silk-like fibres[.]—The Pinna on the coast of Provence and Italy, is called the silk-worm of the sea. Stockings and gloves of exquisite fineness have been made of it. See note 27th to the Œconomy of Vegetation [Erasmus Darwin, *The Economy of Vegetation*, Additional Notes, Note 27—Shell Fish, in *Poetical Works* (London: Johnson, 1806), I, 369–70]. The subsequent lines attempt a description of sea plants, without any correct classification.

Then her terrestial train the Nereids meet,
And lay their spoils saline at Flora's feet.   200

   O! fairest of the fabled forms that stream,
Dress'd by wild Fancy, thro' the Poet's dream,
Still may thy attributes, of leaves and flowers,
Thy gardens rich, and shrub-o'ershadowed bowers,
And yellow meads, with Spring's first honors bright,   205
The child's gay heart, and frolic step invite;
And, while the careless wanderer explores
The umbrageous forest, or the rugged shores,
Climbs the green down, or roams the broom-clad waste,
May *Truth* and *Nature* form his future taste.   210
Goddess! on Youth's bless'd hours thy gifts bestow,
Bind the fair wreath on Virgin Beauty's brow,
And still may Fancy's brightest flowers be wove
Round the gold chains of Hymeneal love;
But most for those, by Sorrow's hands oppress'd,   215
May thy beds blossom, and thy wilds be drest;
And where, by Fortune, and the World, forgot,
The Mourner droops in some sequester'd spot,
("Sad luxury to vulgar minds unknown")
O'er blighted happiness, for ever gone,   220
Yet the dear image seeks not to forget,
But woos his grief, and cherishes regret,
Loving, with fond and lingering pain, to mourn
O'er joys and hopes that never will return,

Line 199. **Nereids**: sea nymphs.

Line 209. **down**: high grassland.   **broom-clad**: the barren, chalky soil supports broom, a shrub with yellow flowers.

Line 214. **Hymeneal**: marital.

Line 219. **Sad luxury … unknown**: A likely reference to a long account of blighted love in an exceptional garden in the fourth book of William Mason's *English Garden*, which concludes with an admonition to those skeptical of the mourners: " … let the scorners learn / There is a solemn luxury in grief / Which they shall never taste, well known to those, / And only those, in solitude's deep gloom / Who heave the sigh sincerely."

Thou, visionary Power, may'st bid him view   225
Forms not less lovely—and as transient too,
And, while they soothe the wearied Pilgrim's eyes,
Afford an antepast of Paradise.

Studies by the sea

Ah! wherefore do the incurious say,
That this stupendous Ocean wide
No change presents from day to day,
Save only the alternate tide,
Or save when gales of Summer glide   5
Across the lightly crisped wave;
Or, when against the cliff's rough side
As equinoctial tempests rave
It wildly bursts; o'erwhelms the deluged strand,
Tears down its bounds, and desolates the land?   10

He who with more enquiring eyes
Doth this extensive scene survey,
Beholds innumerous changes rise,
As various winds its surface sway;
Now o'er its heaving bosom play   15
Small sparkling waves of silver gleam,
And as they lightly glide away,
Illume with fluctuating beam
The deepening surge; green as the dewy corn
That undulates in April's breezy morn.   20

The far off waters then assume
A glowing amethystine shade,

Flora. Line 228. **antepast**: foretaste.

That changing like the Paon's* plume,
Seems in celestial blue to fade;
Or paler colder hues of lead,   25
As lurid vapours float on high,
Along the ruffling billows spread,
While darkly lours the threatening sky;
And the small scatter'd barks with outspread shrouds
Catch the long gleams, that fall between the clouds.   30

Then Day's bright star with blunted rays
Seems struggling thro' the sea-fog pale,
And doubtful in the heavy haze
Is dimly seen the nearing sail;
Till from the land a fresher gale   35
Disperses the white mist, and clear,
As melts away the gauzy veil,
The sun-reflecting waves appear;
So brighter genuine Virtue seems to rise
From Envy's dark invidious calumnies.   40

What glories on the Sun attend
When the full tides of evening flow,
Where in still changing beauty, blend,
With amber light the opal's glow,
While in the East the diamond bow   45
Rises in virgin lustre bright,
And from the horizon seems to throw
A partial line of trembling light
To the hush'd shore; and all the tranquil deep
Beneath the modest Moon is sooth'd to sleep.   50

---

* Paon. The Paon, for peacock, has also the authority of old writers.

Line 29. **outspread shrouds**: the ship's rigging.
Line 31. **Day's bright star**: the sun.   Line 45. **diamond bow**: crescent moon.

Forgotten then the thundering break
Of waves, that in the tempest rise,
The falling cliff, the shatter'd wreck,
The howling blast, the sufferers' cries;
For soft the breeze of evening sighs,   55
And murmuring, seems in Fancy's ear*
To whisper fairy lullabies
That tributary waters bear,
From precipices, dark with piny woods
And inland rocks, and heathy solitudes.   60

The vast encircling seas within,
What endless swarms of creatures hide
Of burnish'd scale and spiny fin!
These, providential instincts guide,
And bid them know the annual tide,   65
When, from unfathom'd waves that swell,[†]
Beyond Fuego's stormy side,
They come, to cheer the tribes that dwell
In Boreal climes; and through his half year's night
Give to the Lapland savage food and light.   70

---

* Whoever has listened on a still Summer or Autumnal evening, to the murmurs of the small waves, just breaking on the shingles, and remarked the low sounds re-echoed by the distant rocks, will understand this.

† The course of those wonderful swarms of fishes that take their annual journey is, I believe, less understood than the emigration of birds. I suppose them, without having any particular ground for my conjecture, to begin their voyage from beyond the extreme point of the Southern continent of America. Many of the Northern nations live almost entirely on fish. Their light, during the long night of an arctic winter, is supplied by the oil of marine animals.

Line 67. **Fuego's stormy side:** Tierra del Fuego, the tip of South America, lies on Cape Horn, meeting place of the Atlantic and Pacific Oceans and notorious for its stormy conditions.

Line 69. **Boreal climes:** arctic regions.

From cliffs that pierce the northern sky,
Where eagles rear their sanguine brood,
With long awaiting patient eye
Baffled by many a sailing cloud,
The Highland native marks the flood,*   75
Till bright the quickening billows roll,
And hosts of Sea-birds clamouring loud
Track with wild wing the welcome shoal,
Swift o'er the animated current sweep,
And bear their silver captives from the deep.   80

Sons of the North! your streamy vales
With no rich sheaves rejoice and sing,
Her flowery robe no fruit conceals,
Tho' sweetly smile your tardy Spring;
Yet every mountain clothed with ling†   85
Doth from its purple brow survey
Your busy sails, that ceaseless bring
To the broad frith and sheltering bay,
Riches by Heaven's parental power supplied,
The harvest of the far embracing tide.   90

And where those fractur'd mountains lift
O'er the blue wave their towering crest,
Each salient ledge, and hollow cleft,
To Sea-fowl give a rugged nest.
But, with instinctive love is drest   95

---

* In the countries where the produce of the sea is so necessary to human life, the arrival of shoals of fish is most eagerly waited for by the hardy inhabitant. Thrown on the summit of an high clift, overlooking the sea, the native watches for the approach of the expected good, and sees with pleasure the numerous sea birds, who, by an instinct superior to his own, perceive it at a far greater distance, and follow to take their share of the swarming multitude.

† Ling, a name given in many parts of England to the *Erica vulgaris*—Common Heath.

Line 72. **sanguine**: carnivorous.   Line 88. **frith**: firth, a narrow inlet from the ocean.

The Eider's downy cradle;* where
The mother bird, her glossy breast
Devotes; and with maternal care
And plumeless bosom, stems the toiling Seas
That foam round the tempestuous Orcades.   100

From heights whence shuddering sense recoils,
And cloud-capped headlands, steep and bare,
Sons of the North! your venturous toils
Collect your poor and scanty fare.
Urged by imperious want, you dare   105
Scale the loose cliff, where Gannets† hide,
Or scarce suspended, in the air
Hang perilous;° and thus provide
The soft voluptuous couch, which not secures
To Luxury's pamper'd minions, sleep like yours.   110

    Revolving still, the waves that now
Just ripple on the level shore,
Have borne, perchance, the Indian's proa,
Or half congeal'd, 'mid ice-rocks hoar

---

* *Anas mollissima.* While many sea-birds deposit their eggs on the bare rocks, the eider Duck lines her nest most carefully with the feathers from her own breast, which are particularly fine and light: the nest is robbed, and she a second time unplumes herself for the accommodation of her young. If the lining be again taken away, the drake lends his breast feathers; but if, after that, their unreasonable persecutors deprive it of its lining, they abandon the nest in despair, the master of the domicile wisely judging, that any farther sacrifice would be useless.

† *Pelicanus Bassanus*, the Gannet, builds on the highest rocks.

° Suspended by a slight rope, the adventurous native of the north of Scotland is let down from the highest cliffs that hang over the sea, while with little or no support, he collects the eggs of the sea fowl, in a basket tied round his waist. The feathers also of these birds gathered from the rocks, are a great object to these poor industrious people.

Line 100. **Orcades:** the Orkney Islands, off the northeast coast of Scotland; pronounced as three syllables.

Line 114. **hoar:** white; i.e. icebergs.

Raved to the Walruss'* hollow roar,   115
Or have by currents swift convey'd†
To the cold coast of Labrador
The relics of the Tropic shade;
And to the wondering Esquimeaux have shewn
Leaves of strange shape, and fruits unlike their own.   120

　　No more then let the incurious say,
No change this World of Water shews,
But as the tides the Moon obey,
Or tempests rave, or calms repose.
Shew them its bounteous breast bestows   125
On myriads life: and bid them see
In every wave that circling flows,
Beauty, and use, and harmony—
Works of the Power supreme who poured the flood
Round the green peopled earth, and call'd it good.   130

---

* *Trichecus rosmarus.* The Walruss, or Morse, a creature of the seal kind, now said to be no longer found on the coast of Scotland, but still inhabiting other northern countries. They are sometimes eighteen or twenty feet long, and roar like bulls.

† Gulph currents are supposed to throw the remains of fruits of the tropical regions on the most northern coast of America, and it is asserted that the same fruits are also found on the coast of Norway. See *Les Etudes de la Nature* [(1784), by Jacques Henri Bernardin de Saint-Pierre].

The horologe* of the fields
Addressed to a young lady, on seeing
at the house of an acquaintance a
magnificent French timepiece

For her who owns this splendid toy,
    Where use with elegance unites,
Still may its index point to joy,
    And moments wing'd with new delights.

Sweet may resound each silver bell,—   5
    And never quick returning chime,
Seem in reproving notes to tell,
    Of hours mispent, and murder'd time.

Tho' Fortune, Emily, deny
    To us these splendid works of art,   10
The woods, the lawns, the heaths supply
    Lessons from Nature to the heart.

In every copse, and shelter'd dell,
    Unveil'd to the observant eye,
Are faithful monitors, who tell   15
    How pass the hours and seasons by.

---

* The sleep of plants has been frequently the subject of inquiry and admiration. "Vigiliæ Plantarum. Botanists, under this term, comprehend the precise time of the day in which the flowers of different plants open, expand, and shut. As all plants do not flower in the same season, or month; in like manner, those which flower the same day in the same place, do not open and shut precisely at the same hour. Some open in the morning, as the lipped flowers, and compound flowers with flat spreading petals; others at noon, as the mallows; and a third set in the evening, or after sun-set, as some Geraniums and Opuntias. The hour of shutting is equally determined. Of those which open in the morning, some shut soon after, while others remain expanded till night." For further information on this subject, see Milne's *Botanical Dictionary* [Colin Milne: *Botanical Dictionary: or Elements of Systematic and Philosophical Botany* (1770, 1778)].

The green robed children of the Spring
   Will mark the periods as they pass,
Mingle with leaves Time's feather'd wing,
   And bind with flowers his silent glass.   20

Mark where transparent waters glide,
   Soft flowing o'er their tranquil bed;
There, cradled on the dimpling tide,
   Nymphæa* rests her lovely head.

But conscious of the earliest beam,   25
   She rises from her humid rest,
And sees reflected in the stream
   The virgin whiteness of her breast.

Till the bright daystar to the west
   Declines, in the Ocean's surge to lave,   30
Then folded in her modest vest,
   She slumbers on the rocking wave.

See Hieracium's various tribe,†
   Of plumy seed and radiate flowers,
The course of Time their blooms describe,   35
   And wake or sleep appointed hours.

---

* *Nymphæa alba.* The flower of this beautiful aquatic opens about seven in the morning, closes about four in the afternoon, and then lies down upon the surface of the water. *Linnæus.*

† All I believe of the solar tribe; the two mentioned by [William] Withering [*A Botanical Arrangement of British Plants*, 3 vols. (1787–92)] are the sabaudum and murorum. The first opens at seven, and shuts between one and two; the other expands at six in the morning, and closes between two and three in the afternoon.

Line 29. **daystar:** sun.

Broad o'er its imbricated cup
 The Goatsbeard spreads its golden rays,*
But shuts its cautious petals up,
 Retreating from the noon-tide blaze: 40

Pale as a pensive cloister'd nun
 The Bethlem-star,† her face unveils,
When o'er the mountain peers the Sun,
 But shades it from the vesper gales.

Among the loose and arid sands   45
 The humble Arenaria° creeps;
Slowly the purple star expands,
 But soon within its calyx sleeps.

And those small bells‡ so lightly ray'd
 With young Aurora's rosy hue,   50
Are to the noon-tide Sun display'd,
 But shut their plaits against the dew.

On upland slopes the shepherds mark
 The hour, when as the dial true,

---

* Goatsbeard. *Tragopogon pratense.* A most unfortunate name for poetry. The yellow sort, which is the most common, opens about three in the morning, and closes between nine and ten. *Withering.*

† Bethlem-star. *Ornithogalum umbellatum.*

° Arenaria. *Arenaria marina.* Flowers open at nine o'clock in the morning, and shut between two and three in the afternoon. [John] Lightfoot's *Flora Scotica* [*: or, a Systematic Arrangement, in the Linnean method, of the native plants of Scotland and the Hebrides,* 2 vols.(London: 1777; 1789)].

‡ *Convolvulus arvensis.* The flowers close in the evening.

Line 37. **imbricated cup**: formed by overlapping petals.
Line 48. **calyx**: outer covering, husk.
Line 50. **Aurora's rosy hue**: first dawn. Line 52. **plaits**: pleats, foldings.

Cichorium* to the towering Lark,   55
    Lifts her soft eyes, serenely blue.

And thou "Wee crimson tipped flower,"†
    Gatherest thy fringed mantle round
Thy bosom, at the closing hour,
    When night drops bathe the turfy ground.   60

Unlike Silene,° who declines
    The garish noontide's blazing light;
But when the evening crescent shines
    Gives all her sweetness to the night.

Thus in each flower and simple bell,   65
    That in our path untrodden lie,
Are sweet remembrancers who tell
    How fast the winged moments fly.

Time will steal on with ceaseless pace,
    Yet lose we not the fleeting hours,   70
Who still their fairy footsteps trace,
    As light they dance among the flowers.

---

* Cichorium. *Cichorium intybus,* Wild Succory, Cichory, or Endive. The flowers open at
eight o'clock in the morning, and close at four in the afternoon. *Withering.*

† Quoted from Burn[s]'s address to the mountain daisy ["Wee, modest, crimson-tipped
flow'r," line 1]. The flowers close at night.

° Silene. *Silene noctiflora.* "Flowers opening in the night, sweet-scented in the summer, not
so in the autumn." *Withering.*

Saint Monica

Among deep woods is the dismantled scite
Of an old Abbey, where the chaunted rite,
By twice ten brethren of the monkish cowl,
Was duly sung; and requiems for the soul
Of the first founder: For the lordly chief,   5
Who flourish'd paramount of many a fief,
Left here a stipend yearly paid, that they,
The pious monks, for his repose might say
Mass and orisons to Saint Monica.

Beneath the falling archway overgrown   10
With briars, a bench remains, a single stone,
Where sat the indigent, to wait the dole
Given at the buttery; that the baron's soul
The poor might intercede for; there would rest,
Known by his hat of straw with cockles drest,   15
And staff and humble weed of watchet gray,
The wandering pilgrim; who came there to pray
The intercession of Saint Monica.

Stern Reformation and the lapse of years
Have reft the windows, and no more appears   20
Abbot or martyr on the glass anneal'd;
And half the falling cloisters are conceal'd
By ash and elder: the refectory wall

Line 1. **scite**: site.

Line 15. **cockles**: A hat with a cockle-shell attached to it signified that the pilgrim had vis-
ited the shrine of St. James of Campostella in Spain.

Line 16. **weed**: garment. **watchet**: an obscure, archaic word, denoting a light blue color;
hence it could designate the hue of the garment as blue-gray or be meant mistakenly to sig-
nify a kind of rough cloth.

Line 19. **Reformation**: When Henry VIII broke with Rome, sensible of the political power
in ecclesiastical hands, he dismantled, and in many cases sacked, the abbeys.

Line 21. **anneal'd**: stained.

Oft in the storm of night is heard to fall,
When, wearied by the labours of the day,   25
The half awaken'd cotters, starting say,
"It is the ruins of Saint Monica."

Now with approaching rain is heard the rill,
Just trickling thro' a deep and hollow gill*
By osiers, and the alder's crowding bush,   30
Reeds, and dwarf elder, and the pithy rush,
Choak'd and impeded: to the lower ground
Slowly it creeps; there traces still are found
Of hollow squares, embank'd with beaten clay,
Where brightly glitter'd in the eye of day   35
The peopled waters of Saint Monica.

The chapel pavement, where the name and date,
Or monkish rhyme, had mark'd the graven plate,
With docks and nettles now is overgrown;
And brambles trail above the dead unknown.—   40
Impatient of the heat, the straggling ewe
Tinkles her drowsy bell, as nibbling slow
She picks the grass among the thistles gray,
Whose feather'd seed the light air bears away,
O'er the pale relicks of Saint Monica.   45

Reecho'd by the walls, the owl obscene
Hoots to the night; as thro' the ivy green

---

* Gill is a word understood in many parts of England, and more particularly in the North, to mean an hollow watercourse, or an hollow overshadowed with coppice and brush wood, such as frequently occur in hilly countries. It has the same meaning as Gully, a deep trench in the earth, so frequent in the West Indies, where the tropic rains tear away the earth and make hollows, which in process of time become overgrown with trees, and the resort of monkeys and other animals.

Line 26. **cotters:** peasants.   Line 38. **graven plate:** brass tomb marking.

Whose matted tods* the arch and buttress bind,   50
Sobs in low gusts the melancholy wind:
The Conium† there, her stalks bedropp'd with red,
Rears, with Circea, neighbour of the dead;
Atropa° too, that, as the beldams say,
Shews her black fruit to tempt and to betray,   55
Nods by the mouldering shrine of Monica.

Old tales and legends are not quite forgot.
Still Superstition hovers o'er the spot,
And tells how here, the wan and restless sprite,
By some way-wilder'd peasant seen at night,   60
Gibbers‡ and shrieks, among the ruins drear;
And how the friar's lanthorn will appear
Gleaming among the woods, with fearful ray,
And from the church-yard take its wavering way,
To the dim arches of Saint Monica.   65

The antiquary comes not to explore,
As once, the unrafter'd roof and pathless floor;
For now, no more beneath the vaulted ground
Is crosier, cross, or sculptur'd chalice found,
Nor record telling of the wassail ale,   70
What time the welcome summons to regale,
Given by the matin peal on holiday,

---

* A judicious friend objected to this expression as obscure; but it has the authority of Spencer. "At length within an Ivy tod /There shrouded was the little God." *Shepherd's Calendar.* Ecl[ogue] 3 [March, lines 67–68]. And I think I could quote other poets as having used it.

† Conium. *Conium maculatum.*

° Atropa. *Atropa belladonna* [a poison also called deadly nightshade].

‡ The word Gibber has been also objected to; but besides that it appears to me very expressive, I have for its use the example of Shakspeare: "—the sheeted dead / Did squeal [squeak] and *gibber* in the streets of Rome." *Hamlet* [I.i.106, Q2].

Line 50. **tods**: masses of foliage, like bushes.

The villagers rejoicing to obey,
Feasted, in honour of Saint Monica.

Yet often still at eve, or early morn,   75
Among these ruins shagg'd with fern and thorn,
A pensive stranger from his lonely seat
Observes the rapid martin, threading fleet
The broken arch: or follows with his eye,
The wall-creeper* that hunts the burnish'd fly;   80
Sees the newt† basking in the sunny ray,
Or snail that sinuous winds his shining way,
O'er the time-fretted walls of Monica.

He comes not here, from the sepulchral stone   85
To tear the oblivious pall that Time has thrown,
But meditating, marks the power proceed
From the mapped lichen, to the plumed weed,
From thready mosses to the veined flower,
The silent, slow, but ever active power   90
Of Vegetative Life, that o'er Decay
Weaves her green mantle, when returning May
Dresses the ruins of Saint Monica.

Oh Nature! ever lovely, ever new,
He whom his earliest vows has paid to you   95
Still finds, that life has something to bestow;
And while to dark Forgetfulness they go,
Man, and the works of man; immortal Youth,

---

* wall-creeper. *Certhia muraria.* This bird frequents old towers, castles, and walls, feeding on insects.

† newt. *Lacerta vulgaris.* This reptile in its complete state lives among rubbish and old walls. It is the Wall Newt of Shakspeare, as part of the food of poor Tom: "The wall newt and the water newt, / With rats and mice and such small deer, / Have been Tom's food for many a year."[*King Lear,* III.iv.127–28; 136–37; freely quoted.] And [the newt] is commonly known by the name of Evett or Eft; and from its ugliness is held in abhorrence, and is supposed to be venomous, though perfectly harmless.

Line 88. **mapped:** flat and multicolored, therefore resembling a map.

Unfading Beauty, and eternal Truth,
Your Heaven-indited volume will display,   100
While Art's elaborate monuments decay,
Even as these shatter'd aisles, deserted Monica!

A walk in the shrubbery*

To the cistus† or rock rose, a beautiful
plant, whose flowers expand, and fall
off twice in twenty-four hours

The Florists, who have fondly watch'd,
    Some curious bulb from hour to hour,
And, to ideal charms attach'd,
    Derive their glory from a flower;

Or they, who lose in crouded rooms,   5
    Spring's tepid suns and balmy air,
And value Flora's fairest blooms,
    But in proportion as they're rare;

Feel not the pensive pleasures known
    To him, who, thro' the morning mist,   10
Explores the bowery shrubs new blown,
    A moralizing Botanist.—

---

* The extravagant fondness for the cultivation of those flowers which the art of the gardener can improve, such as Tulips, Auriculas, and Carnations, has excited laughter and contempt; and was, I think, sometimes confounded with the Science of Botany, with which it has little to do. A Florist, however, has very different pursuits and purposes from a Botanist.

† cistus. *Cistus ladaniferus,* Gum cistus. This plant took its trivial name from its having been supposed to produce the ladanum of the shops, and ought to have been changed when the mistake was detected. [Labdanum, used in perfumes and medicines, is in fact an extract from the rockrose or cistus.]

Saint Monica. Line 100. **Heaven-indited volume:** laws of nature written by God.
Line 9. **pensive:** thoughtful.

He marks, with colours how profuse
    Some are design'd to please the eye;
While beauty some combine with use,   15
    In admirable harmony.

The fruit buds, shadow'd red and white,
    Amid young leaves of April hue;
Convey sensations of delight,
    And promise fruits autumnal too: 20

And, while the Thrush his home and food,
    Hails, as the flowering thorns unfold,
And from its trunk of ebon wood,
    Rears Cytisus* its floating gold;

The Lilac, whose tall head discloses   25
    Groups of such bright empurpled shade,
And snow-globes form'd of elfin roses,†
    Seem for exclusive beauty made:

Such too art thou; when light anew
    Above the eastern hill is seen,   30
Thy buds, as fearful of the dew,
    Still wear their sheltering veil of green.

But in the next more genial hour
    Thy tender rose-shaped cups unfold,
And soon appears the perfect flower,   35
    With ruby spots and threads of gold.

---

* Cytisus. *Cytisus laburnum.* This beautiful tree, of which there are many sorts, attains great
perfection in this country. The wood is black, of a fine grain, and takes a polish like Ebony.
The French call it from thence, L'Ebene; the Ebony tree.

† elfin roses. *Viburnum,* commonly called Guelder Rose. A shrub of great beauty, of which
the globular groups are composed of single monopetalous flowers: it is a cultivated variety of
the *Viburnum opulus,* Water-elder of the hedges, sometimes called The Wayfaring Tree.

That short and fleeting hour gone by,
 And even the slightest breath of air,
Scarce heard among thy leaves to sigh,
 Or little bird that flutters there;   40

Shakes off thy petals thin and frail,
 And soon, like half-congealing snow,
The sport of every wandering gale,
 They strew the humid turf below.

Yet tho' thy gauzy bells fall fast,   45
 Long ere appears the evening crescent;
Another bloom succeeds the last,
 As lovely and as evanescent.

Not so the poet's favourite Rose,
 She blooms beyond a second day,   50
And even some later beauty shews—
 Some charm still lingering in decay.

Thus those, who thro' life's path have pass'd,
 A path how seldom strewn with flowers!
May have met Friendships formed to last 55
 Beyond the noonday's golden hours.

While quickly formed, dissolv'd as soon,
 Some warm attachments I have known
Just flourish for an hour at noon,
 But leave no trace when overblown.   60

Minds that form these, with ardent zeal
 Their *new* connexions fondly cherish,
And for a moment keenly feel
 Affection, doomed as soon to perish;

Incapable of Friendship long,   65
    Awake to every new impression,
Old friends, becoming *ci-devant!*
    Are still replaced by a Succession.

Hope. A rondeau

A parody on Lord Strangford's
"Just like love is yonder rose"

Just like Hope is yonder bow,
    That from the center bends so low,
Where bright prismatic colours shew
    How gems of heavenly radiance glow,
            Just like Hope!   5

Yet if, to the illusion new,
    The pilgrim should the arch pursue,
Farther and farther from his view,
    It flies; then melts in chilling dew,
            Just like Hope!   10

Ye fade, ethereal hues! for ever,
While, cold Reason, thy endeavour
Soothes not that sad heart, which never
            Glows with Hope.

Walk in the shrubbery. Line 67. **ci-devant**: lit. heretofore; hence, former.
Hope. Line 1. **bow**: rainbow.

Evening

Oh! soothing hour, when glowing day,
    Low in the western wave declines,
And village murmurs die away,
    And bright the vesper planet shines;

I love to hear the gale of Even   5
    Breathing along the new-leaf'd copse,
And feel the freshening dew of Heaven,
    Fall silently in limpid drops.

For, like a friend's consoling sighs,
    That breeze of night to me appears;   10
And, as soft dew from Pity's eyes,
    Descend those pure celestial tears.

Alas! for those who long have borne,
    Like me, a heart by sorrow riven,
Who, but the plaintive winds, will mourn,   15
    What tears will fall, but those of Heaven?

Line 4. **vesper planet:** the evening star, Venus.

Love and Folly

From the Fables of La Fontaine

"Quand on eut bien considéré
L'interêt du public, celui de la patrie,
Le résultat enfin de la suprême cour
Fut, de condamner la Folie
A servir de guide à l'Amour."*

Love, who now deals to human hearts,
Such ill thrown, yet resistless darts,
 That hapless mortals can't withstand them,
Was once less cruel and perverse,
Nor did he then his shafts disperse,   5
                        So much at random.

It happened, that the thoughtless child
Was rambling thro' a flowery wild,
 Like idle lad in school vacation;
Where sauntering now, and now at rest,   10
Stroll'd Folly, who to Love address'd
                        His conversation.

On trifles he had much to say,
Then laughing he propos'd to play,
 And stake against Love's bow his bauble;†   15

---

* This is called the most elegant of the Fables of La Fontaine, though it is perhaps told with less simplicity than is generally his perfection. But the close is admirable. Book XII, Fable 14, 27–31. [When the public interest and that of the state had been carefully considered, the final sentence of the supreme judge was to condemn Folly to serve as guide to Love.]

† When kings and great men, to divert the tedious hours of those who have nothing to do, kept about them a fool, one who either really was deficient in understanding, or abject enough to pretend to a degree of idiotism for the amusement of his patron; the insignia of the office were, a cap with feathers, or sometimes a cock's head fastened to the top, and with bells round it, while in their hands was carried a short wooden truncheon, on which was rudely carved a human head with asses ears. There are several passages describing this in Johnson's or Stevens' Notes on Shakespeare.

Line 11. **Love:** Cupid.   Line 14. **play:** gamble.

The quiver'd gamester smil'd and won,
But testy Folly soon began
                    To fret and squabble.

Loud and more loud the quarrel grows;
From words the wrangles went to blows,   20
    For Folly's rage is prompt to rise;
Till bleeding Love a martyr stood—
A stroke from Folly's weapon rude,
                    Put out his eyes.

Then wild with anguish, Venus pray'd,   25
For vengence on the idiot's head,
    And begg'd of cloud-compelling Jove,
His swiftest lightening, to destroy,
The mischievous malignant boy
                    That blinded Love.   30

"Folly is immortal," Jove replied,
"But, tho' your prayer must be denied,
    An endless penance is decreed him;
For *Love*, tho' blind, will reign around
The world; but still where-ever found,   35
                    Folly shall lead him."

On the aphorism
"L'Amitié est l'Amour sans ailes."*

Friendship, as some sage poet sings,
Is chasten'd Love, depriv'd of wings,
Without all wish or power to wander;
Less volatile, but not less tender:
Yet says the proverb—"Sly and slow   5
Love creeps, even where he cannot go;"
To clip his pinions then is vain,
His old propensities remain;
And she, who years *beyond* fifteen,
Has counted *twenty,* may have seen   10
How rarely unplum'd Love will stay;
He flies not—but he coolly walks away.

To my lyre

Such as thou art, my faithful Lyre,
For all the great and wise admire,
    Believe me, I would not exchange thee,
Since e'en adversity could never
Thee from my anguish'd bosom sever,   5
    Or time or sorrow e'er estrange thee.

Far from my native fields removed,
From all I valued, all I loved;
    By early sorrows soon beset,

---

* L'Amitié est l'Amour sans ailes: Friendship is love without wings.

Annoy'd and wearied past endurance, 10
With drawbacks, bottomry, insurance,
    With samples drawn, and tare and tret;

With Scrip, and Omnium, and Consols,
With City Feasts and Lord Mayors' Balls,
    Scenes that to me no joy afforded; 15
For all the anxious Sons of Care,
From Bishopsgate to Temple Bar,
    To my young eyes seem'd gross and sordid.

Proud city dames, with loud shrill clacks,
"The wealth of nations on their backs,") 20
    Their clumsy daughters and their nieces,
Good sort of people! and well meaners,
But they could not be my congeners,
    For I was of a different species.

Lines 10–13. These are all terms employed in the West-Indian import business of Smith's father-in-law, terms Smith learned when early in her marriage she agreed (in the place of her husband) to help him with his books and correspondence.

Line 11. **drawbacks**: remitted duty on goods for export. **bottomry**: a loan secured by the value of a ship.

Line 12. **samples drawn**: a commercial term, probably used to indicate compensation for samples given out. **tare and tret**: deductions in gross weight, for the container of goods and incidental refuse, in calculating net weight.

Line 13. **Scrip**: a receipt or certificate of stock shares. **Omnium**: the aggregate value of all components of a loan. **Consols**: Consolidated Annuities, British government securities. These are terms, it appears, often used in tandem: the *Oxford English Dictionary* cites Charles Jenner's comedy, *The Placid Man* of 1760: "Her head was as full with wealth, scrip, omnium, consols, and lord-mayor shews."

Line 14. **City ... Balls**: Gala entertainments frequented by successful businessmen and their families.

Line 17. **Bishopsgate ... Bar**: financial and legal centers of London.   Line 19. **clacks**: chatter.

Line 20. **nations**: Smith alludes with irony to Adam Smith's economic treatise, which was published after the experiences she is recounting, in 1776.

Long were thy gentle accents drown'd,   25
Till from the Bow-bells' detested sound
    I bore thee far, my darling treasure;
And unrepining left for thee
Both calepash and callipee,
    And sought green fields, pure air, and leisure.   30

Who that has heard thy silver tones—
Who that the Muse's influence owns,
    Can at my fond attachment wonder,
That still my heart should own thy power?
Thou—who hast soothed each adverse hour,   35
    So thou and I will never sunder.

In cheerless solitude, bereft
Of youth and health, thou still art left,
    When hope and fortune have deceived me;
Thou, far unlike the summer friend,   40
Did still my falt'ring steps attend,
    And with thy plaintive voice relieved me.

And as the time ere long must come
When I lie silent in the tomb,
    Thou wilt preserve these mournful pages;   45
For gentle minds will love my verse,
And Pity shall my strains rehearse,
    And tell my name to distant ages.

Line 26. **Bow-bells**: The Bow church is located in the central business area of London, the City, where the Smiths lived in the first years of their marriage.

Line 29. **calepash … calipee**: West Indian terms for the dorsal and ventral shells of the tortoise; but, here the prized turtle meat served at City functions.

TEXTUAL NOTES

As mentioned in the Introduction, the base text for Sonnets 1 through 59, inclusive, and for the sequence of poems between the "Ode to despair" and "Verses intended to have been prefixed to the novel of Emmeline" is the ninth edition of *Elegiac Sonnets,* Volume I (London: Cadell and Davies, 1800); Sonnets 60 through 92, and the sequence between "The dead beggar" and "Lydia," derive from the second edition of *Elegiac Sonnets,* Volume II (London: Cadell and Davies, 1800). Textual variants for Volume I are cited from its second edition (*ES²*), 1784; third edition (*ES³*), 1786; fifth edition (*ES⁵*), 1789; sixth edition (*ES⁶*), 1792; eighth edition (*ES⁸*), 1797; and ninth edition (*ES⁹*). Textual variants for Volume II are cited from its first (*ES2¹*), 1797, and second (*ES2²*) editions. Variants of poems that first appeared in other Smith publications are likewise noted where appropriate: *The Banished Man* (*BM*), 1794; *Celestina* (*C*), 1791; *Conversations Introducing Poetry* (*CIP*), 1804; *Emmeline* (*Em*), 1788; *Letters of a Solitary Wanderer* (LSW), 1802; *Marchmont* (*Ma*), 1796; *Montalbert* (*Mo*), 1795; *Minor Morals* (*MM*), 1798; *The Old Manor House* (*OMH*), 1793; *Rambles Farther* (*RF*), 1796; *Rural Walks* (*RW*), 1795; *The Young Philosopher* (*YP*), 1798. *The Emigrants* (*Emi*) is printed from its single London edition (Cadell, 1793); the Dublin edition later that year is without authority. *Beachy Head, with Other Poems* (*BH*) (London: Joseph Johnson, 1807), was published posthumously, and so where one can establish an alternative text printed in Smith's last years or, as seems the case with her other posthumous work *The History of Birds* (*HB*) (1807), a text can reasonably be thought to have been prepared for the press by her, such versions have been preferred. The three manuscript epilogues to the drama *What is She?* are designated by successive letters on the basis of the order in which they are placed in the autograph of the play in the Larpent Collection of the Huntington Library (LA 1253). Epilogue [A] is the original epilogue. Epilogue [B], though it is a tipped-in appendage, was the one printed. This volume uses the second edition (1799b) as the copy text, noting substantive variants from the first edition (1799a).

313

Elegiac Sonnets

Dedication. last line. *ES²:* Bignor Park / May 10, 1784
Preface, 3rd–4th eds. last line. *ES³:* Woolbeding / March 22d, 1786
1.10.   *ES²–ES⁶:* ills   *ES⁸–ES⁹:* hills
2.11.   *ES²:* passions
3.8.   *ES²:* fate.   *ES⁵⁻⁹:* fate?
3.11.   Say—hast   *ES²:* Or hast
3.12.   *ES²:* thou martyr
5.7.   first six editions spell it soothe: restored throughout poems.
7.6.   *ES²⁻⁹:* you   *HB:* thou
7.9.   *ES²:* steps
8.9.   *ES²:* torturing bosom pain
8.10.   *ES²:* shaft,
8.12.   *ES²:* prospects
8.13.   sounds   *ES²:* notes
9.5.   felt   *ES²:* known
11.14. *ES²:* breast,   *ES⁵⁻⁹:* breast;
12.7.   *ES⁸:* me,   *ES⁹:* me.
14.2.   Forming   *ES²:* And form'd
14.7.   beauteous   *ES²:* lovely
14.11. Yet   *ES²:* But
15.10. anguish   *ES²:* sadness
15.13–14. *ES²⁻⁴:*

        Ah! wherefore should you mourn, that her you love,
        Snatch'd from a world of woe, survives in bliss above.

16.4.   Behold   *ES²:* Ah! see
17.5.   darker   *ES³:* sombre
20.6.   send!   *ES³⁻⁵:* lend;
22.12. *ES²:* Thy own sweet plaintive songstress weeps my fate.
23.1.   To   *ES³:* Towards
24.8.   o'er   *ES²:* for
24.10. *ES²⁻⁸:* bed,   *ES⁹:* bed.
24.11. tears   *ES²⁻⁸:* tear
28.7.   *ES³:* While the frail summer-friendship fleets away,
29.2.   gay   *ES³:* laughing

30.5–6. *ES³:*

> Thy shadowy rocks, unhappy love shall seek,
> Where mantling loose, the green clematis flaunts,

30.11.fn. 1, line 1:

> probably   *ES³:* I should imagine

31.Title. *ES⁹:* in   *ES³⁻⁸:* on

31.2.fn. 2 *ES³:* others with which I am but imperfectly acquainted.

34.9.   *ES³:* thy sanction crowns my simple lays,

36.6.   lose;   *ES³:* loose;

37.Title. *ES⁵:* O'Niell

46.8.   *ES⁵:* heron!

49.7.   *C:* hope

49.8.   wild   *C:* lone

51.9.   Summer suns   *C:* the bright sun

58.1.   If   *ES⁶⁻⁹:* When

58.4.   *ES⁶⁻⁹:* heath-bell

58.14.   *CIP:* turns

60.5.   a shadowy veil   *RW:* its modest veil

60.11.   that turns   *RW:* and turns

60.12.   *RW:* And seeks

60.13.   With such unconscious   *RW:* So in unconscious

60.14.   *RW:* Miranda still shall charm—Nature's ingenuous child.

61.13–14. *OMH:*

> But aid me, Heaven, my real ills to bear,
> Nor let my spirit yield to phantoms of despair.

62.4.   quiet   *OMH:* repose

62.13.   *OMH:* vicissitude

63.13.   *ES2¹:* fleeting dreams

64.6.   stain'd   *BM:* dy'd

66.14.   *Mo:* And flees the wretch, who only 'wakes to weep!'

75.1–3. *Ma:*

> Where with incumbent night the forests frown,
> The care-worn pilgrim seeks his doubtful way;
> Till weary on the grass he throws him down,

75.9.   *Ma:* fountain's

75.10.   *Ma:* Ideal forms of Nymphs

75.11. *Ma:* And Naiads

79.14. *ES2¹:* Ocean's

81.3–4. *RF:*

> Where shadowy forests, and the coppices green,
> By summer's glowing hands are newly drest:

81.11. current,   *RF:* stream,

81.12. bad   *RD:* vain

81.13–14. *RF:*

> Learns, in retir'd seclusion, to possess
> With friendship sweeten'd—rural happiness!

82.13. *ES2¹:* Associate,

85.11. youth's   *YP:* life's

85.12 While   *YP:* When

86.2. Night on   *YP:* Night o'er

86.8. *ES2²:* bell,"

Origin of flattery

22. or threw   *ES²*, *ES⁵:* and threw

30. *ES²:* Cupid sighing fled

35–44. *ES²:*

> Too surely feeling that the blasts of care
> Would blight each blooming face, and plough deep wrinkles there,
> Sore sigh'd the goddess at the mournful view,
> Then try'd at length what heavenly art could do
> To bring back pleasure to her pensive train,
> And vindicate the glories of her reign.
> From Mars's head his casque, by Cupid borne,
> (That which in softer wars the god had worn)
> She smiling took, and on its silver round
> Her magic cestus three times thrice she bound;

36. *ES⁵:* joy.   *ES⁸⁻⁹:* joy,

44. Weaved   *ES⁵:* Wreath'd   *ES⁵:* round.   *ES⁸⁻⁹:* round,

76. *ES²:* Zephyr's stronger breath

97–115. *ES²:*

> She governs fashion, and becomes the *ton*.
> By thee dim-sighted dowagers behold
> The record where their conquests are enroll'd;

> They see the shades of ancient beaux arise,
> Who swear their eyes exceeded modern eyes,
> And scenes long past, by memory fondly nurs'd,
> When GEORGE the Second reign'd, or GEORGE the First;
> Compar'd to which, degenerate and absurd
> Seems the gay world that moves round GEORGE the Third.

119.   soothing   *ES²:* dulcet

The peasant of the Alps

3.   *C:* Down the chasms,

Verses intended to have been prefixed to the novel of Emmeline...
"To my Children," *Emmeline,* first edition (1788)

6.   *Em:* Of every hope
8.   *Em:* And dress
11.   anxious   *Em:* tender
17.   solicitudes   *Em:* anxieties
20.   sorrows   *Em:* evils   ills arise   *Em:* sorrows, rise.
22.   some   *Em:* still
24.   sorrows   *Em:* miseries
29.   you   *Em:* ye

Written for the benefit of a distressed player...

5. fn.   *ES2¹:* From an idea that the wheat-ear of the Southern downs is the becca-fica of Italy. I doubt it; but have no books that give one any information on the subject.

A descriptive ode

5.   frown'd   *Ma:* scowl'd
8.   giant   *Ma:* hideous
12.   Hears ... voices   *Ma:* He seems to hear the murmurs
15.   shade   *Ma:* hide
27.   *Ma:* Zephyrs'
30.   Blasting   *Ma:* And blast
37.   Perchance ... ruins   *Ma:* Forlorn, among these ruins
41.   *Ma:* sails
43.   On ... tombs,   *Ma:* Long on these tombs,
44.   may   *Ma:* will

49.   Hence   *Ma:* Here
74.   *Ma:* rustic's

Verses supposed to have been written in the New Forest…
Title.   *CIP:* Verses Written in Early Spring
18.   *ES2²:* When Love shall dress for him
20.   *ES2²:* past, or

Song from the French
1.   Louisa   *RF:* Miranda
19.   *RF:* amid the autumnal

Apostrophe to an old tree
5.   *ES2¹:* That clothes the bark in
20.   relics   *ES2¹:* relicts

The forest boy
28.   soft   *ES2¹:* wild
74.   *ES2¹:* And it seem'd as each blast of wind fearfully told
80.   *ES2¹:* soon she
127.   *ES2¹:* She sits by the river and weaves
132.   *ES2¹:* Ye statesmen! ne'er dreading a scar;

Verses on the death of [Henrietta O'Neill] …
6.   these   *BM:* those
31.   that   *BM:* thy

Ode to death
15.   *ES2¹:* To lose the anguish of ungrateful love?

Stanzas
9.   Liberty   *YP:* freedom once
11–15. *YP:*

        Think! mid the gloomy haunts of gain
        Reluctant days I pass in pain,
        And all I once desired resign;
        Ah! let me then at length obtain
        One soft, one pitying sigh of thine.
17.   will   *YP:* shall

To the winds

12.   *YP:* Laments

44.   rocky   *YP:* desart

50.   *YP:* may'st thou

The Emigrants

II.22.   A single endnote in the 1793 text conflates this line and line 78, crediting Shakespeare as source. For the second allusion the attribution is correct; but it is unlikely that Smith would have mistaken Shakespeare for the author of the first phrase, which is one often cited during this period as Waller's.

II.256–81; 292–312. This passage was excerpted in 1797 and republished in *ES2*[1] as "Fragment Descriptive of the Miseries of War"; the revised text of those lines is here substituted for the original.

II.260.   they die   *Emi:* it dies

II.265.   quick throbbing   *Emi:* hard-heaving

II.269.   *Emi:* repentant

II.272.   *Emi:* soldier's

II.274.   sudden   *Emi:* sullen

II.298.   stillness!   *Emi:* silence

II.301.   *Emi:* casements

Prologue to What is She?

Text from second edition (1799b); variants from first edition (1799a) as follows:

1.   various. 1799a; author's handwritten correction in presentation copy of 1799b (Huntington Library KD-631). sev'ral. 1799b.

4.   then to childhood we return

7.   moral display'd [printer's error]

14.   Auxiliary light'ning,

20.   Cupid hover'd

21.   To

22.   Blue-beard

30.   And slung

32.   just when

34.   fall—to

35.   To night an Authoress

42.   and. 1799a; author's handwritten correction in presentation copy of 1799b (Huntington Library KD-631).

Epilogue [A] to What is She?

2.   *1799a:* the Vot'ry still of
3.   *1799a:* fashion's round
16.   *1799a:* Women's ... their tongues &
18.   *1799a:* perdition to

The hedge-hog seen in a frequented path
21.   *CIP:* thee;

The moth
7.   *CIP:* feast,

Wild flowers
Title.   *MM:* The Kalandar of Flora
9.   There   *MM:* Then
11.   *MM:* cowslips
12.   *MM:* Receive in jasper cups
14.   *MM:* Maia's genial beam;
25.   in   *MM:* o'er
30.   the Brionia ... scollop'd   *MM:* pale brionia ... scallop'd
32.   *CIP:* Clemati's
46.   the Corn flower   *MM:* cyanus
52.   Sink   *MM:* Shrink
53.   *CIP:* food,   *MM:* use,   *CIP:* or pleasure   *MM:* for pleasure

An evening walk by the sea-side
24.   *CIP:* beams

The heath
20.   *CIP:* mantle,
21.   *CIP:* honey,)
24.   *CIP:* Whole,

Ode to the missel thrush
4.   *CIP:* ground.

Ode to the olive tree
6.   *CIP:* pale.

Lines composed in passing through a forest in Germany

Title.   *LSW:* untitled

16.   love   *LSW:* heart

17.   *LSW:* would

Fables

In 1807 appeared two posthumous publications of Charlotte Smith. *The History of Birds*, the last of her children's books, contained five poems in its two volumes. Those of the second volume were reprinted in somewhat altered form that year in the *Beachy Head* collection; but the two poems of the first volume, "The dictatorial owl" and "The jay in masquerade," were overlooked or simply omitted. They are here restored to the context of the other fables, and since the texts of "The truant dove" and "The lark's nest" in *The History of Birds* are in numerous particulars more polished than those in *Beachy Head*, all four fables are taken from the same original source, with minor emendations from *Beachy Head* adopted in the case of the latter two. On the other hand, the fifth poem about birds, "The swallow" ("To the swallow" in *The History of Birds*) seems a more advanced text in its *Beachy Head* version (among other refinements is an additional stanza); that printing has here been adopted as copytext.

The truant dove

13.   *HB:* seem

15.   *HB:* The twins

29.   *BH:* peas

40.   *BH:* friend's

87.   your   *BH:* thy

128.   *HB:* repast,   *BH:* repast;

129.   *HB:* flow'r: *BH:* flower,

144.   *BH:* be long

179.   *BH:* It silence

224.   *HB:* him, earnest

The swallow

23.   What   *HB:* All

25.   came   *HB:* come

27.   wing,   *HB:* flight,

29.   above   *HB:* across

30.   *HB:* charioteer?

31–35. *HB:*

>Do Afric's plains, where ev'ry gale
>Bears odors from the palmy grove,
>Hear the loud cuckoo's frequent tale?
>There did you meet the vagrant rail?
>   Or the low murmuring dove?

38.   in sorrow   *HB:* incessant

42.   vast and pathless   *HB:* wide and stormy

44.   to build anew.   *HB:* anew, to build

46.   as   *HB:* when

49.   *HB:* In some tall cliff's encaved brow.

51–55. *HB:*[omitted]

56.   *HB:* What wondrous instinct bids you know

57.   *HB:* food?

58.   To isles and   *HB:* If to the

60.   *HB:* dimpled

61–65. *HB:*

>How there, while cold waves eddying flow
>   Your transitory tomb above,
>Learn ye when winds more mildly blow,
>And the propitious moment know,
>   To rise to life and love?

Flora

30.   *BH:* Enwove   *CIP:* Enwoven (The original text disturbs the iambic
pentameter by adding a syllable to it.)

45.   *BH:* Scandix'   *CIP:* Scandix's

46.   *BH:* And graced a shining knot, her head behind—

117.   *BH:* The Honeysuckle rears his scallop'd horn;

129.   *BH* is stiffly rewritten to avoid the grammatical solecism: "See a fair
pyramid the Chesnut rear,"

152.   *BH:* grew,   *CIP:* grow,

185.   *BH:* Fancy   *CIP:* Fancy,

Studies by the sea

10.   *BH:* land?   *CIP:* land.

113.   *BH:* prow   *CIP:* proa (The errata sheet for *CIP* supplies Smith's pre-
ferred spelling; the pronounciation is unaffected.)

Hope and *Evening*

Charlotte Smith sent copies of "Hope" and "Evening" to her faithful correspondent Sarah Rose on 30 July 1805: these appear to be the only poems that have survived in authorial manuscript. The text of "Hope" has only slight differences in punctuation, but the text of "Evening" is written (as "To Evening") in a less polished form than that eventually published. Variants by permission of the Henry W. and Albert A. Berg Collection, New York Public Library, Astor, Lennox and Tilden Foundations.

Evening

1.	gorgeous day—
5.	T'is then I love the gale
6.	That breaths shadowy copse,
7.	While slow the silver dews
8.	Descend in light and lucid drops
10.	That balmy breeze to me
11.	While as
12.	Seem those cold celestial
13.	And Ah!
14.	an heart
15.	mourn?

To my lyre

Charlotte Smith's last poem, on the authority of her sister Catherine Anne Dorset, was printed as part of her memoir, published by Walter Scott in 1829. The text is taken from Scott, *Prose* (Edinburgh: Ballantyne, 1834), XI, 29–31.

INDEX OF FIRST LINES

INDEX OF TITLES